HOW
PEOPLE
LIVE

3 1901 03986 7629

DK Publishing

LONDON, NEW YORK, MUNICH,
MELBOURNE, AND DELHI

Senior Editor Penelope Arlon
Senior Art Editor Claire Patané

Editorial Team Lorrie Mack, Zahavit Shalev
Design Team Laura Roberts, Venice Shone,
Cathy Chesson, Tory Gordon-Harris
Editorial Assistant Fleur Star
Picture Research Lorna Ainger, Kathy Lockley
US Editor Margaret Parrish

Publishing Manager Sue Leonard
Managing Art Editor Clare Shedden
Production Shivani Pandey
DTP Designer Almudena Díaz
DTP Assistant Pilar Morales

Written and researched by Penelope Arlon,
Lorrie Mack, Zahavit Shalev

Consultant Team:
Dr. Dena Freeman: Chief Consultant and Africa
Dr. Leo Howe: East Asia
Dr. Mark Jamieson: North America
Dr. James Leach: Australia and the Pacific
Dr. Perveez Mody: West Asia
Dr. Valentina Napolitano: South America
Dr. David Sneath: West Asia
Dr. Jaro Stacul: Europe
Bryan Alexander: Arctic

First American Edition, 2003

Published in the United States by DK Publishing, Inc.
375 Hudson Street, New York, NY 10014

03 04 05 06 07 10 9 8 7 6 5 4 3 2 1

A Cataloging-in-Publication record for this book is
available from the Library of Congress.

ISBN: 0-7894-9867-7

Color reproduction by GRB Edrice S.r.l., Verona, Italy
Printed and bound in Spain by Artes Gráficas Toledo

Discover more at
www.dk.com

THERE ARE MANY MANY different
groups of people in the world, so
many, in fact, that they could not
possibly all fit into one book.
How People Live
gives an initial understanding of
the enormous diversity of cultures
in the world today and celebrates
the common bonds that link
us all together.

CONTENTS

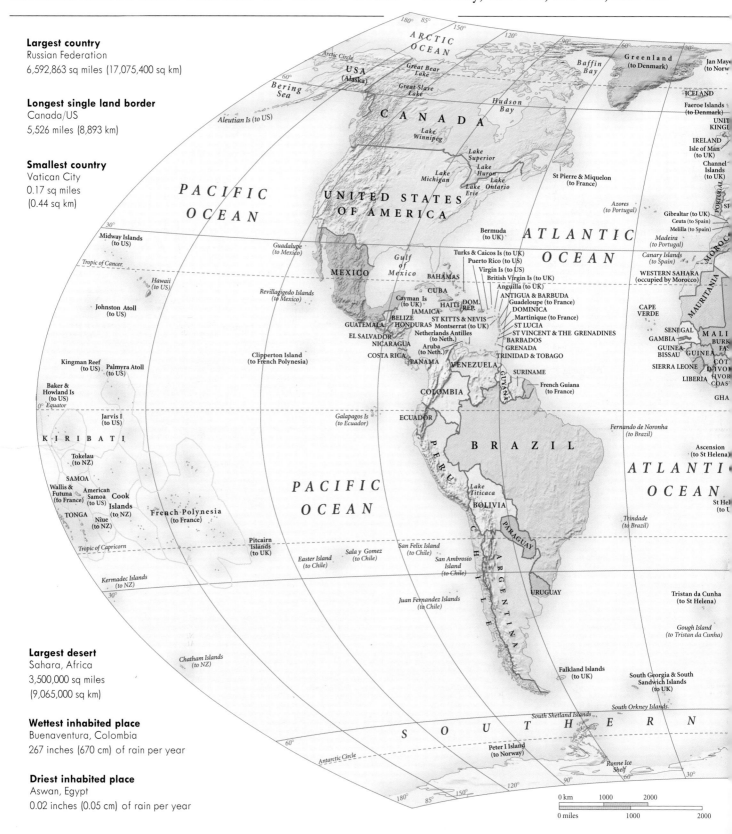
WORLD MAP

THERE ARE 193 INDEPENDENT COUNTRIES on Earth today. There are over 50 dependent territories that are administered by any one of: France, Australia, Denmark, New Zealand, Norway, the UK, the US, and the

INTERNATIONAL BORDERS OF THE WORLD

Largest country
Russian Federation
6,592,863 sq miles (17,075,400 sq km)

Longest single land border
Canada/US
5,526 miles (8,893 km)

Smallest country
Vatican City
0.17 sq miles
(0.44 sq km)

Largest desert
Sahara, Africa
3,500,000 sq miles
(9,065,000 sq km)

Wettest inhabited place
Buenaventura, Colombia
267 inches (670 cm) of rain per year

Driest inhabited place
Aswan, Egypt
0.02 inches (0.05 cm) of rain per year

Netherlands. Every piece of land is owned by a country with the exception of Antarctica. Australia, Argentina, Britain, Chile, France, New Zealand, and Norway have all laid claim to sections of it, but the 1961 Antarctic Treaty, signed by 39 nations, agreed that no one country could own it. The extreme climate has meant that no one has ever permanently settled there and the only settlements today are scientific bases.

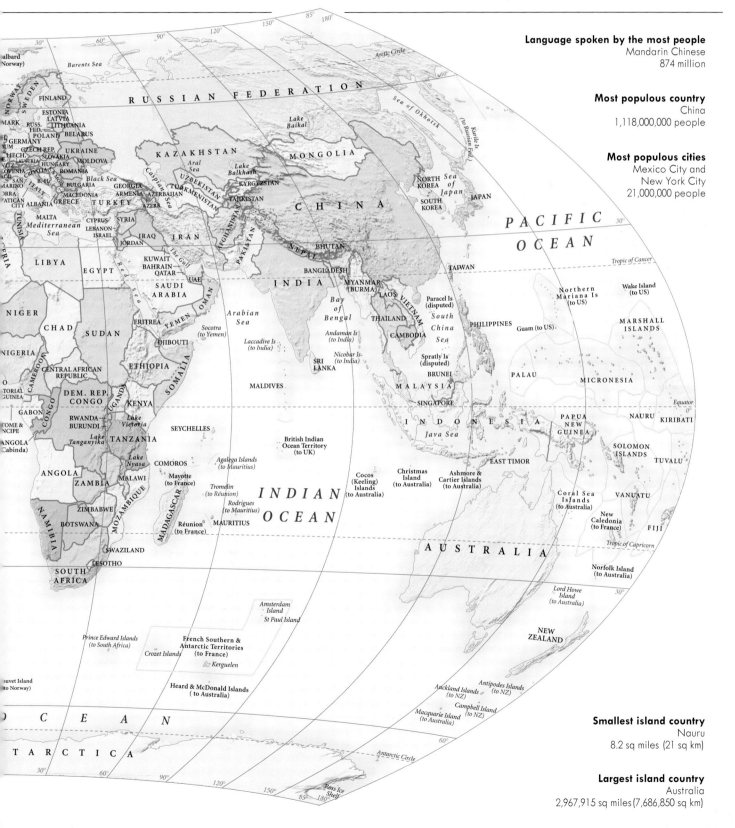

Language spoken by the most people
Mandarin Chinese
874 million

Most populous country
China
1,118,000,000 people

Most populous cities
Mexico City and
New York City
21,000,000 people

Smallest island country
Nauru
8.2 sq miles (21 sq km)

Largest island country
Australia
2,967,915 sq miles (7,686,850 sq km)

On October 12, 1999, the six billionth

THE GLOBAL VILLAGE

person was born on Earth, and by 2002 there were 6,200,000,000 people in the world. Numbers this huge

If the world was a village of 100 people

FOOD

The global village of 100 people has many animals that are a source of food. There are:

31 sheep
23 cows, bulls, oxen
15 pigs
3 camels
2 horses
189 chickens

There is no shortage of food in the global village. If it were divided equally everyone would have enough to eat. But the food isn't divided equally:

60 people always go hungry and, of these, 26 are severely undernourished.

16 people go to bed hungry some of the time. Only 24 people have enough to eat.

EDUCATION

There are 38 people in the global village who are of school age, but only 31 go to school.

88 people are old enough to read:
71 can read at least a little.
17 cannot read at all.
In the global village of a 100 people there are:

5 soldiers
7 teachers
1 doctor

NATIONALITY

The village people come from all over the world.
There are:

61 from Asia
13 from Africa
12 from Europe
8 from South and Central America
5 from North America
1 from Oceania

are difficult to understand, so to make it easier, on the next four pages we are reducing the whole world down to a village of 100 people so that the statistics are easier to absorb. The 100 villagers live in many different ways. They are different nationalities, they speak different languages, and practice different religions, but deep down they all strive for the same things: enough food and water, and a happy, healthy life.

RELIGION

Most people in the world belong to a religion. In the village there are:

32 Christians
19 Muslims
13 Hindus
12 Shamanists, animists, and other folk religions
6 Buddhists
2 belong to global religions such as Confucianism
1 Jew
15 non-religious

LANGUAGE

It is estimated that there are 3,000 languages spoken in the world. In the village:

22 speak a Chinese dialect
9 speak English
8 speak Hindi
7 speak Spanish
4 speak Arabic
4 speak Bengali
3 speak Portugese
3 speak Russian
40 speak other languages

AIR AND WATER

In most of the village the air and water is healthy and clean, but in some areas it is polluted, which is unhealthy for the villagers. Water is also in short supply for some people.

WATER
75 people have access to safe water in their homes or within a short distance.

25 people must spend a large part of each day collecting safe water.

SANITATION
60 people have access to public and household sewage control.

AIR
68 people breathe in clean air.
32 people breathe in polluted air.

Only half of the children in the village are immunized against infectious diseases.

THE EARTH AT NIGHT

ELECTRICITY IN THE GLOBAL VILLAGE

ELECTRICITY HAS CHANGED PEOPLE'S LIVES, so much so that many people cannot imagine life without it. Yet only 76 people in the global village of 100 people

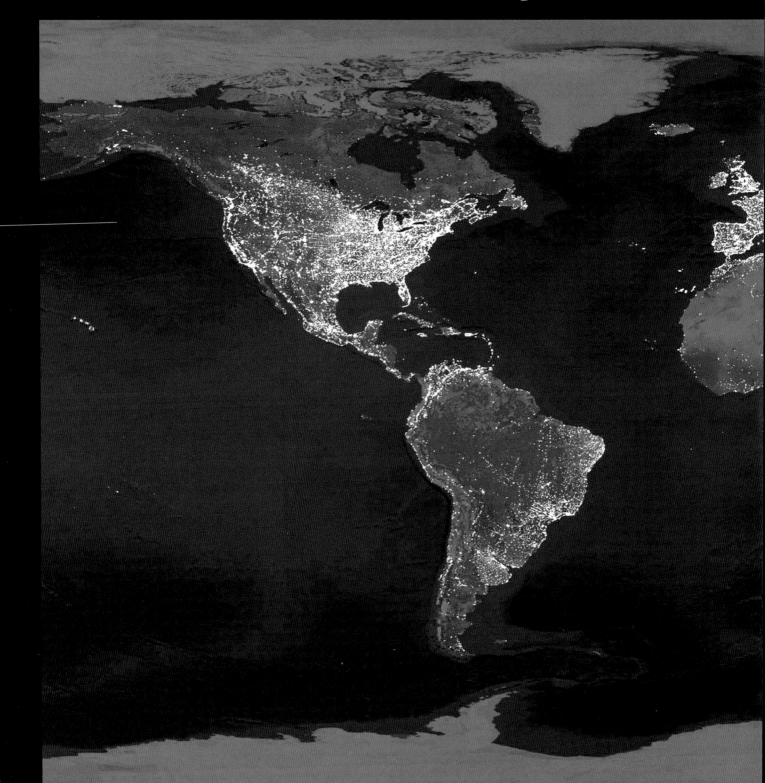

have electricity. Of these, most use it only for light at night, rather than for all the luxuries some people are used to. In the village there are only 42 radios, 24 televisions, 14 telephones, and, surprisingly, 7 computers. This satellite image of the Earth at night gives a very rough idea of the distribution of light electricity in the world. You can also spot where the heavily populated cities are.

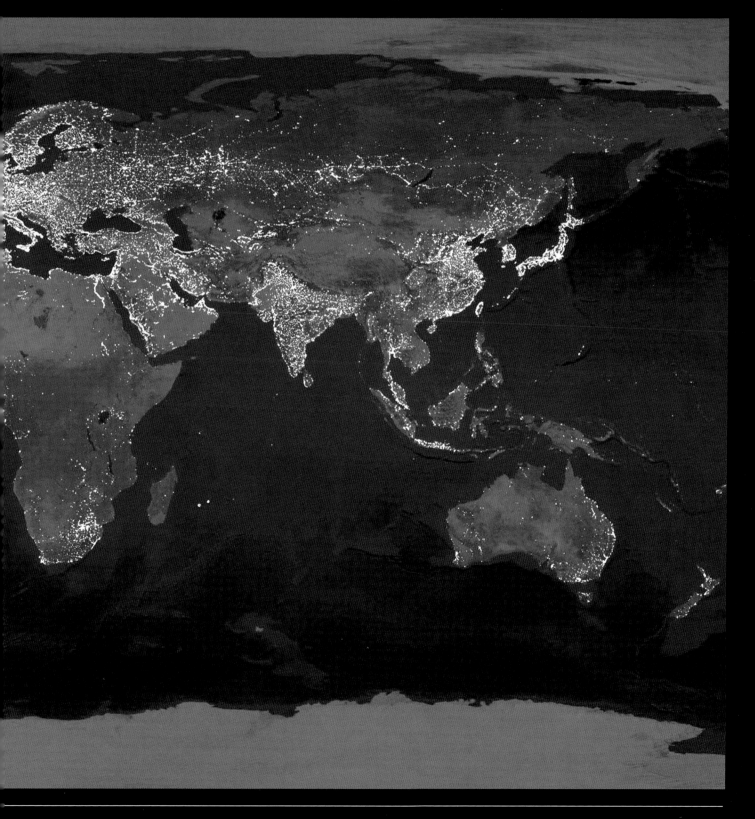

PEOPLE AND CULTURE

WHAT MAKES AN ETHNIC GROUP?

Belonging to a group

There are many reasons why people feel that they belong to an ethnic group. They often have lots of things in common, such as a shared race, language, or culture. Ethnic groups can be large or small, and these days they can live together or can be spread all over the world.

SHARED RELIGION

Religion often creates a sense of cultural distinctiveness and can be a key factor within an ethnic group. Some religions, such as Christianity, can stretch across very diverse ethnic groups, for example, from the European communities to South Africa.

THE SOCIAL ANIMAL

People are social beings, those that live near each other often create communities and societies. During their lives they almost always socialize, or interact, with a large amount of people from other ethnic groups for various reasons, such as trade.

The Miao people are one of 55 Chinese ethnic minorities. Within the Miao there are many different clans.

forests of Papua New Guinea there are societies who live traditional lifestyles, while in nearby Australia the cities buzz with the latest technology and fashions. Some people believe that cultures and languages are disappearing due to the influence of the modern world—globalization. However, it is clear from this book that people still value the cultural variations that make our world all the more interesting.

WHO ARE INDIGENOUS PEOPLE?

The word "indigenous" is sometimes used in this book. Indigenous people are those who are "native to," or originate in, a country. Often a country is taken over by another culture or nation and the indigenous population is then governed by different people. This is what happened in Australia where the indigenous people were initially conquered by the British and are now governed by the independent Australian nation.

There are very few indigenous people with little contact with the rest of the world. There are, however, some rain forest communities in Papua New Guinea that are totally isolated.

NATIONALITY

The world is divided into countries that have their own nationality. There can be many ethnic groups within a country, as in Canada, or in some cases, as in Japan, they are almost entirely made up of one.

In many countries children are educated together regardless of their ethnic or cultural differences.

SIMILARITIES

In many countries today people from different ethnic groups live and work together, thus creating the vibrant mix that makes up the modern world. Although people may seem different, we all have a lot of things in common—all people have the need to work, value family and relations, and like to feel a sense of community. People may have their differences, but we are at our core essentially the same—we are all human.

MIGRATION

PEOPLE ARE CONSTANTLY MOVING. THERE ARE MANY reasons why people relocate to a different place. Sometimes people are forced to migrate, by, for example, conflict or a natural

WHY DO PEOPLE MOVE AROUND?

WAR

Conflict between nations or peoples often forces people to move to escape danger. Here, hundreds of thousands of Afghans are on the move, fearing for their lives. They are refugees in their own country.

IMMIGRATION

Many people yearn for a better life or job and move to find them. There are, for example, Chinese communities in many of the world's major cities.

SLAVERY

During the 16th and 17th centuries many European powers took people from Africa and shipped them all over the world as slaves. The Portuguese shipped over 3.5 million Africans to Brazil and today many of their descendents live in Bahia, Brazil. They have created a new culture based on an African origin with South American and European influences.

Dance troupe in Salavador, Brazil practicing an Afro-Brazilian dance.

NEW DIAMOND RESTAURANT

disaster, and sometimes people choose to migrate, perhaps for a better life or for work. As a result, different people come into contact with each other, languages and ideas spread, and over time ways of life change and in their place new fashions and ideas are formed. These pages look in detail at some of the reasons why people choose to migrate or are forced to move.

Sakurajima volcano, in Japan, hurls rocks down daily on the nearby town. For protection the children wear hard hats to school.

COLONIZATION
In the 16th, 17th, and 18th centuries Europeans conquered huge areas of the world, and large amounts of people moved to some of these areas, such as Australia. Many countries have since become independent but still keep in contact with their colonizing power and have in some cases adopted their language.

URBANIZATION
Cities often attract people from the surrounding countryside who are tempted by work. The city of Dubai, situated on the shores of Dubai Creek in the United Arab Emirates, has become a sprawling place due to businesses growing up around the oil industry. A valuable natural resource will attract people to an area.

NATURAL DISASTER
An earthquake, an eruption of a volcano, or a hurricane can be a reason for people to move. The aftermath of a natural disaster can often bring with it terror and chaos, forcing people to take up their belongings and leave. In 1995, a volcano on the island of Montserrat in the West Indies erupted and many people had to flee the island. Much of the island is still buried under ash today.

CHANGING POLITICAL BOUNDARIES
Some regimes place tight restrictions on movement. Until the late 1980s much of Europe, including East Germany, was ruled by the former communist power, the USSR. The people were unable to move freely until 1989, when the Berlin Wall came down, allowing movement once again.

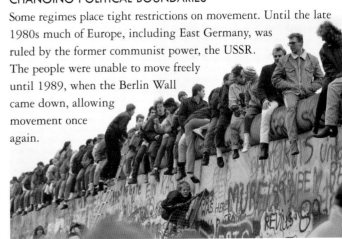

THE PEOPLE OF
North and
Central
America

THE CONTINENTS OF NORTH AND CENTRAL AMERICA include 23 countries plus a number of dependent territories.

NORTH AND CENTRAL AMERICA

FROM THE ARCTIC TO THE TROPICS

Deep chill
Recorded in 1971, the coldest-ever recorded temperature in Alaska is -80 °F (-62 °C).

Lots of latitude

Some parts of Greenland, Canada, and Alaska lie far inside the Arctic Circle, while the southern tip of Panama extends almost as far as the Equator.

Distant relation
The 50th state of the US, Hawaii, is far to the west of this map, halfway to Australia.

Under pressure
The huge ice sheet pushing down on Greenland has caused the island's center to sink to 1,000 ft (300 m) below sea level.

Coastal record
At 151,394 miles (243,638 km), Canada has the longest coastline of any country in the world.

Water power
Over 40 million gallons (180 million liters) of water rush over Niagara Falls every minute.

Greenland (the largest island in the world) belongs to Denmark, for example, and the small islands of St. Pierre and Miquelon, near the east coast of Canada, belong to France. Several of the the Caribbean islands (such as Martinique and Guadeloupe) also belong to France, while others are territories of the Netherlands (like Aruba), the United Kingdom (Cayman Islands), or the United States (Virgin Islands).

Statistics

LANGUAGES
French features prominently because it is spoken widely in the Caribbean, as well as being one of Canada's two official languages.

English	236 million
Spanish	160 million
Indigenous langs	81.3 million
French	14.5 million

RELIGIONS
Because of the high incidence of immigration in this region, virtually every world religion is practiced here somewhere.

Roman Catholic	156 million
Protestant	104 million
Jewish	6.2 million
Muslim	5.5 million

URBAN POPULATION
In each case, the figures given include suburbs as well as inner city areas, which contain considerably fewer people.

New York City	21 million
Mexico City	21 million
Los Angeles	16 million
Chicago	9 million

POPULATION BY COUNTRY
Despite having the biggest land mass in the region (and the second biggest in the world), Canada has just 32 million people.

US	280.5 million
Mexico	103.4 million
Canada	32 million
Guatemala	13.3 million

POPULATION

The island of Barbados, which is only 166 sq miles (430 sq km) in size, has the region's highest population density—1,658 people per sq mile (640 people per sq km).

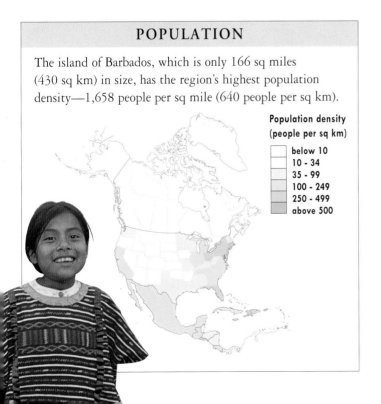

Population density
(people per sq km)

	below 10
	10 - 34
	35 - 99
	100 - 249
	250 - 499
	above 500

NORTH & CENTRAL AMERICA FACTS

PLACES
Number of countries ....23 (plus dependencies)
Highest point ....Mt. McKinley (Denali), Alaska, US, 20,321 ft (6,194 m)
Lowest point ....Badwater, Death Valley, California, US, 282 ft (-86 m)
Biggest country ....Canada, 3,560,216 sq m (9,220,970 sq km)
Smallest country ....Grenada, 131 sq m (340 sq km)

PEOPLE
Total population ....490 million
Proportion living in urban areas 72%

LITERACY RATE
90% of the population

HEALTH
People per doctor 719
Proportion with access to clean water 93%

The People of North America

COVERING A VAST LAND MASS that has attracted immigrants from every corner of the globe, this region—which reaches from Greenland to Mexico—is home to a greater and more diverse variety of intermingled peoples, cultures, and religions than anywhere else on Earth.

CITY LIFE

The great cities of North America all provide important public spaces that define both their physical and their human landscapes. During the winter months, and especially at Christmas, New Yorkers flock to the huge skating rink at Rockefeller Center.

FAITHS AND FESTIVALS

In North America, the most extravagant celebrations tend to be religious. Here, Mexican Catholics mark the festival of Our Lady of Guadalupe (December 12) outside the grand 18th-century Basilica de Guadalupe in Mexico city.

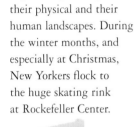

Changes of scene

Indigenous peoples and recent immigrants, old customs and modern trends, treasured handicrafts and modern technology, formal ceremonies and casual entertainments—all nourish the richly diverse cultures of North America. Each decade, new arrivals add their own color and detail to the constantly changing scene.

MOVING WITH THE TIMES

Today, the indigenous people of North America combine a wide range of elements from the modern world with their own customs and traditions. Here, a Canadian Inuit family navigates the forbidding conditions around their home on a high-speed snowmobile.

COMMON HERITAGE

Native Americans celebrate their shared history and tradition. Here, at the Red Earth Festival in Oklahoma City, two children display symbols of their diverse ancestry: between them, they have Kiowa, Cherokee, Comanche, Choctow, and Navajo roots.

CULTURAL

North American cityscapes reflect the many influences that shape them. In Toronto, Canada's largest city, the City Hall and adjoining square sit between its bustling Chinatown and the glass towers of the business district. The dramatic complex was designed and built in the 1960s by the Finnish architect Viljo Revell.

PLAYING TO WIN

From major-league events, to college and high-school playoffs and casual street games, sporting activities play a major part in North American life. Baseball is more than a sport, though; it has become an international symbol of the United States. Across the country—even in the far-flung state of Hawaii—children don the uniform of their local Little League team to express their passion for their national game.

THE UNITED STATES OF AMERICA is a place where people from many countries have come together to form a unified culture. Following the country's independence

THE PEOPLE OF THE US

A RICH "MELTING POT" OF CULTURES

A symbol of freedom

The Statue of Liberty was erected on an island in New York harbor in 1886 as a symbol of the city's role as a gateway to the "land of the free and the home of the brave." Near the statue lies Ellis Island, where more than 12 million immigrants first landed in their new country in order to be processed.

INDEPENDENCE DAY
On July 4, 1776, after the American War of Independence, the Declaration of Independence was drawn up. Each year on this date Americans celebrate their freedom with barbeques, picnics, and family gatherings.

AFRICAN-AMERICANS
During the 17th and 18th centuries, hundreds of thousands of people were shipped to the US from Africa as slaves. Today, many African-Americans are descended from these slaves.

IRISH-AMERICANS
In 1845 the great potato rot and subsequent famine in Ireland started a mass migration to the US. Starving families who could not pay landlords faced no alternative but to leave the country in hopes of a better future.

St. Patrick's Day is celebrated on March 17 each year. On this day the Chicago River is dyed green for the celebrations!

The Statue of Liberty was a gift from the French to the American people.

in 1776, immigrants started to arrive in enormous numbers, attracted by a better life, or the "American Dream." Today, the United States still accepts about one million immigrants annually. The mix of cultures has enriched the country and has become its defining quality. In cities such as New York, pockets of established ethnic communities manage to maintain the culture of their homeland as well lead American lives.

HISPANIC COMMUNITY

Twelve percent of the US population is Hispanic, which means they, or their ancestors, came to the US from Mexico, Spain, Puerto Rico, or one of the other countries in South or Central America. This young girl holds a Puerto Rican flag while participating in Chicago's Puerto Rico Day Parade.

CHINATOWN

By the 1880s the Chinese began to arrive, attracted by available jobs—many built the railroads out to the West. Today over 80,000 Chinese-Americans live in New York City in an area known as Chinatown, which has remained a self-contained community with countless restaurants and seven Chinese newspapers.

AMERICAN JEWS

The first Jewish immigrants in the United States are said to have arrived around 1650. During the late the 1800s Jews began to move in substantial numbers to the United States from Europe and Asia. Today, there are about 5.5 million Jews in the country. The largest synagogue in the world is the Temple Emanu-El on the Upper East Side, New York City.

ITALIAN-AMERICANS

The first Italians, many of them from northern Italy, arrived in the US in the 1830s and 1840s. Later, during the 1870s, poverty forced many more to move. Over 11 days each September, about three million people converge on the neighborhood known as Little Italy in New York City for the Feast of San Gennaro—a massive festival to celebrate the patron saint of Naples, Italy.

The Marathon

THE LARGEST RACE ON EARTH

THE VERY FIRST NEW YORK MARATHON was held on September 13, 1970. One hundred and twenty seven runners started, only 55 finished, and fewer than 100 people watched. By the year 2000, more than 32,000 people finished the race successfully, and it is now the world's largest marathon. The course is 26 miles (41 km) and covers all five of New York City's boroughs. People from all over the world take part, and the amounts raised for charity have a huge impact worldwide.

East coast

THE FIRST REGION OF THE US to be colonized by Europeans, the East coast takes in the cosmopolitan buzz of New York City, the historic centers of Boston and Philadelphia, and the picturesque landscapes of New England, with its fiery fall foliage, popular winter resorts, and traditional industries such as farming and fishing.

NEW YORK, NEW YORK

Times Square, where it meets the lights of Broadway, forms the heart of New York City, an international center of business and culture, and one of the world's most exciting cities. Broadway was originally an American Indian woodland path.

NATURAL HERITAGE

Most of the pretty, old buildings in New England (like this rural Vermont church) are made of wood. There are two main reasons for this: the early British settlers were familiar with timber-frame construction, and the forested landscape provided plenty of free building material.

MAPLE SYRUP

For hundreds of years, New Englanders have been using the sweet sap from the local trees to make maple syrup. There is only one short season a year when sap can be collected, and the earlier in this season the sap is drawn, the higher its sugar content, and therefore its quality.

WINTER WONDERLAND

The hilly terrain and crisp, snowy weather in Vermont make it an ideal ski resort. The world's first rope-tow ski lift was invented here, and early versions were powered by Model-T Ford engines. Ski lifts revolutionized the sport since they multiplied dramatically the number of runs enthusiasts could make in one day.

LOBSTER RACE

The Great International Lobster Crate Race is part of the Maine Lobster Festival. Each competitor runs repeatedly along 50 crates strung across Boothbay Harbor. The winner is the one who covers the most crates before falling in.

BOSTON SKYLINE
The largest city in New England, Boston was named after the town of the same name in Lincolnshire, England. Established in 1624, it is the capital and principal port of Massachusetts and a leading center of education, with 35 colleges and universities (including Harvard) in the greater Boston area.

Harvest from the sea

Fishing is a major industry along the northeastern coast, which is particularly famous for shellfish of all kinds. Lobster is the best-known product, but crawfish, crab, and clams are important as well. Clam chowder, a thick, nourishing soup enjoyed all over the world, was invented in Maine.

LOBSTER FISHING
In the state of Maine alone there are nearly 6,000 licensed lobstermen. The trade tends to run in families, with some men "lobstering" exactly the same waters as their fathers and grandfathers before them.

Lobstermen tie colored buoys to their traps so they know where to find them.

1 Setting traps
Lobsters are caught in bait-filled traps. Once they have been lured inside they cannot escape. Most lobstermen check their traps every 3-4 days.

2 All at sea
Each trap (which can weigh as much as a small person when it is full of lobster) is pulled up by hand. The men who do this develop very muscular forearms.

3 Good catch
The smallest commerical lobsters are called "chickens"; the largest are known as "jumbos."

The Gulf Coast

CROWNING THE GULF OF MEXICO, this region (which overlaps slightly with that of the Southern states) includes Florida, Alabama, Mississippi, and Louisiana. Here, the Gulf itself—and the waterways connected to it—dominate many aspects of culture and industry, from local foods and festivals to water sports, fishing, and tourism.

MIAMI STYLE

Surrounded by the heavy-duty glitz of Miami, South Beach is famous for its multicolored Art Deco buildings, now immaculately restored to their original condition. The pink-and-chrome perfection of a classic 1950s car perfectly matches the hotel's style, if not its period.

CALLE OCHO CARNIVAL

Miami's vast Cuban population is centered around Eighth Street. Their annual festival, the biggest Latino celebration in the US, is called *Calle Ocho*—Eighth Street in Spanish.

WALT DISNEY WORLD

This huge theme park near Orlando is one of the world's most profitable tourist destinations. Florida's government has given Disney the right to enforce laws with its own security force.

The inviting beaches that line Alabama's coast are seldom overcrowded.

MAGNOLIA STATE

Dominated by the vast and powerful river that shares its name, the state of Mississippi was once wealthy and prosperous, its huge cotton industry providing a firm economic foundation. Today, although Mississippi is still a major cotton producer, it also depends on the revenue it receives from oil and and natural gas. Another important source of income is the tourist trade: every year, thousands of visitors come here to see the birthplace of Elvis Presley and the Delta Blues, and to ride on one of the paddle wheel steamers that have been negotiating the great waterway for generations.

JAMBALAYA

Particularly associated with Louisiana, Cajun food is spicy and rich. One of the best-known dishes, jambalaya, is made from rice fried up with spices, vegetables, sausages, shrimp and crawfish, known locally as "poor man's lobster."

The *American Queen*, one of the world's largest paddle wheelers, travels along the Mississippi near Natchez.

STORMY WEATHER

This region is vulnerable to violent storms called hurricanes. People are advised to make their homes as safe as possible, watch for warning signs, and—if necessary—leave the area quickly.

TEEMING WATERS

The seas around the Gulf coast provide fishermen with striped bass, herring, shad, and lesser-known species such as menhaden, bluefish, weakfish, and butterfish. There are plenty of catfish farms (catfish tastes a little like trout) near the mouth of the Mississippi, and oyster, shrimp, and crawfish farms all along the Gulf.

Small fish intended for use as live bait thrash around in this fine net.

Southern states

FROM COTTON FIELDS to country music and curly wrought iron, the images connected with the American South are uniquely characterful and romantic. Carrying a huge historical legacy from the days of plantations, slavery, and the Civil War, this region is also home to such quintessentially modern phenomena as the oil industry and jazz music.

LAND OF COTTON

The US is the world's leading producer of cotton. Most of this yield is grown in the South, where Spanish colonists introduced the first cotton plants. Originally, cotton was picked by hand, but today the job is done mechanically. In cotton country, the fluffy harvest is known as "white gold."

DRILLING FOR OIL

First discovered in Texas in 1901, oil has provided vital revenue to the state ever since; at the beginning of the 21st century, this region was supplying one-third of the country's oil.

Children in New Orleans make music in the street.

HORSE RACING IN KENTUCKY

The celebrated Kentucky Derby was first held in 1875. Each year, thousands of enthusiasts fill the main spectator area (the infield) shown here; wealthy patrons use the grandstand. The event's success inspired the local breeding of thoroughbreds for which the state is now famous.

Music

Many major musical styles were born in the South, including gospel, jazz, blues, rock and roll, and country. Music permeates the region's culture, and inspires much of its tourism—thousands of people every year visit New Orleans, Nashville, and Memphis for their musical associations alone.

GOSPEL SOUNDS

Nurtured in Southern churches, gospel music resonates with the passion and expressiveness of early African-American Christians. The name "gospel" comes from combining "God" with "spel," the old English word for story.

NEW ORLEANS

Affectionately nicknamed "the big easy" or "the city that care forgot," New Orleans symbolizes charm, pleasure, and general indulgence. Founded by French explorers in the 18th century, it was later colonized by the Spanish, and it's this influence that is most evident in the city's distinctive architecture.

New Orleans is famous for its *Mardi Gras* celebrations, when merrymakers fill the streets.

Friends and neighbors join in by beating the rhythm on empty cardboard boxes.

COUNTRY NOTES

The hub of the country-music universe is Nashville, Tennessee. Influenced by the ballad and folk traditions of early British immigrants, country music uses melodic guitar, fiddle, and voice to express basic emotion. Since it first became popular in the early 20th century, the style has spawned several related genres such as country-rock, western, bluegrass, and rockabilly music.

Western states

BIRTHPLACE OF SUCH POWERFUL American icons as the cowboy and the movie star, the Western region of the US also contains some of the most breathtaking landscapes in the world: the Rocky Mountains, the Grand Canyon, the Death Valley desert, and the stunning national parks of Yellowstone and Yosemite.

MOVIE CITY

Gwyneth Paltrow poses for photographers at Hollywood's annual Academy Award ceremony. California's film industry has spread the influence of American culture to almost every corner of the world.

WATER WONDERLAND

California's climate and location make it ideal for water sports. Windsurfing was invented here in 1968 when two friends—a surfer and a sailor—decided to combine their passions.

WINTER SCENE

Colorado is North America's premier destination for skiers. Famous for its celebrity visitors and residents, the pretty resort of Aspen (shown here) is totally surrounded by mountains.

LAS VEGAS

The extravagant glamour of Las Vegas has made this Nevada city one of the world's gambling meccas. Here, fabulous hotels offer 24-hour gaming in opulent casinos where drinks are always on tap, and where there are no windows or clocks to remind players of the outside world.

WEST COAST METROPOLIS

San Francisco is built on rugged terrain that dominates its landscape. The cable car was designed in 1873 by Scots-born Andrew Hallidie to replace the carriage-pulling horses that were often injured on the treacherous slopes.

WINE LAND

Northern California, the heart of America's wine country, produces a number of vintages that equal Europe's finest. Here, skilled workers in the Napa Valley harvest Cabernet Sauvignon grapes for one of the region's celebrated red wines.

THE FIFTH OF MAY

Mexicans living in the US celebrate their countries' friendship at the *Cinco de Mayo* (5th May) festival. Held in various cities (this one is San Diego), it honours a Mexican victory over the French in 1862.

As part of the *Cinco de Mayo* festival, dancers in long ruffled dresses take to the streets, twirling gracefully to traditional guitar music.

THE ALOHA STATE

Admitted to the union in 1959, modern-day Hawaii provides a tourist paradise for visitors from all over the world. Here, adorned with flowery *leis* around their necks, local girls perform their ancient ritual dance, the *hula*.

Back at the ranch

One of the industries on which Arizona was founded, cattle ranching is still important to the state's economy. Today, in addition to working ranches, there are many that cater to tourists wanting to experience cowboy life first hand. This one is in the Coconino National Forest.

RIDE 'EM COWBOYS

Virtually everywhere that cattle ranching is established, its essential skills—often in extreme and specialized form—are displayed as some kind of entertainment. Here, at the Green Days Rendezvous Rodeo in Wyoming, a courageous cowboy rides a bucking bronco.

The wild ones

SAVING OREGON'S FERAL HORSES

WHEN EARLY PIONEERS BEGAN RAISING HORSES in the Oregon desert, a number of spirited creatures regularly broke through their restrictive fencing and headed for the open range. Also, when times were so hard that desperate ranchers could not afford to buy feed, they would release their prize stock to fend for themselves rather than allow them to starve. For decades, the wild herds doubled in size every few years, and thousands were captured by opportunists and sold off for slaughter. Finally, in 1971, Oregon's legislature passed the Wild Free-Roaming Horses and Burros Act, which assigned responsibility for their care to the state Bureau of Land Management. Today, the BLM manages the rangeland so it is able to support the herds, and makes sure that sick and injured animals are cared for. Every year, they also gather in hundreds of healthy horses and burros (donkeys) and find permanent homes for them under the hugely successful "Adopt-a-Horse" program.

The Midwest

SOMETIMES CALLED "HEARTLAND US," the Midwestern region includes the legendary plains that roll across states like Nebraska and North and South Dakota, the fertile farming lands that typify Kansas, Iowa, Oklahoma, and Wisconsin, and the Great Lakes states lying farther east, with their huge industrial centers.

TWIN CITIES
Spanning the Mississippi River, the Minnesota cities of Minneapolis and St. Paul are collectively known as the Twin Cities. Traditionally called "the last city of the East," St. Paul sits directly opposite Minneapolis (shown here), "the first city of the West."

ALL THAT JAZZ
The establishment of a strong jazz culture in the large Midwestern cities came from the huge migration of Southern black workers in the early 20th century. Here, the tradition is carried on in a Chicago jazz club.

Traditional American footballs are made from pigskin.

Iowa is a predominantly agricultural state containing hundreds of small farming communities like this one.

FOOTBALL
Like most small boys, these Micro League players are passionate about football. This is a fairly violent sport, but all participants wear tough helmets and thick padding. Football fans tend to support their local team; important Midwest teams include the Green Bay Packers (Wisconsin), the Cleveland Browns (Ohio), the Chicago Cubs (Illinois), and the St. Louis Rams (Missouri).

Farming country

The image of the agricultural Midwest is so firmly established that it has its own place in popular culture: Rodgers and Hammerstein's *Oklahoma* celebrates corn that grows "as high as an elephant's eye," while the farmlands of Kansas play a featured part in both *The Wizard of Oz* and *Little House on the Prairie*.

MAJOR CROPS

Although a wide range of crops is grown in this area, the three most important are wheat, soy beans, and corn. Historical evidence suggests that grain of some kind has been planted here since about 1840.

1 Wheat
Kansas—"the wheat state"—is the country's leading producer of the grain, with roughly one-third of the state's farms devoted to this crop alone.

2 Soy beans
Half the entire world soy-bean crop comes from the United States, and most of this is grown in the Midwest. This large farm is in Wisconsin.

3 Corn
Over a third of all the corn grown worldwide comes from the Midwest region, which is sometimes known as the "Heartland."

DAIRY FARMING

Widely known as "Dairyland," Wisconsin is home to as many cows as people—about four million in each case. As well as milk, vast amounts of butter and cheese are made here, often by farming families descended from the Swedish and German immigrants who poured into the state at the end of the 19th century.

Organic farming as practiced by these Wisconsin-based enthusiasts is the fastest-growing agricultural sector in the country.

Alaska

LIVING IN THE NORTHERNMOST PART OF THE US

THE ARCTIC IS AN UNLIKELY PLACE FOR MAN TO LIVE. The extreme weather and temperature conditions make it very difficult to survive there. Thousands of years ago the Inuit people mastered the art of survival in the cold and learned to lived successfully off the land. Life for the Inuit, however, started to change following the purchase of Alaska by the US in 1867. In the 20th century, technology made it possible for others to live comfortably in Alaska, and people started to arrive when it was discovered that the area was rich in natural oil and gas as well as gold. The oil and mining companies moved in and the trans-Alaska oil pipeline—which carries millions of gallons of oil every day across the country—was built. The challenge for the Alaskan people today is to reclaim their cultural identity as well as move forward in the modern world. The clash continues over oil retrieval and the preservation of the polar environment.

AMISH

THE PLAIN PEOPLE

ORIGINALLY PART OF THE PROTESTANT MENNONITE church, the Amish order originated in Switzerland in the 16th century. Persecuted cruelly in a Catholic age—even martyred in some countries—many of their people headed for the United States, whose founders promised freedom of religion. Today, there

GETTING AROUND

The Amish are not permitted to own motorized vehicles, so they drive horses and buggies instead of cars. This limits the distance they can travel easily from their stable, fairly insular, communities. If they do need to visit far-flung relatives, they are happy to make the journey by plane, train, or bus.

Home on the farm

Amish people live in small farming communities. Their pretty white homes are cozy and practical, with heat from wood or coal stoves, power from low-voltage generators, and light from gas lamps. There are no private telephones, but groups of neighbors often install a single, communal phone for emergencies.

ALL FOR ONE

When people need a new house or barn, their friends all join together to help them build it.

1 Making plans
Amish Elders plan a barn-building session for a newlywed couple. The construction itself is called a "raising"; the whole gathering is called a "frolic."

2 Team effort
During the morning, neighborhood men assemble the frame of the traditional barn. Amish women contribute by preparing meals for the workers.

3 Final result
By the end of the work day the task has been completed. The design of Amish barns, with their steeply pitched roofs, has not changed for over a century.

The Amish believe that working with animals is part of God's plan for them to be close to nature.

LIVING ON THE LAND

The Amish work mainly in agriculture or related trades like blacksmithing and saddlery. Although their farm machinery is often modern in design, it is always horse powered. Some of the yield they produce is consumed within the community, but much of it is traded with outsiders (or *Englishers* as the Amish call them).

are no Amish in Europe, and over 80 percent still live where their ancestors settled, in the states of Pennsylvania, Indiana, and Ohio. The order was named after one of their early leaders, Jacob Amman, who laid down their

defining principles: living apart from the world, remaining close to the land, supporting one another, and shunning any form of adornment. This last rule has led the Amish to be known as "the plain people."

HOME LIFE

Families are usually large and closely knit. Discipline is strong, but Amish parents recognize and allow a limited period of adolescent rebellion. The term they use for this—*rumm-shpringa* (meaning running around)— is the equivalent of "sowing wild oats."

NIMBLE FINGERS

Apart from things like underwear and men's suits, which tend to be bought from specialty stores, an Amish family's clothing is made by the women. The sewing machines they use are powered by treadle rather than electricity. The Amish are also known for their patchwork and quilting skills, and their quilts are widely sold to bring in extra money.

Young girls learn how to sew from their mothers.

Amish clothing is plain and dark. Single women wear nothing on their heads (except to church); married ladies wear white caps.

LEARNING BY EXPERIENCE

Children go to Amish schools until they're about 13. After that, they gain the skills they need through on-the-job training: boys are apprenticed on a farm or in a workshop; girls work at home.

AMERICAN INDIANS

EXPERTS AGREE THAT THE INDIGENOUS PEOPLES OF North America originally came from Siberia, trekking across an Ice-Age land bridge

THE FIRST INHABITANTS OF THE US

BRAVE WORDS

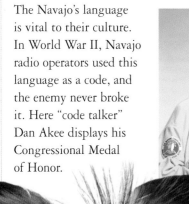

The Navajo's language is vital to their culture. In World War II, Navajo radio operators used this language as a code, and the enemy never broke it. Here "code talker" Dan Akee displays his Congressional Medal of Honor.

Proud nations

Native Americans are usually categorized according to the regions they first settled: Plains, Northeastern Woodlands, Southwest, etc. Within each category, there are a number of separate groups, or nations. Across the country though, these groups are linked by a deep pride in their heritage and a fierce determination to keep their cultures alive.

PAINTING IN THE SAND

As part of their healing ritual, the Navajo people of the Southwest create delicate and beautiful sand paintings. Once, these were destroyed as soon as they were created, but now many are preserved, or their designs captured on special rugs and textiles.

HONORED CRAFT

Navajo textiles have been highly valued since the 19th century, and all the relevant skills and tools are passed down from mother to daughter. Typical blankets have strong graphic designs interpreted in bright colors.

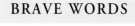
Traditional Navajo houses are called hogans.

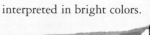
Navajo craftspeople make intricate silver-and-turquoise jewelry.

to present-day Alaska. Later, they spread across the continent and formed separate groups. Today, surviving American Indians communities vary widely, both in their customs and rituals, and in the degree to which they have preserved their traditional ways. Many exploit the widespread interest in their history by becoming involved in the tourist trade—often by selling objects they produce using unique and time-honored craft skills.

IMAGE AND REALITY

The Sioux Nation is the most like Hollywood Indians. Together with the Cheyenne, these Plains people defeated the 7th US Cavalry at Little Big Horn in 1876, killing its leader, General Custer. In 1890, Custer's men took revenge when they slaughtered the Sioux at Wounded Knee, South Dakota. These modern descendents are visiting the site, which has come to symbolize Indian rights.

WEARING THE PAST

Historical Sioux dress involves many of the elements associated with American Indian clothing: feathered headdresses, fringed leather, beadwork, quillwork, and moccasins. Today, most American Indians wear casual clothing for every day, and save their full regalia for ceremonial occasions or tourist display.

PRINCIPAL PEOPLE

Native to the Southeast region, the Cherokee Nation—who, in their own language, call themselves the "principal people"—practice a number of traditional crafts, perhaps the best known of which is basket-making; they are also skilled potters, carvers, and weavers.

CHEROKEE CHIEF

Principal Chief of the Cherokee Nation of Oklahoma from 1985 to 1995, Wilma Mankiller was the first female in modern history to lead a major American Indian people. Her family name is an old military title given to the honored figure entrusted with protecting a Cherokee village.

LIVING HISTORY

This re-created Cherokee settlement in North Carolina provides a popular attraction for tourists, and helps the people to preserve their centuries-old heritage. Here, a young Cherokee girl uses traditional skills and designs to weave a collection of colorful belts.

MEXICANS

THERE ARE MORE PEOPLE IN MEXICO THAN in any other Spanish-speaking country in the world, including Spain, and its population is still increasing rapidly. Of the total number, about 60 percent are *Mestizo*

MULTI-COLORED CULTURE

New World mix

In common with much of South America, Mexico has a culture that blends influences from its indigenous population with those of the Spanish who defeated the Aztecs and colonized the country during the 16th century. Mexico remained under Spanish rule for 300 years, achieving total independence only in 1821.

LOOKING TOWARD THE PAST
Deceptively modern in feel, these shops in the city of Oaxaca have been built in an early colonial style distinguished by simple shapes, flat roofs, and wide doors and windows with contrasting borders.

ART FOR ALL

During the 20th century, Mexican artists led a movement to bring art to the people by putting it on public buildings. This Mexican culture mosaic is at the University Library in Mexico City.

Mexican women buy fresh fruit and vegetables daily at the local market, like this one in Mérida, Yucatán.

(of Amerindian and Spanish descent), 30 percent are Amerindian, and 10 percent are European—mostly Spanish. Through most of its history, Mexico has been strongly agricultural (the people of this land were among the first to cultivate crops rather than hunt and gather). Today, relatively few Mexicans are involved in agriculture; some work in industry, while over half are employed in the service sector.

INDUSTRY
Electronic equipment is one of Mexico's top exports to the US. In this small southern factory, components are being assembled.

WEAVING
Many traditional textiles are woven on backstrap looms, named for the belt support that fits around the weaver's waist.

MARIACHI MUSIC
Often associated with romance (the name comes from the French word for marriage), *mariachi* bands date from the 19th century. They play at weddings and parties, and ardent suitors hire them to serenade their *enamoradas* (lovers).

THE CULTURE OF THE HORSE
Mexican cowboys are called *charros*, and their special skills and rituals are known as *charrería*. *Charreadas* are rodeo-style events that involve impressive displays of horsemanship, and related skills like lassoing from the saddle, all performed in elaborate costume.

FAMILY LIFE
Mexican families tend to be large and close, with grown-up children living at home. Many women have outside jobs, and while middle-class mothers often have domestic help, poorer mothers do not.

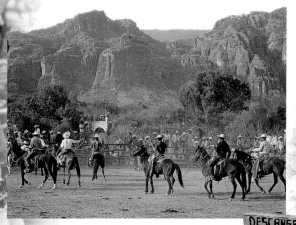

Today, most performing *charros* are wealthy ranchers.

THE DAY OF THE DEAD
According to ancient Amerindian belief, the dead come back to visit their loved ones on one day each year: the *Día de los Muertos*, or Day of the Dead. Despite strong efforts, the Spanish were unable to destroy this belief or the rituals associated with it, but they did give it a Catholic veneer by moving it to All Saints' Day on November 1. Here, a family group keeps a graveside vigil on that day.

SOMETIMES SEEN AS A PALER VERSION OF THE UNITED STATES,

CANADIANS

A CULTURAL MOSAIC

Canada (the second largest country in the world after Russia) actually has a strong national and cultural identity of its own. Apart from bountiful natural

Mix and blend

Most Canadians are of French or British descent, but large Italian, Ukranian, German, and Asian communities are established here too, along with those of other cultures and native ("First Nations") groups. While the US takes pride in blending nationalities (the "melting-pot" effect), Canada has a mosaic-style multiculturalism that respects the identity of each people.

PLAYING TO WIN
While lacrosse is Canada's national sport, ice hockey inspires a public passion that makes it top unofficial contender. Here, with the speed and energy that characterize the game, a Canadian player competes against the USSR in the Calgary Olympics.

INDUSTRIAL STRENGTH
During the 20th century, manufacturing overtook agriculture and the exploitation of natural resources to dominate Canada's economy. Here, a skilled worker adjusts components at a Ford car plant in Ontario.

CITY FISHING
With the Vancouver skyline as a backdrop, two intrepid fishermen position their nets in English Bay, near the city center. Canada's waters, both inland and coastal, are ideal for fishing, a hugely popular recreational activity as well as an important commercial venture.

A TASTE OF EUROPE

In the province of Quebec, not only is the language French, but the culture and the urban landscapes that support it also feel very European. This typical street scene in the old part of Quebec City, for example, could almost be set somewhere in France.

resources, stunning landscapes, and a famously tolerant, law-abiding society, for example, it offers one of the highest standards of living anywhere in the world. Canada was first colonized in the 17th and 18th centuries by France and Britain. While both influences are still obvious, modern Canada (a parliamentary democracy) is a member of the British Commonwealth, with Queen Elizabeth II as its head of state.

GROWTH INDUSTRY

Lumber is one of Canada's most important natural resources; for the western province of British Columbia, lumber (and related trades like the pulp-and-paper business) constitutes the main industry.

1 Tree felling
On Lyell Island, in BC's Queen Charlotte group, a logger cuts down a large tree. Evergreen trees from British Columbia make up about half of all Canada's timber.

2 Water ride
Felled logs are usually transported to the lumber or paper mill by water. Here, the driver of a "winder boat" rounds up loose logs on their way for processing.

3 Cutting up
Instead of being transported to a mill, cut tree trunks are sometimes trimmed into posts or planks on a portable sawmill taken to the forestry site.

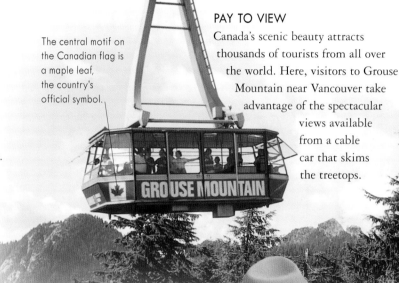

The central motif on the Canadian flag is a maple leaf, the country's official symbol.

PAY TO VIEW
Canada's scenic beauty attracts thousands of tourists from all over the world. Here, visitors to Grouse Mountain near Vancouver take advantage of the spectacular views available from a cable car that skims the treetops.

ROYAL CANADIAN MOUNTED POLICE
Originally based in northwestern Canada (and called Northwest Mounted Police), this famous force gained its Royal Charter in 1904. In 1920, their responsibilities were expanded to include the enforcement of federal laws countrywide, and they became the RCMP. Today, the familiar uniform is purely ceremonial.

MUSICAL RIDE
Developed by early Mounties to amuse themselves and show off their riding skills to the community, the RCMP Musical Ride is based on cavalry drills. This theatrical display is performed across the country during the summer months.

Cowboy carnival
CALGARY STAMPEDE

FOR 10 DAYS IN THE MIDDLE OF JULY, the city of Calgary in southern Alberta plays host to one of the biggest rodeos in the world, the Calgary Stampede. Although the Stampede is a major tourist attraction, the competitors are genuine cowboys and cowgirls, as opposed to fringed and beaded performers, and some of the events are extremely dangerous; this is widely considered to be the roughest of all rodeos. Among the best-known and most popular attractions are the heart-stoppingly treacherous chuck-wagon races that are held every night of the competition; the World Championship final provides the traditional highlight of the Stampede's last evening.

OF THE MORE THAN 30 MILLION PEOPLE WHO LIVE in

FIRST NATIONS

CANADA'S NATIVE PEOPLES

modern-day Canada, only about two percent are aboriginal. This category is divided into three: the First Nations, or Indians (like the

The world of the Iroquois

The Iroquois are a federation of First Nations people (Mohawk, Oneida, Cayuga, Onondaga, Seneca, and Tuscarora) who originally inhabited the forests of the northeastern United States and southeastern Canada. Today, more than half live in Canada. The Iroquois call themselves *Haudenosaunee*, meaning "people of the longhouse," after their large, traditional dwellings.

BADGES OF HONOR

Two generations of Mohawks attend a traditional ceremony. Although historically Iroquois men wear feathers as a badge of their nation, the style of headdress (and shirt) shown here is usually associated with Plains Indians. Today, many groups have adopted Plains dress to express their pan-Indian identity.

SIX NATIONS POW WOW

Throughout much of North America, the pow wow—a festive meeting between the members of one or more nations—is a native tradition. This one, held at the Six Nations Iroquois Reserve near Brantford, Ontario, features all the singing, dancing, feasting, and color that characterize these celebrations.

NATIVE SPORT

The ancient Iroquois game of *tewaarathon*, known as lacrosse, is widely enjoyed in many countries. Today, the Iroquois Nationals are the only indigenous team in the world to take part in an international sporting competition. Here, a group of Mohawk boys play informally.

Haida and the Tlingit in the west, and the Iroquois, Algonquin, and Cree in the central and eastern regions); the Métis, a mixed-race group that originated from unions between French-Canadian fur traders and native women; and the Inuit in the north. All these people have very individual cultures, but they share a strong and growing pride in their indigenous heritage.

WITHOUT FEAR

Since many apparently lack a fear of heights, Iroquois men often work on building sites. Iroquois crews have helped to build such celebrated projects as the Empire State Building, the Golden Gate Bridge, and the world's tallest free-standing structure—the CN Tower in Toronto (left).

Haida life

Unlike many peoples, the Haida have always had rich natural food resources, which encouraged them to trade with other groups. As a result, elaborate social ceremonies—many concerned with skills and status—developed between the various trading groups.

BUTTON BLANKETS

These dancers are wearing ceremonial button blankets, which were once made by sewing shell fragments onto blankets traded from the Europeans. Now, bought buttons and blankets fulfill the same functions.

Headdresses are stylized figures of sea creatures, animals, birds, and mythical beings.

TOTEM POLES

For the native people who make them, totem poles are important cultural and historical documents. They are created to record a family's history, or to mark significant milestones such as the death of a leader.

1 Carving
The animals carved on a totem tend to be mythical figures that represent families or clans. Human figures often portray the pole's owner.

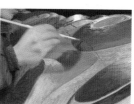

2 Painting
Of all the totem poles made by indigenous Northwestern people, those of the Haida feature the most beautiful and intricate painting.

3 Raising
The heavy poles are hauled upright by large groups of people. They use four sets of ropes in each direction, and a supporting X-frame.

FLOATING TREES

The Haida also carve and paint beautiful dugout canoes, which they once traded to other Pacific-coast peoples. The giant cedars that make the best canoes grow in the Queen Charlotte Islands off British Columbia. The Haida know this territory—their homeland—as *Haida Gwaii*—"islands of the people."

INUIT

THE RETURN OF "OUR LAND"

IN 1999 THE CANADIAN GOVERNMENT GAVE BACK part of the Northwest Territories to the Inuit. The new land, called Nunavut, which means "our land," has been occupied by the Inuit for 4,000 years. For centuries the Inuit lived

IGLOOLIK

Igloolik is a small town on an island in Foxe Basin. In 1932 the Hudson's Bay Trading Company built the town as a trading post and the Inuit were lured away from their nomadic settlements to the Western luxuries of the town. Although Western food, even junk food, is available in Igloolik, the local people still like to rely on meat from the land, such as caribou (wild reindeer), walrus, seal, whale, and birds.

LANGUAGE—INUKTITUT

The Inuit language, *Inuktitut*, is widely used in the North with varying dialects. In *Inuktitut* there are 125 different words for snow and ice! This is actually essential when snow conditions are vital for survival.

Inuktitut characters	Inuktitut word	Meaning
◁⊃ᶜ	aput	snow
ᴦ d	siku	ice
ᖃᵃᖕᓂᖅ	qanniq	falling snow
∧ᖅᴦᖅ	piqsiq	blowing snow
◁▷ᐱᖅ	auviq	snow ideal for igloos

Here are some familiar *Inuktitut* words:

Igloo - *house*

Anorak - *windproof coat*

Kayak - *long, thin boat suitable for one person*

CARIBOU SPOOKS

The Inuit sometimes build a structure, called an *Inukshuk*, on raised ground to help them navigate. They also use it as a caribou spook in the hope that the caribou will think it is a man and run in the opposite direction toward the hunter.

Inukshuk

THE IGLOO MYTH

Contrary to popular belief, the Inuit do not live in igloos. The snow houses that we know as igloos are only temporary shelters for hunters. However, igloo actually means "house" in *Inuktitut* so technically they do live in igloos!

1 Building an igloo
The hunter must find a site containing snow that is perfect for making an igloo. Blocks of snow of the same size are cut using a snow knife.

2 Starting the wall
The skillful builder stands the bottom blocks upright, slightly leaning inward. He shapes and fits each block so that there are no gaps between them.

3 The finished shelter
As the walls rise, the angle of each block increases, and a large fitted cap-block completes the domelike structure.

without much outside contact and developed a tough way of life that suited their frozen environment. Since their integration into the political structure of Canada, their lives have modernized in many aspects.

However, the Inuit make efforts to keep their traditions—old superstitions combine with Christianity, dogsleds run alongside skidoos, and raw meat is eaten along with prepackaged meals.

The modern hunt

The Inuit still hunt out on the ice for valuable meat and fur, and can be away from home for a month or more. They use snowmobiles or dogsleds, and guns. The hunters talk to each other over radios, known as *uvaq*, which means "over," named after the word they heard so often during transmissions.

LIFE ON THE LAND
It is a difficult and not very prosperous life as a full-time hunter. However, there are some families who have returned to the land to live in camps all year round. The Canadian Government now helps financially in an effort to try to regain some of the Inuit traditions.

ON THIN ICE
The hunter takes a flat-bottomed boat out onto the ice floe so that when he has shot an animal in the water he can paddle to retrieve it. It is essential to use a boat since the ice can break up easily.

An igloo may keep out some cold, but in temperatures of -40°F (-40°C), the inside will still be a chilly -14°F (-10°C).

GREENLANDERS

MOST OF THE PEOPLE WHO LIVE ON THE WORLD'S biggest island (it's more than three times the size of Texas) are descended from Inuit groups and from

MODERN LIFE IN A FROZEN WORLD

Proud land

Although it's part of Denmark, Greenland has had wide-ranging powers of self-rule since 1979. Elected every four years, the Greenlandic parliament, called the *Landsting*, oversees most domestic legislation, including the country's modern and efficient health, welfare, and education systems.

MIXED FEELINGS
On the first day of school, children wave their national flag—the flag of Denmark. Greenland is very dependent on Denmark: most of its money comes from the Danish government, which also runs its foreign affairs and legal system. Some people resent this, though, and want to be totally independent.

SUMMER CRAFT
Hunting is an important industry in Greenland. Some Inuits still catch seals, walruses, and small whales from traditional boats called kayaks. To make them light enough for one man to carry, these were originally covered with seal skin. Today, this has been replaced by plastic-coated canvas.

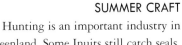

RELIABLE TRANSPORTATION
These strong huskie dogs are harnessed up to pull an old-fashioned sled. While snowmobiles are sometimes used to travel across icy terrain, they are not allowed in many places because the noise they make frightens animals and scares away game. For this reason, and because machines tend to break down and run out of fuel, traditional transportation is often the best.

Polar bear pants.

RULES OF HUNTING
Federal law dictates which animals can be hunted with guns. Hunters, who are mainly Inuit (Greenlandic Inuit are called *Inughuit*) cannot shoot narwhal, for instance, but they can shoot *nanuq*, the great polar bear. There are also limits on the numbers that can be killed. Such legislation not only protects species, but it also acknowledges the Inuit view that animals have spirit owners who demand respect.

Scandinavians: Greenland is a largely self-governing territory owned by Denmark. Since almost all the land is permanently covered with thick ice, only about 57,000 people live there, mainly scattered along the southernwestern fringe. Greenland has two official languages: Danish and Greenlandic, an Inuit dialect peppered with Danish words. Many locals, however, feel strongly that only Greenlandic should be recognized.

COMMUNITY LIFE

Greenlanders live mainly in urban centers like the pretty harbor town of Ilulissat. Within each town or city, there are conventional roads, but these do not usually link one center with another—people travel long distances by air. Housing is modern and well insulated, and shopping is done in ordinary supermarkets. Most produce is imported, though, and meat from seabirds, seals, and whales is sold alongside beef and lamb.

FISHY PROFITS

Greenland's fishing industry produces 95 percent of its commercial revenue. There are more than 200 species of fish and seafood in the island's waters, but the principal trade is in cold-water prawns and halibut. Fishermen sell most of their produce through wholesale companies like this one, where halibut is being packed for shipment.

HISTORIC CRAFT

Greenland attracts large numbers of tourists, many of whom take home traditional *tupilak* figures carved by the Inuit from soapstone, caribou antler, or whale tooth. Typical examples like these represent mythical creatures from Inuit legend.

COLORFUL CLOTHING

Greenlandic dress is one of the few national costumes that involve pants for women. Featuring intricate motifs, beading, and sometimes even lace, the outfit always includes high boots: white ones for young unmarried girls; red for those who are married; and blue or yellow for older women.

The People of Central America & the Caribbean

THE NARROW LAND MASS and the sprinkling of islands that lie between North and South America are home to a wide variety of peoples. In general, they are *Mestizo* or *Ladino*—a mix of indigenous American and immigrant ancestry.

Red, gold, and green are the colors of Rastafarianism.

RASTAFARIANS

The ancestors of today's Afro-Caribbeans were taken to the islands from Africa as slaves. The Rastafarian religion, founded in Jamaica in 1930, involves the beliefs that Emperor Haile Selasse of Ethiopia is the Messiah, and that his followers will one day return to their homeland. The word Rastafarian comes from "Ras Tafari," Haile Selassie's given name.

PANAMA CANAL

Opened on August 15, 1914, the Panama Canal took nearly 8,000 miles (13,000 km) off the journey from New York to San Francisco, and brought money and jobs to Central America. Its construction, paid for by the US and France, took 34 years and involved the loss of over 30,000 lives.

THE WAY TO SAN JOSÉ

Most large cities in Central America were founded centuries ago by the first colonists; their modern face blends this historic past with hallmarks of the modern world such as glass-walled buildings, and massive public sculptures. Shown here is downtown San José, the capital city of Costa Rica.

Danger in paradise

The beautiful Caribbean islands (this idyllic beach is in Cuba) attract thousands of visitors with considerable spending power. The same landscapes, though, are also vulnerable to severe weather conditions such as hurricanes, which regularly destroy lives and property.

The islands of the Caribbean feature white sandy beaches fringed with graceful palm trees.

HOME AND AWAY

British colonists introduced the game of cricket to the islands they settled. West Indian players, like these in Barbados, are now among the best in the world.

GROWING THINGS

A wide range of fruit and vegetables is grown in the region. Some of this produce is sold for export, but much of it ends up in colorful street markets like this one on Grand Bahama Island.

CELEBRATION

Catholicism is the dominant religion in Central America. To celebrate Good Friday in Antigua, Guatemala, the streets are covered with *alfombras*, or "carpets" made from painted sawdust.

MAKING MUSIC

This region has produced some of the most influential musical styles of recent years, from the *ranchera* sounds of Central America, to styles as diverse as mambo, rumba, calypso, and reggae from the West Indies. This traditional steel-drum band is performing in Soufriere, Saint Lucia.

Steel drums evoke the Caribbean wherever they're played.

THE ORIGINAL INHABITANTS OF THE WEST INDIES WERE the Carib Indians (after whom the Caribbean Sea was named). Apart from isolated pockets, though, they have long since disappeared, and today the islands are populated mainly by the descendents of unions

CRÉOLES

TROPICAL MIX

COLORFUL CAPITAL

In Port au Prince, capital of Haiti, the towering Roman Catholic cathedral is clearly European in style. The exterior, though, is painted bright tropical pink, which forms a perfect backdrop to the vibrant cityscape constantly moving around it.

Best of both worlds

Créole society reflects both French and African culture. Buildings tend to be European in style, with distinctively tropical touches. On the whole, clothing has a conventional Western look that is often interpreted in brilliant sunshine hues. And the Créole language is a unique and expressive blend of African sentence structure and French vocabulary.

SPECIAL DAY

Decked out in frothy white dresses with gloves and veils, these young girls in St. Lucia pose proudly for the camera on the day they take their first communion. Catholicism is the dominant religion in the French West Indies, and people take great pride in observing its rites.

SPIRITS OF THE PAST

A follower of the Vodun religion performs a ritual dance. Strongly associated with Haiti, Vodun arrived with West-African slaves. Like Christianity, it is spirit based, with one supreme God and many lesser dieties (Vodun means "spirit"). Its traditions bear little relation to those of the bizarre fictional cult of Voodoo. ("Voodoo" is an older spelling of Vodun.)

CASH AND CARRY

Many Créole people are very poor, and women regularly walk for days to sell their wares at the nearest market, bearing heavy loads on their head all the way. These Haitian peddlers in Port au Prince have high hopes of selling their precariously stacked supplies of plastic basins and household towels.

between colonists who arrived there in the 15th century and African slaves. The word "creole" originally referred to anyone of European parentage born in the New World. Now, of its several different meanings, the most common, spelled Créole, refers to the people of this heritage who live in the French West Indies (such as St. Lucia, Martinique, Guadaloupe, Dominica, and Haiti), and whose colorful culture reflects their dramatic past.

CRÉOLE SOUNDS

Music is an integral part of Créole culture, and many local rhythms have become popular worldwide: zouk and beguine from Martinique and Guadaloupe, for example, and meringué from Haiti and Dominica. Another dominant musical style is American jazz, as interpreted with a strong Caribbean flavor by this small but enthusiastic band in Guadaloupe.

TABLE TOURNAMENT

Créole men take their dominoes seriously and often play for money. Here, intense concentration shows on the faces of both competitors and observers at an outdoor match in St. Lucia.

SEDUCTIVE LANDSCAPES

The islands of the West Indies are actually the tops of underwater—often volcanic—mountains. Because of this, the landscape of each one consists of central hills or highlands that slope down to lush coastal plains ending in white sandy beaches. These attract visitors from all over the world, and the resulting tourism is one of the two most important industries in the region; the other is farming.

Exotic blooms that grow wild in the Caribbean provide this young girl with all the carnival finery she needs.

SPRINGTIME CELEBRATIONS

Virtually every Créole island supports its own colorful carnival involving parades, street parties, costumes, masks, dancing, and feasting. Although preparations begin in January, the festivities themselves are crowded into the few days just before Lent. These happy children are all ready to take part in one of the carnival processions on Guadaloupe.

Traveling by tap-tap
THE PAINTED BUSES OF HAITI

WHEN HAITIANS NEED TO GET ACROSS THEIR SUNNY island or make their way around the capital city, Port au Prince, they hop aboard one of the rickety local buses called tap-taps, which are covered with brightly painted folk motifs. Passengers who want to get off tap several times on the vehicle's wooden side to let the driver know, and this is how the buses got their name. Travel by tap-tap is crowed and noisy (music often blares from loud speakers), but it's also friendly and courteous: in crowded conditions, women and children sit inside, while men cling to the sides and the top, where the baggage is stored.

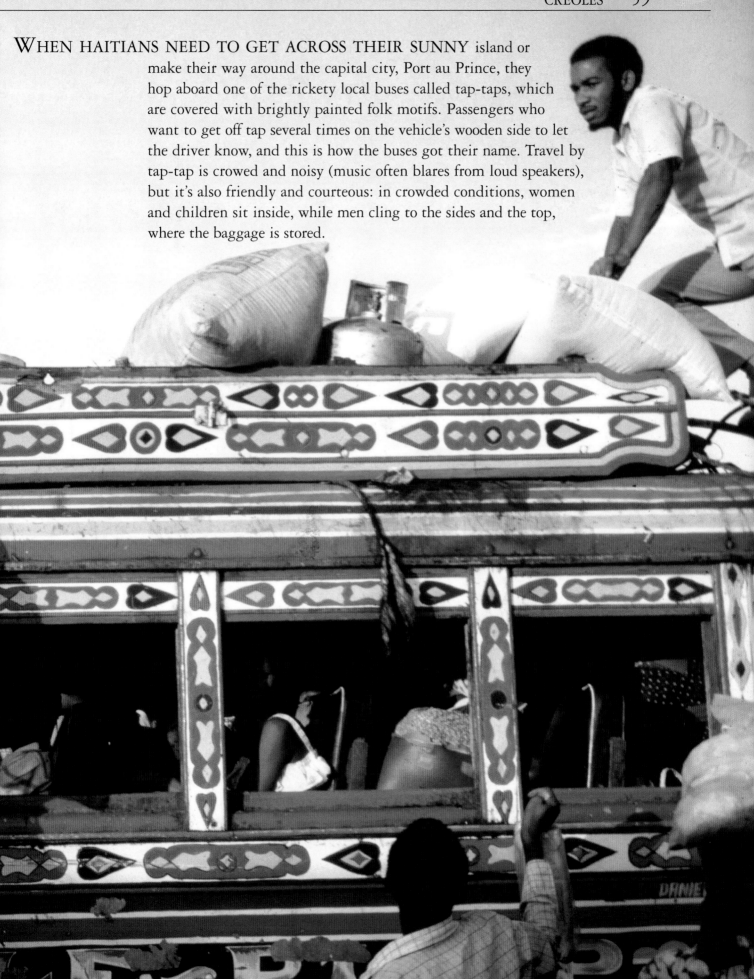

WHILE SOME GROUPS (LIKE THE KOGI IN SOUTH AMERICA)

MISKITU

EMBRACING OTHER WAYS

value cultural purity, the Miskitu people of Central America are almost defined by the exotic mix of peoples they've absorbed. Originating from unions between Indians and Afro-

People of the coast

The Miskitu make their home along the Caribbean coast of Nicaragua and Honduras. This territory, known as the Mosquito Coast, is rich in natural resources, yet the people are poor, and many make their living from subsistence farming, fishing, and hunting. They have their own language, also called Miskitu, and many people speak English and Spanish as well.

MISKITU CAYS

These groups of small cays (islands) off the coast also belong to the Miskitu. People don't live on them, but they regularly hunt for turtles, collect coconuts, and shelter from stormy seas there.

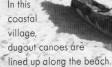
In this coastal village, dugout canoes are lined up along the beach.

TURTLE PEOPLE

The Miskitu were once known as the "turtle people" and green turtles are still a major source of food. Hunters kill them on the beach and leave the tide to wash them clean. These turtles are for domestic consumption only—exporting them is illegal.

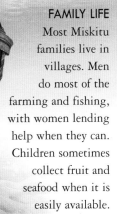

FAMILY LIFE

Most Miskitu families live in villages. Men do most of the farming and fishing, with women lending help when they can. Children sometimes collect fruit and seafood when it is easily available.

Caribbeans, the Miskitu are an assimilating people—they choose partners from a variety of groups, and consider any children to be Miskitu. During the 1800s, Moravian missionaries brought Protestantism to the people, and this is still the main religion. The origin of the name Miskitu is uncertain. It may have been inspired by the English word "musket," since 17th-century pirates supplied the Miskitu with these weapons.

BUILDING A HOUSE

All Miskitu men know how to build a house, since few women would marry a man without this skill. To protect their families from the region's frequent flooding, they usually build their homes on stilts.

1 Making planks
To prepare the lumber, large pine logs are hoisted up onto a platform. A two-man team then uses a long saw to cut each log into planks.

2 Roofing material
Women gather a special kind of palm leaf called *papta* that is used for thatch. When they get to the site, they will tie it into bundles for the men to work with.

3 Taking shape
At this point in the construction process, the frame is up and work has begun on one of the walls. During the dry season, the roof can safely be left until last.

COOL AND DRY

Miskitu houses allow plenty of cool air to flow underneath, across the open porch, and through the windows. Simple shutters swivel into place when it is cold or rainy.

Traditional buildings have thatched roofs like this one, but some modern homes are roofed with zinc.

PASSING THE TIME
In some communities, unemployment runs as high as 85 percent, partly because only 14 percent of the population have access to secondary education.

CROWNING THE KING

In the 17th century, inspired by the English, the Miskitu created their own king; called Jeremy I, he was crowned in 1687. The last king was deposed by the army in 1894. Today, to commemorate their royal line, many communities crown a symbolic king for one day a year.

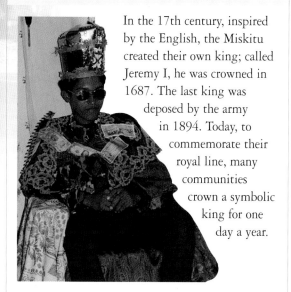

WESTERN INFLUENCE
The culture of the West (especially the US and the English West Indies) has a strong influence on Miskitu life. These boys from the village of Awastara are playing marbles.

KUNA

FRAGMENTS OF A LOST WORLD

AMONG THE LAST OF THE INDIGENOUS PEOPLES who once populated the Panama coast, the Kuna people now live mainly in the islands of the nearby San Blas archipelago. Some elements of their culture are probably of ancient origin; reflecting a

Independent nation

The land inhabited by the Kuna people is known as the Comarca of Kuna Yala ("Kuna Yala" means "Kuna Land"). Since 1938, it has been a self-governing area within the country of Panama, making this the first indigenous group in modern Central America to exercise political control over its own territory.

WOMEN'S WORLD

Kuna society places great value on women—female children are highly desired, daughters tend to inherit family houses, and a husband moves in with his wife's family. One clear expression of this attitude is the fact that women's dress is much more elaborate, colorful, and symbolic than men's clothing.

DIVING FOR GOLD

One uniquely modern tradition involves the luxury ships that constantly cruise the Caribbean. Kuna youngsters row out to meet them, and the passengers throw coins in their direction.

Gold nose rings indicate a woman's status.

From the time of puberty, Kuna girls have their arms and legs tightly bound in beaded wrappings.

DANCING WITH THE PAST

The Kuna value tradition highly, and their culture provides customs and rituals for most life events. Often, these customs are passed along the generations through chants and dances.

ISLANDS IN THE SUN

Kuna Yala consists of 365 islands like this one, and a strip of land on the adjacent Atlantic coast. With the help of environmental groups, the Kuna have established a 232 sq mile (600 sq km) forest reserve on their territory.

spiritual relationship with nature, for example, they create sanctuaries for plants and animals, called Galu, near many of their settlements. Other customs though—such as the colorful way they dress—did not emerge until the 19th century. The Kuna have their own language, also called Kuna. Spanish is their second tongue, and some people—mostly those who trade with tourists—speak a few words of English.

LOBSTER FISHING

At one time, lobster provided the Kuna with dietary protein as well as export revenue. Now, supplies are dwindling, and lobster has become so expensive that local people can't afford it.

SUGAR CANE

Largely agricultural people, the Kuna farm plots of waterside land. Main crops include coconuts, plantains, bananas, and sugar cane, which this matriarch is processing while she puffs on her traditional pipe.

WOVEN CULTURE

One of the best-known Kuna traditions is the making of colorful *molas*—hand-woven panels appliquéd with beautiful patterns or pictures. Although many of them feature authentic folk-art designs, the craft itself is a relatively modern one, inspired by access to both commercial fabrics and, to some degree, images from Western media.

TRADING IN TRADITION

Molas (which were originally intended to be set into women's blouses) are strongly symbolic of Kuna cultural identity, but they are widely valued too by souvenir-hunting tourists and lovers of textile art. Patterns range from graphic shapes and stylized plants and animals, to interpretations of poster images, labels, illustrations, and logos. Resourceful traders use the same technique to produce smaller, more saleable items like bags and pot holders.

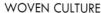

MAYA

PRESERVING THE PAST

THE ANCIENT MAYA HAD ONE OF THE MOST SOPHISTICATED civilizations that ever existed. As well as a practical calendar, a written history, an intricate system of mathematics, and a complex rule of law, they had a hugely impressive arts and crafts tradition. But, by the 10th

The modern way

About six million Maya live in Central America. Like their ancestors, many of them survive by growing maize (Indian corn) or other crops on their land, or by producing woven textiles for sale. In some villages, the men have to leave their families to find work in the cities, or on coffee and cotton plantations in other areas.

Some Mayan textile designs are hundreds of years old.

FEEDING THE FAMILY

Maize is an essential crop for the Mayan people, and it forms a major part of their diet. This busy mother uses ground maize to make *tortillas* (pancakes) over a wood fire, but it can also be served baked, boiled, and made into bread. Supplementing this basic fare are other vegetables (like beans and squash), fruit, and small amounts of meat and fish.

LIVING LEGENDS

Formed by a group of writers, and based in Chiapas in Mexico, the *Sna Jtz'ibajom* theater company brings Mayan myths, legends, and history to life through elaborate plays and puppet shows that tour widely. Their name, *Sna Jtz'ibajom*, means "The House of the Writer."

century, their society had collapsed and split into small groups that were easily overpowered by the Spanish a few centuries later. The people did, however, keep control of both their land and their cultural heritage, both of which have survived into the 21st century. Today, there are over 30 Mayan groups in Central America, mainly in southern Mexico. Some of them even speak a version of the ancient Mayan language.

COMING HOME

Typical Mayan houses are made of locally available materials like wattle and daub (rubble and clay), plaster, and wood. They are usually painted white. In areas with heavy rainfall, homes have palm- or grass-thatched roofs that are steeply pitched, with overhanging eaves to protect the walls. The small plot of land this cottage stands on is enclosed by a stone wall and a length of rush fencing.

The front door has a coat of fresh blue-and-white paint.

Woven checks are a popular choice.

FANCY FEMALES

These days, Mayan men and boys tend to wear plain Western clothing, while women's dress reflects decorative historical elements such as bold borders and colorful embroidery. This barefoot mother-and-daughter pair have chosen traditional skirts and blouses in bright cotton fabrics.

MAYAN MUSIC

The modern marimba, similar to the xylophone, is part of the Mayan musical tradition. Originating from a primitive instrument brought to Central America by early African slaves, it was adopted and developed by the indigenous Mayan people.

HAPPY NEW YEAR

Mayan culture sets great store by New Year. This Guatemalan group is holding a mountainside ceremony to wash away the past and prepare for the year ahead. Mountains have special meaning for the Maya, who believe they house protective spirits.

FIRED EARTH

The entire Mexican village of Amatenango is dominated by its famous women potters. Using the local *terra-cotta* clay, and passing on skills from mother to daughter, these Mayan women have been producing decorative pots and bowls here for centuries.

Terra-cotta means fired earth.

WINTER FESTIVAL

The people of Chichicastenango, Guatemala, commemorate the arrival of the white man in a ceremonial Dance of the Conquistadors, part of their annual winter-soltice festival. This costumed participant wears the mask of Tecum Uman, last Mayan emperor of Guatemala.

THE PEOPLE OF
South
America

Latin America *noun* those parts of either American continent where Spanish and Portuguese are the dominant cultures
Mestizo *noun (and adj)* person of mixed Spanish or Portuguese and Amerindian descent

SOUTH AMERICA

THE CONTINENT OF SOUTH AMERICA COMPRISES 12 countries, plus the dependency of French Guiana. Offshore territories include the Galapagos Islands (Ecuador),

HOME OF THE DISAPPEARING RAIN FOREST

Global position

Joined to Central America by the Isthmus of Panama, South America lies across the equator. Because it is rapidly being destroyed, the vast tropical rain forest around the Amazon River is one of the world's most environmentally sensitive sites.

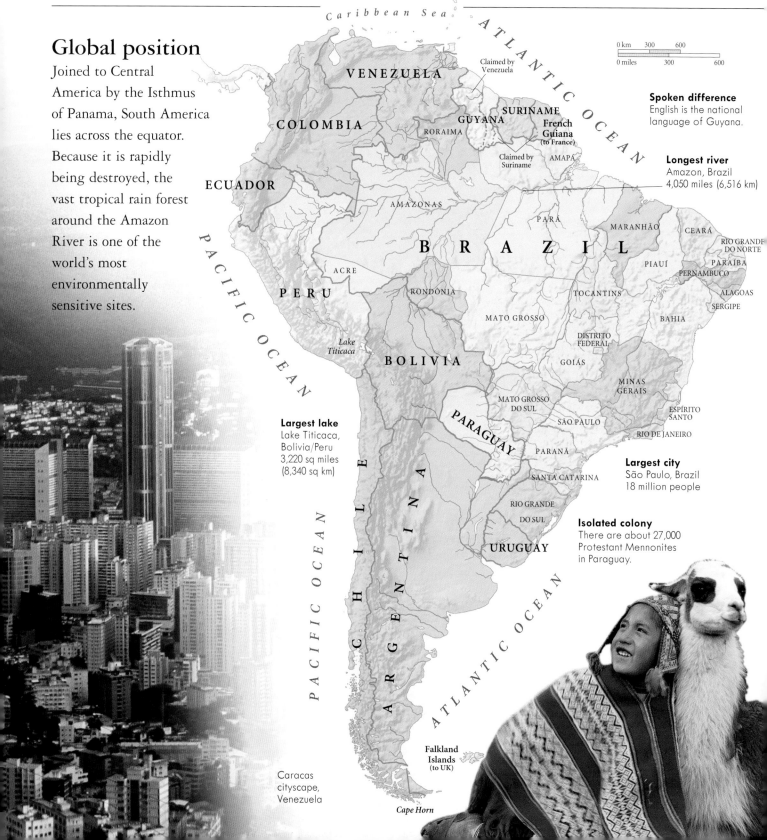

Caribbean Sea

ATLANTIC OCEAN

0 km 300 600
0 miles 300 600

VENEZUELA

Claimed by Venezuela

COLOMBIA

GUYANA SURINAME
French Guiana (to France)

RORAIMA

Claimed by Suriname

AMAPÁ

ECUADOR

AMAZONAS

PARÁ

BRAZIL

MARANHÃO CEARÁ
RIO GRANDE DO NORTE
PIAUÍ PARAÍBA
PERNAMBUCO
ACRE

PACIFIC OCEAN

PERU

RONDÔNIA

TOCANTINS

ALAGOAS
SERGIPE

BAHIA

MATO GROSSO

DISTRITO FEDERAL

Lake Titicaca

GOIÁS

BOLIVIA

MINAS GERAIS

MATO GROSSO DO SUL

ESPÍRITO SANTO

SÃO PAULO

PARAGUAY

RIO DE JANEIRO

PARANÁ

SANTA CATARINA

PACIFIC OCEAN

CHILE

ARGENTINA

RIO GRANDE DO SUL

URUGUAY

ATLANTIC OCEAN

Falkland Islands (to UK)

Cape Horn

Spoken difference
English is the national language of Guyana.

Longest river
Amazon, Brazil
4,050 miles (6,516 km)

Largest lake
Lake Titicaca, Bolivia/Peru
3,220 sq miles (8,340 sq km)

Largest city
São Paulo, Brazil
18 million people

Isolated colony
There are about 27,000 Protestant Mennonites in Paraguay.

Caracas cityscape, Venezuela

the Juan Fernández Islands and Easter Island (Chile), the Fernando de Noronha Archipelago (Brazil), and the Falkland Islands, a British dependency claimed by Argentina as the Islas Malvinas. In terms of both size and population, the biggest country is Brazil. Most people in South America are descended from indigenous Indians, Portuguese or Spanish colonists, African slaves, or a mixture of these groups.

South American statistics

LANGUAGES
Reflecting the region's colonial past, European languages are the most widely spoken. Quechua and Guarani are indigenous tongues.

Portuguese	153 million
Spanish	117 million
Quechua	5 million
Guarani	2.5 million

RELIGIONS
South America is unusual in its religious uniformity. Roman Catholicism, another colonial legacy, dominates significantly.

Roman Catholic	268 million
Protestant	4.3 million
Jewish	889,000
Hindu	365,000

URBAN POPULATION
South America's cities are constantly growing in population. Most of the big urban centers are near the coast.

São Paolo	18 million
Buenos Aires	12 million
Rio de Janeiro	11 million
Lima	8 million

POPULATION BY COUNTRY
Over half the continent's population live in Brazil. French Guiana has the smallest number of people.

Brazil	176 million
Colombia	41 million
Suriname	436,500
French Guiana	182,000

POPULATION

The population of South America is about 350 million, with 76 percent of these people living in urban areas. Currently, the continent's population is growing at a rate of about 7 percent every five years.

Population density (people per sq km)
- below 4
- 4 - 9
- 10 - 14
- 15 - 19
- 20 - 30
- above 30

SOUTH AMERICAN FACTS

PLACES
Number of countries ....12 (plus dependencies)
Highest point ....Cerro Aconcagua, Argentina, 22,833 ft (6,959 m)
Lowest point ....Valdés Peninsula, Argentina, -151 ft (-40 m)

LITERACY RATE
90% of the population

HEALTH
People per doctor 1,100
Proportion of people with access to clean water 86%

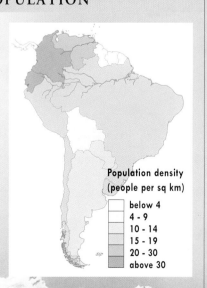

The People of South America

THIS LONG, VAGUELY TRIANGULAR continent was first settled thousands of years ago by adventurous migrants from North America. Descended from the same prehistoric race as the Inuit, First Nations, and American Indian peoples, they wandered across the spectacularly varied landscape they discovered, and eventually inhabited almost every part of it.

HIGHLAND PEOPLE

These Andean shepherds in Bolivia belong to the large Aymara Amerindian group. This people—and their language, which is also called Aymara—live mainly in the highlands of Bolivia, Chile, and Peru.

SPACE-AGE CITY

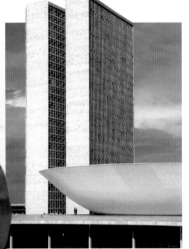

While many South American cities have a historical look, Brasilia, the capital of Brazil, is a strikingly modern metropolis. Here, a tiny human figure enhances the monumental proportions of the city's Congress and Senate Building, designed by Brazilian architects Oscar Niemeyer and Lucio Costa.

FIGHTING FOR THEIR HOME

The number of people living in isolation from the industrial world is dwindling rapidly. Many of those who are left make their home in the vast Amazon rain forest, which is under serious threat from developers who cut down its trees and plunder the region's natural resources.

This Matses Indian boy lives in a small village near the Galvez River in Peru.

AFRICAN ORIGINS

When the European colonizers arrived (see opposite), they built huge plantations and brought over millions of slaves from Africa to work on them. In many parts of South America, particularly in the northeast, descendants of these slaves survive in large numbers.

Clearly of African descent, this mother and child are Maroons from Suriname.

European influences

During the 16th century, the human landscape of South America changed dramatically with the arrival of colonists from southern Europe. Their influence spread quickly and completely, and today many aspects of culture in South America are still dominated by ideas and traditions that originated in Spain and Portugal.

MUSIC

Now an important part of South American music, the guitar was brought over by early Spanish explorers. Their instruments helped them to pass the time on long voyages.

LIQUID HISTORY

Early Europeans who settled in South America brought with them wine making skills from Spain and Portugal. The vines they planted are now the basis of flourishing wine industries in countries like Chile and Argentina.

LACES AND NETS

The skill of lace making arrived in Brazil with the wives of Portuguese fishermen who settled there. The Portuguese word for lace makers is *rendeiras*.

OLD-WORLD DRESS

The traditional clothing worn by Taquile islanders in Lake Titicaca developed from the garments worn by Spanish settlers when they first arrived in Peru.

A MATTER OF FAITH

Roman Catholicism replaced the original belief systems of nearly all the indigenous peoples in South America. This dominance is reflected in the elaborate church architecture that is a feature of virtually every town and city on the continent. Built on the site of an old Inca temple, for example, this cathedral in Cuzco, Peru, clearly reflects Spanish influences.

RELIGIOUS FESTIVAL

Like most indigenous peoples, the Otavalens of Ecuador are largely Catholic. Here, the devout gather for worship on Palm Sunday, their bright costumes contrasting dramatically with the jungle of pale green leaves they have brought to church to mark this special day.

KOGI

GUARDIANS OF OUR WORLD

NATIVES OF THE HIGH SIERRA NEVADA de Santa Marta mountains in northern Colombia, the Kogi are one of the few indigenous Amerindian groups who were not conquered by the Spanish. Descended from the sophisticated Tairona civilization that flourished

MINIATURE WORLD

The 8,000 sq miles (17,000 sq kilometers) of the Sierra Nevada are home to an astonishing variety of ecosystems, from turquoise waters and coral reefs to deserts, plains, rain forests, and glaciers.

ON THE MOVE

Kogi families do not stay in one place, but move between different levels, according to the natural rhythm of the seasons and the fertility of the land. Horses provide the main means of transportation in this steep landscape, which is crisscrossed with narrow paths instead of roads.

The place of creation

The land of the Kogi is set apart from the rest of the continent, in a mountain range near the Caribbean coast. These enlightened people have spent centuries exploring the realms of mind, body, and spirit. They believe that if the rest of humanity (what they call the "younger brother") does anything to harm their sacred homeland, then the whole world will be doomed as well.

NATURE'S CARERS

The Kogi people are convinced that their crops will grow less successfully if the plants are cultivated by men, since women have a stronger and more direct link with fertility and growth. Families move around from season to season so they are able to get the best from all the land they farm without exhausting its goodness.

SHELL SEEKER

An elder gathers shells on the beach for use in one of the main Kogi rituals: the chewing of coca leaves by adult males. Burned shells produce fine white lime powder. When mixed with leaves and saliva in the mouth, it helps the chemical stimulant in the plant to be absorbed.

over 1,000 years ago, the Kogi believe their mountain be the "place of creation" and "the heart of the world." They see themselves as "elder brothers of humanity," and accept the care of our planet as their sacred responsibility. A deeply spiritual people, they place great value on communicating with everything around them— including animals, plants, and even rocks—by thought and intuition as well as with words and actions.

GUIDES AND RULERS

The leading figures in Kogi life are called "mamas" (from *mamos* meaning "sun")—they are always male. Acting as healers, priests, and judges, these figures are chosen from birth. They undergo 18 years of training, much of it spent in caves, where they are deprived of daylight. This mama is holding a *popora*—a hollowed-out gourd used to hold lime powder.

SEPARATE LIVES

Kogi families gather in villages when they want to exchange news or make community decisions. When they are there, the men spend much of their time in the *nuhue* ("men's house" or "world house"), the largest and finest building. Even when they are working their land, Kogi families live separately—the men in one hut, and the women and children in another one close by.

SYMBOLIC BUILDINGS

The construction of Kogi huts is closely linked with the people's spirituality. For instance, because their belief system states that the universe has nine levels, every roof has nine layers of thatch, which are meticulously laid in alternating directions.

CARRIER BAGS

Kogi women grow cactus fiber, then weave it into bags called *mochilas*. Worn slung across the chest by the men, these bags hold coca leaves, which are shared with other men as part of the greeting ritual.

TUCKED HIGH IN THE ECUADORIAN ANDES, the valley town of Otavalo has been attracting visitors to its market for hundreds of years. The local people, known as Otavalens, speak Quichua, one of the languages of the old

OTAVALENS

TRADITIONAL TRADERS

A lasting culture

The Otavalens have prospered through their dealings with both the *Mestizo* population (*Mestizos* are of mixed Spanish/Amerindian origin) and the wider commercial world, yet they have kept a powerful sense of their own identity. Not only their language, but also their houses, their clothing, their crafts, and their basic culture are rooted in native tradition.

TEAM SPIRIT

Working outdoors on a simple elevated frame, these country laborers are using a two-man handsaw to turn huge eucalyptus logs into long, straight planks. The lumber they are producing is intended for the roofs of village houses in the Otavalo valley.

Otavalan men dress their hair in a long braid or *shimba* that hangs down almost to their waist.

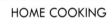

HOME COOKING

Ecuador is a fertile land whose rich soil nourishes a plentiful supply of fruit and vegetables. This girl prepares *calabash*, a long gourd grown there for thousands of years. Inedible when fully grown, the young gourd can be cooked and eaten in a wide variety of ways.

PANPIPES

Popular throughout the Andes, native panpipes are made from reeds of different lengths tied together with plant fiber. This Otavalan man is playing a relatively small set, but some larger versions have as many as 30 pipes.

Inca empire, and many of their customs and rituals are rooted in this ancient and powerful culture. Later, they were heavily influenced by the Spanish colonists, who exploited their traditional craft and weaving skills, taught them new ones, and provided access to extensive markets in other parts of the world. Today, the Otavalen people are among the most prosperous indigenous groups in the whole of South America.

Saturday shopping

There are two main markets in Otavalo—one that supplies food, animals, and household goods to the local people, and one that sells textiles and crafts to the tourists. Saturday is market day, and many of the stalls are open for business before dawn. By midmorning, the local market is closing down, and by noon, even the tourists have drifted away.

PIG FOR THE POT
Otavalen shoppers take special care when it comes to choosing one of their most important purchases—live guinea pigs, known as *cuys*. These animals, which slightly resemble large rabbits with small ears, are kept almost like pets until a special occasion arises. Then they are killed and cooked for the celebration feast.

WORKING TRADITION
Both clothing and domestic textiles play an important part in Otavalo craft heritage. Here, a busy tailor makes practical use of a mechanized sewing machine at his market stall. Behind him hangs a selection of colorful rugs woven from the wool of llamas and alpacas. Both these Andean creatures are distant relatives of the camel.

This flower seller, like many other traders, travels a long way to buy and sell goods at Otavalo market.

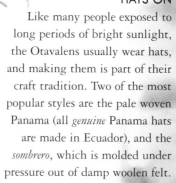

HATS ON
Like many people exposed to long periods of bright sunlight, the Otavalens usually wear hats, and making them is part of their craft tradition. Two of the most popular styles are the pale woven Panama (all *genuine* Panama hats are made in Ecuador), and the *sombrero*, which is molded under pressure out of damp woolen felt.

YAGUA

AIMING POISON DARTS

NATIVE TO THE AMAZON RIVER BASIN in northeastern Peru, the Yagua Indians are one of the last rain-forest people to use blowgun-fired darts for hunting and defense. The darts are tipped with curare, an ancient and deadly poison brewed up from forest roots and leaves. Curare kills almost instantly by causing widespread paralysis—as soon as it reaches the lungs, the victim suffocates. The long blowguns take several days to make and involve a number of different tree and plant materials, but the Yagua get maximum mileage from the specialized skills involved. Like many other isolated groups, they are a focus of increasing interest for intrepid tourists. Taking full advantage of this, their craftspeople have begun to turn out suitcase-sized model blowguns (supplied without poison darts), which they sell to earn ready cash.

YANOMAMI

THE YANOMAMI PEOPLE OF THE AMAZON BASIN are one of the largest and most remote rainforest groups in South America, where they have lived for 50,000 years. Their way of life consists of hunting and fishing,

CARETAKERS OF THE RAINFOREST

Ancient world

The large Yanomami population (there are thought to be over 20,000) live in hundreds of villages scattered through the dense rain forest near the Brazil/Venezuela border. The greatest number live deep inside the forest, while some have settled along the banks of major rivers, including the Negro and the Orinoco.

COMMUNITY LIFE

Between 40 and 300 people live in each Yanomami village; the journey between villages can take anything from a few minutes to several days. Neighboring settlements are independent, yet they keep in constant touch.

MAGIC LIQUID

To make beer from *manioc* (also called sweet cassava), the creamy white root is first mashed, then chewed by village women until it is mixed with their saliva. At this stage, all the women spit it into one large jar where, after a few days, it begins to ferment. Eventually, it turns into a potent drink that is highly valued for both social and ceremonial purposes. This boy hopes his bowl of beer will ward off evil spirits.

FAMILY HOMES

Yanomami communities, which are usually made up of extended family groups, live in huge dwellings called *yanos*; some house up to 400 people, but most are smaller than this. Each *yano* is built in the shape of a large ring, with an open courtyard in the middle for group celebrations and ceremonies.

FOOD AND DRINK

This girl carries a bundle of fruit from the spiny palm tree on her back. The Yanomami diet consists mostly of vegetables and fruit, which the women gather from the forest. These are usually supplemented by meat of some kind, but this is becoming increasingly scarce, since large areas of forest have been destroyed, and with them the habitat of many birds and animals.

HOME COMFORTS

Inside the *yano*, each family has its own area, which is centered around an open fire. Most people sleep in hammocks hung in layers from the ceiling, but some younger Yanomami sleep under the stars.

gathering wild food, and the small-scale farming of subfertile plots. Today the future of the Yanomami is uncertain. Since gold was discovered on their territory during the 1970s, they have endured violence, greed, and infectious diseases at the hands of big business interests intent on exploiting the land. Both multinationals and poor migrants have also caused serious damage to the environment in their desperate search for gold.

RITUAL FOR THE DEAD
The Yanomami include fierce displays in many of their rituals. During funeral ceremonies, for example, warriors perform fantastic dances. Later, the deceased's body is burned and the ashes, along with ground-up bones, are mixed with soup and drunk by friends and family. In this way, they believe, the dead person becomes part of the living.

Ritual warriors cover their heads with white down.

LIVING OFF THE LAND
There isn't much room for farming in the rain forest, but clearing small plots allows the people to grow basic crops. Since most communities move on every few seasons to get the best from the soil, this task is repeated regularly. The working party shown here includes a youngster observing the process; knowledge has to be passed on in practical ways, as the Yanomami have no written language.

DECORATIVE PIERCING
Like some people in Western cultures, the Yanomami use piercing as a form of adornment. According to custom, thin wooden sticks are used; males perforate their bottom lip in the middle only, while females add an extra stick on each side.

KAYAPO

SPEAKING TO THE WORLD

LIKE MANY NATIVE PEOPLE IN THE AMAZON BASIN, the Kayapo Indians are afraid for their rain-forest home, which is steadily being destroyed by the reckless harvesting of its trees. To communicate their fears to the world, they have appointed a unique messenger—a chief called Raoni who travels tirelessly from continent to continent pleading their case. Certainly, Raoni's appearance makes him hard to ignore: on his head is a circle of perfectly matched parrot feathers, handed down through generations like a precious crown. Dominating his face completely, though, is his huge lower lip, stretched since childhood over a series of bigger and bigger balsawood discs. For the Kayapo, this extraordinary feature is an ancient symbol of strength, a quality they value highly. Now, in order to stop the destruction of the rain forest, they need all the strength they can gather.

AS WELL AS BEING THE LARGEST COUNTRY IN South America

BRAZILIANS

LIFE IN THE LAND OF CARNIVAL

by far (it's even bigger than the continental United States), Brazil has one of the world's longest coastlines. Founded in the 16th

City mix

Nearly 80 percent of Brazilians live in cities —the largest are São Paulo and Rio de Janeiro. Most people are Hispanic, but a significant number belong to immigrant communities from Europe, Africa, and the Middle and Far East; there are more Japanese in São Paulo than in any city outside Japan. Each city contains both wealthy, Westernized districts, and areas that are very poor.

STREET LIFE

Clinging to the steep hills behind it, Rio de Janeiro's shantytowns or *favelas* are a triumph of human spirit over deprivation. Assembled from found materials like plastic, sheet metal, and odd bricks, these precarious structures support a complex and lively street culture.

AIMING FOR A GOAL

Soccer was introduced to Brazil by Scottish engineers at the end of the 19th century. Since then, the game has become not just a symbol of patriotic pride, but almost a national obsession, and Brazilian players are among the best in the world. The small boys kicking a ball around this São Paulo *favela* know that becoming a sports hero is one way to escape their bleak surroundings.

CARNIVAL

The exuberant street festival known as Carnival is the most important event in the Brazilian calendar. Once a year, in the days leading up to Ash Wednesday, thousands of costumed revelers pour through the cities, singing, dancing, and playing musical instruments. The most famous of all Brazilian Carnivals is in Rio de Janeiro; here, a fantastic fruity float makes its way down one of the wide thoroughfares.

century by Portuguese colonists and given its independence in 1822, the Federative Republic of Brazil consists of 26 states plus a federal district that, since 1960, has been the setting for a specially created capital city, Brasilia. Together, they accommodate the region's highest population. The name Brazil is believed to come from a Portuguese word for the distinctive red color of brazil wood—*brasa* means "glowing coals."

MAKING COFFEE

Drunk in virtually every country on Earth, coffee is second only to oil as an international commodity, and Brazil is its leading producer worldwide. The raw crop undergoes several stages before it can be exported.

1 Picking

The cherries (fruit) on the coffee plant turn dark red when they are ready to be harvested. Handpicking is labor intensive, but it produces a high-quality crop.

2 Winnowing

Using a large sieve, the cherries are tossed into the air to remove dirt and leaves. This process (called winnowing) prepares them for drying and husking.

3 Tasting

Special tasters process a few of the beans into coffee, then sample it for acidity, body, aroma, and flavor before the rest of the batch is blended and roasted.

FRUIT FOR SALE

Although the Brazilian economy is no longer dominated by agriculture (manufacturing and service industries are also very important), one-third of its workforce is still employed on the land. Some of the country's most profitable exports are fruit crops, especially oranges and bananas.

A DREAM OF URBAN PLANNING

Curitiba in southern Brazil is one of the world's most efficient cities. Uniquely friendly to the environment (two-thirds of all garbage is recycled), it also provides extensive social welfare; here, street children are employed in an urban park.

"MARVELOUS CITY"

People who live in Rio de Janeiro call it the *Cidade Marvilhosa*, or marvelous city. Overlooking Rio, arms outstretched in welcome, stands the famous Statue of Christ the Redeemer, conceived and built in the Art Deco style by engineer Heitor da Silva Costa, and inaugurated in 1931.

ALONG THE NORTHERN COAST OF BRAZIL lies a fertile crescent of

BAHIANS

GRANDCHILDREN OF SLAVERY

land where, in the 16th and 17th centuries, Portuguese settlers established large and wealthy plantations of sugar cane, coffee, and tobacco. To work in the fields, over 3.5

CRUEL HISTORY

Salvador, Bahia's capital, was once the capital of Brazil. Its ultrafashionable Pelourinho district was originally named for the slave-beating sites located here—*pelourinho* means pillory, or whipping post.

Unique hybrid

There are more people of African descent in Brazil than in any other country except Nigeria, and most of them live in Bahia. While the region's culture is rooted in an African past, it has a uniquely seductive Afro-Brazilian identity that draws visitors from all over the world. Today, tourism is Bahia's leading industry.

CARNIVAL

The Salvador carnival, with its exuberant music, dancing, and feasting, is the largest street festival in the world. When it's on, up to three million people— tourists as well as locals—flock into the city. As part of the celebrations, percussion groups called *Blocos Afros* take to the streets.

SUGAR CANE

Ropelike stalks of sugar cane are piled high in a Salvador market. For the workers, the task of harvesting canes is just as backbreaking as it was for their ancestors, as it is still largely done by hand with a machete.

FOOD FOR FRIENDS

Preparing meals by hand is important, since every dish is believed to carry energy from the person who made it. Like many migrant cuisines, Bahian food was created from local produce prepared in the traditional style of the mother country. Here, fish and seafood are particularly plentiful.

million slaves—more than seven times the number that went to the United States—were shipped in from West Africa and sold through teeming human markets. Although slavery was abolished in Brazil in 1888, the direct descendants of these early workers still dominate the present-day state of Bahia. In its early days, this region was known as "the province of the bay"; the name "Bahia" comes from *baia*, the Portuguese word for bay.

Candomblé

The slaves who landed in Bahia were forbidden from practicing their African faith. In order to keep hold of their beliefs, therefore, they resorted to disguise—ancient gods were hidden behind Catholic saints, and familiar customs dressed up as Christian ritual. The new religion that grew out of this strange mix is called Candomblé. Today, it defines not only the spirituality, but also the culture of Bahian life.

SISTERS IN FAITH
Allied to Candomblé is a female society called the Sisterhood of the Good Death. Devoted to the Assumption of the Virgin, its followers (who are all over 40) express their spirituality through street processions, samba dancing, and feasting. This sister is completely clad in white, the color of Candomblé.

Worship takes place in *terreiros*, or houses of Candomblé.

FIRE DANCE
African gods are called *orixás*. Passing a bowl of fire from head to head is part of the Candomblé ritual devoted to Xango, the fire *orixá*. Dancing is another important element of the ceremony: when the movements become wild and frenzied, some believers go into a trance.

GOD OF THE SICK
Contemporary followers of Candomblé summon a grass-shrouded figure of their god Omolú, who they believe causes and cures illness. At one time, Omolú was linked with the Catholic Saint Lazarus.

CAPOEIRA

Cushioned by soft ground, young Bahian men practice *capoeira*, a blend of martial arts and dancing that warrior slaves brought with them from Africa. This move—where one person tosses the other into a midair somersault—is performed on beaches and streets all over the state.

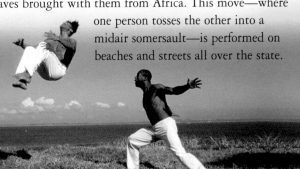

UROS

PEOPLE OF THE WATER

AT THE PERUVIAN END OF LAKE TITICACA lie over 40 tiny masses called the Uros floating islands. Unlike ordinary islands, which are part of the Earth's surface, these are man-made from the hollow tortora reeds that thrive in the shallow waters of the lake. The lives of the Uros

Floating nests

The Uros islands look like huge straw nests floating in the bright blue waters of Lake Titicaca. Each one is formed from layer on layer of tortora reeds, woven by hand into mats and bound tightly together. The reeds rot very quickly, however, so new ones are constantly being added on top to renew the surface.

1 Collecting
The reeds that the Uros people use are pulled away from the bottom of the lake by its moving waters. This woman is collecting them in her reed boat.

2 Drying
Before they can be woven, the long reeds are laid out to dry in the sun. This doesn't take long, since its strong rays are intensified by the lake's glassy surface.

3 Weaving
Here, reeds are bound into bundles that form one of the small, simple boats the Uros people use to transport themselves and their possessions.

REED HOMES
Uros families live in huts made completely from tortora reeds. Wooden stakes support the bases, which are raised slightly off the ground. The walls and the roof are formed from sheets of bound reeds known as *quesana*. A few of these huts are equipped with solar panels as a power source.

WOVEN CURRENCY
Like many South American peoples, the Uros weave beautiful textiles. They sell these to the tourists and trade them on the mainland for clothing and household supplies.

TROUBLE UNDERFOOT
The Uros people are very used to walking on the spongy, uneven surface of their islands. Visitors and children, though, can easily fall through a weak patch. The ground is constantly being renewed, but accidents do happen.

Indians who live here (there are about 800 of them left) are bound up completely with these reeds. They not only use them to form the ground they walk on, but also bind them together to construct simple shelters, weave them into mats, build rafts and boats with them, burn them as fuel, drink a healing tea made with their flowers, and even prepare their soft hearts as an asparagus-like vegetable to accompany their meals.

MENDING NETS

A few decades ago there was a thriving fishing industry in the Uros Islands, but this, like many other traditional trades and customs, has been eroded by technology and tourism. Today, any fish the people catch is mainly for their own meals, or to use as barter on the mainland.

NATURAL PRESERVATION

Fresh fish would quickly spoil in the strong sun, so the Uros people preserve some of their catch by cleaning it, then spreading it out on the ground to dry.

COLD AND BRIGHT

Because Lake Titicaca is so far above sea level— about 12,500 ft (3,800 m)—it is chilly all year round, so the people wrap up well in woolen clothing. Hats keep their heads warm and protect them from the sun.

Observation platform

DESCENDED FROM AN ANCIENT PRE-INCA PEOPLE called the Huari, the Ayacucho (the name means "purple soul"), like the Otavalens, share their name with an Andes region and city. During the colonial era, the territory

AYACUCHO

BUILDING ON THE PAST

Inspiring setting

Inhabitants of a city that features some of the most outstanding colonial architecture in South America, the urban Ayacucho population, like so many others, reflects two main influences—from their Amerindian ancestors and from the Europeans who dominated their land for so long. The craft objects for which they are best known include brilliantly hued textiles, stone and wood carvings, and fine filigree silver.

POSITIVE ATTITUDE

Many crumbling walls in Ayacucho still display faded traces of terrorist graffiti that date from the 1980s. The people are trying hard to move on from these bitter memories, though, and focus their attention on the color and vitality that define their city today.

Ayacucho women wear the bright skirts, white blouses, and felt hats typical of Andes dress.

EASTER LAMB

In the strongly Roman Catholic Ayacucho culture, Easter is the most important celebration, and Holy Week (*Semana Santa*) dominates the life of the people. During this time, the scent of incense is everywhere, prayers are murmured constantly, and solemn processions fill the streets. As her contribution, this young girl is carrying a living symbol of the Lamb of God.

flowered as a center of commerce and culture. In 1824, the bloody conflict that liberated Peru from Spain was fought here, and remembered as the Battle of Ayacucho. Again during the 1980s, the people were caught up in violence between the army and terrorists rebelling against it. Today though, the warmth of the Ayacucho people, together with their exquisite craft skills, have made their home a hugely popular visitor attraction.

COLORFUL SCENES

The Ayacucho are known for producing *retablos*, painted wooden boxes framing papier mâché scenes—religious or historical. This simple one shows a Palm Sunday gathering, but some are very complex, with several stories like a house.

MAKING MERRY

In Ayacucho, February is carnival time, when the streets overflow with dancers, singers, musicians, and high-spirited revelers. Here, a brilliantly costumed troup of players (note the glowering devil on the left) makes its leisurely way through the crowd.

SOLID HERITAGE

Many of the city's important buildings were constructed using rose-colored stone, quarried locally, which is called the "marble of Peru." The structure that dominates this cityscape is the Town Hall.

MODERN INFLUENCES

Ayacucho people in urban areas enjoy wearing traditional dress on special occasions. Many of them, however—especially children—prefer modern clothing for every day.

ARGENTINES

OF ALL THE COUNTRIES IN SOUTH AMERICA, Argentina reflects the strongest European (as opposed to Amerindian) influence. This is due not only to early Spanish colonization, but

NEW-WORLD NATION: OLD-WORLD CULTURE

Land of diversity

South America's second largest country, Argentina has a hugely diverse population. As well as the Hispanic majority, there is a significant Italian sector here, and small, proud, pockets of French, Jewish, British, Japanese, and Polish people. The name Argentina comes from *argentum*, the Latin word for "silver"; early explorers mistakenly thought there were large deposits of the mineral here.

TEATRO COLÓN

The glittering Teatro Colón in Buenos Aires is one of the world's finest opera houses. Since it was built in 1908, the leading opera and ballet stars of every generation have performed here—from Enrico Caruso to Placido Domingo, and from Anna Pavlova to Mikhail Barishnikov.

TWO TO TANGO

Born in the slums of Buenos Aires near the turn of the 20th century, the slow and sensual dance called the tango has since taken the flavor of Argentinian life to almost every country in the world.

NATIONAL INSTRUMENT

Invented in 1830 and shaped like a large, square concertina, the *bandonón*—an important element of tango culture—is Argentina's national instrument. Its name is believed to come from a combination of "Band," the last name of an important musical-instrument dealer of the day, with the word "acordeón" (accordion). People who play this instrument are known as *bandoneonistas*.

MODERN CITY

The wide Avenida 9 de Julio that runs through the heart of Buenos Aires was named in honor of Argentina's Independence Day. People who live in this huge waterfront city are known as *Porteños*—literally, "people of the port."

also to the heavy immigration of other Europeans in the late 19th and 20th centuries. Today, these settlers have almost swamped the indigenous peoples: the prevailing culture in Argentina is Hispanic, Spanish is the national language, and Roman Catholicism is the dominant religion. Nearly 90 percent of the population live in cities, and more than one-third are in or near the capital, Buenos Aires.

GATHERING GRAPES
The heart of Argentina's prosperous wine industry is the western province of Mendoza. The country's first vines were planted in this area in order to provide communion wine to colonists from Chile. Here, local grape pickers bring in another year's harvest.

OFF THE HOOF
The production of beef (in the form of both cattle and meatpacking industries), dominates Argentina's economy. Because of this, the *asado*, or barbecue—always a male domain—is an important social ritual. Locals tend to prefer their roasts and steaks well cooked.

ROMANCE OF THE RANGE
Cattle ranching is centered in the flat, fertile, farmland region known as the Pampa. Historically, the work is done by nomadic horsemen called *gauchos*, whose almost mythical status parallels that of the American cowboy. Bucking tradition, these Hereford cows are being herded by a lady *gaucho*, or *gaucha*.

Artists' colors

PAINTING THE TOWN RED, BLUE, YELLOW, GREEN ...

IN THE SOUTHEASTERN CORNER OF BUENOS AIRES, near the waterfront, lies the historic working-class *barrio,* or neighborhood, of La Boca; *boca* means mouth, and the district was named for the mouth of the Riachuelo River, which winds along its southern border. Full of ancient cobbled streets and rickety houses made of wood and tin, La Boca grew up as the city's Italian quarter during its first flush of prosperity at the end of the 19th century. Soon, the immigrant families who lived here began to adopt an appealing custom from the port of Genoa, where people brightened their streets with paint left over from the building and refitting of ships in the harbor. Today, the streets of La Boca are inhabited by a lively colony of artists and bohemians who take great delight in carrying on this tradition—every corrugated sheet, plank of wood, wrought-iron balustrade, and fretwork panel sings out in dazzling crimson, cobalt, aqua, or saffron.

TAQUILEÑOS

THE GLITTERING WATERS OF LAKE TITICACA—the highest

LIVING AT THE TOP OF THE WORLD

navigable lake in the world—span the border between Peru and Bolivia. On the Peruvian side is a small but very beautiful island called Taquile, which

Island in the sun

Taquile is an enchanting place whose exquisite setting and gentle way of life attract more and more tourists every year. There are fishermen and farmers here, but most people make their living from the tourist industry. Society is completely communal on Taquile, and everyone, whatever they do, shares in any profits the visitors bring.

BUSY NEEDLES

Textile crafts provide considerable tourist income for the Taquileños, and many elements of their traditional dress (which they wear every day) are hand made on the island as well. Knitting forms a major part of this heritage—but only the men do it. Here, an industrious worker is turning out one of the stocking caps, or *chulos*, worn by adult males—with red pom-poms if they are married, and white ones if they are single.

THE LANGUAGE OF DRESS

Like the men, the women of Taquile reveal their marital status through their clothing—navy or black skirts if they are married, brightly colored ones if they are not. Heavily embroidered waist sashes are common to both sexes.

ANCIENT ARCHWAY

The main entrance to Taquile is through a graceful archway over 500 steps up from the lake and harbor below. This arch, like most of the paths, ruins, and terraces on the island, is made from warm, reddish local stone.

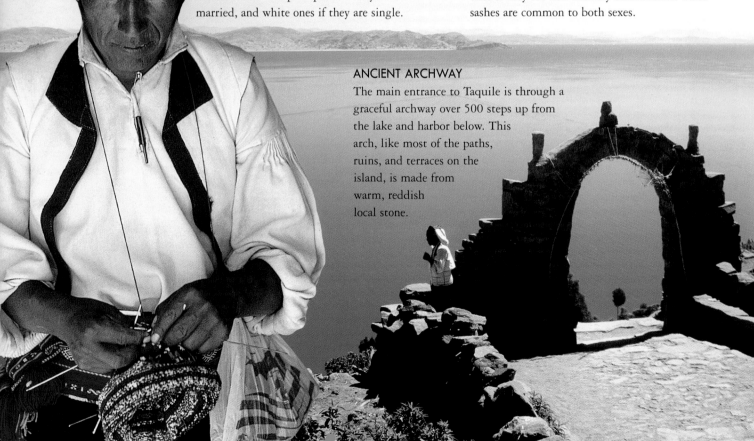

has been inhabited for over 10,000 years. Named after the Count of Taquila, a Spanish nobleman who once owned it, Taquile has remained almost untouched by modern life: it has no cars, no paved roads, no electricity or telecommunications—and no police force. There is virtually no crime on the island because the people live by a strict and simple moral code: *Ama suwa* (do not steal), *Ama llulla* (do not lie), *Ama quella* (do not be idle).

Carnival

There are three main festivals a year on Taquile: the first is around Easter; the second is when the harvest comes in; and the last is at new year. At these times the islanders bring out their finest costumes and jewelry, and create joyous celebrations with music, dancing, and feasting.

SACRED PLANT
A group of islanders gather and bless fresh coca leaves, which grow abundantly on Taquile. To make sure each journey they make is a peaceful one, they will offer these to the ancient gods of their lake and its surrounding mountains before they depart.

MANY LAYERS
At carnival time, Taqueliños parade through the island playing festive music and performing special dances. As the women twirl, they reveal the full glory of their costumes, which have up to 16 layered skirts.

FOR HUNDREDS OF YEARS, MAPUCHE CULTURE (their name means

MAPUCHE

ADAPTING AND SURVIVING

"people of the Earth") dominated the rugged landscapes of present-day Chile and northern Argentina. When the Spanish arrived, the Mapuche refused to be overpowered by them,

Masters of their universe

Mapuche territory is not only harsh, but it is also remarkably varied, from jagged peaks and valleys in the mountains to coastal lowlands and plains. The Mapuche have remained stable and prosperous because they have adapted to these diverse terrains, learned to hunt and farm them skillfully, and established strong community structures based on extended family units called *lofs*.

FEMALE SHAMAN
Mapuche priests or shamans, called *machis*, are usually female. This one stands in front of a small hill that has been a sacred site since before the Spanish arrived. On top is a statue of Caupolican, a revered Mapuche chief.

HOME LIFE
Inside a family dwelling, called a *ruca*, meals are prepared over an open fire. Domestic chores like cooking and childcare are the sole responsibility of Mapuche women, who also take charge of preserving valued customs and passing them on.

COLONIAL LEGACY
The introduction of horses and cattle by the Spanish had a huge influence on the Mapuche. Most importantly, horses provided greatly increased mobility, which made them much more effective hunters and fighters. Also, both horses and cattle ran wild on the plains, which led to the livestock trading that is still a major source of income for the Mapuche.

FAMILY HOUSE
Rucas have steeply pitched roofs covered with reed thatch that extends all the way down the walls. Traditionally, *rucas* are built facing east. According to Mapuche belief, the east, from where the sun, moon, and stars rise, is the source of all life forces.

yet they quickly adapted for their own purposes the unfamiliar horses and cattle their invaders brought with them. Finally losing their independence to military force in the mid-19th century, this proud people still maintain their own strong identity, religion, family structure, and language. The Mapuche call their homeland Waj Mapu, meaning "all the Earth," and their language Mapudungun—"the language of the Earth."

YEARLY BLESSINGS

Once a year the Mapuche celebrate their main festival called *Nguillatun.* At this time, they offer thanks for the community's well-being, pray for its continuing safety, and ask the gods to grant abundant harvests and healthy, fertile livestock.

MEN'S WORK

All work outside the home is undertaken by Mapuche men in their role as head of the family. Here, at harvesttime, a hard-working farmer gathers sheaves of ripe wheat from one of the small agricultural plots that surround a collection of *rucas.* As well as wheat, corn, potatoes, beans, vegetable marrows, and peppers are all widely cultivated crops.

PLAYING TOGETHER

Team activities like this game of *palin* link Mapuche communities and provide a focus for their identity. Similar to field hockey, *palin* involves a curved stick, or *weño,* and a small ball. Matches are played by friendly opponents, or used to settle differences between quarreling parties.

SOCIAL STRUCTURE

Mapuche society is organized into groups of related families, called *lofs,* rather than into towns and villages. Each *lof* consists of 15-20 families under the leadership of a *lonko,* or head man. Here, two generations of Mapuche males set forth in simple woolen garments, which, by tradition, are woven by the women and girls of their *lof.*

The clear, bright blue of the boy's shirt represents sky and spiritual purity to the Mapuche.

THE PEOPLE OF
Africa

African *adj* of Africa - *n* a native of Africa; a person of black race, especially one whose people live now, or lived recently, in Africa.

AFRICA

CRADLE OF THE HUMAN RACE

HUMAN LIFE BEGAN IN AFRICA with apelike creatures who started to become recognizably human about 200,000 years ago. Africa is home to the world's longest river, the Nile, and its biggest desert, the Sahara, which

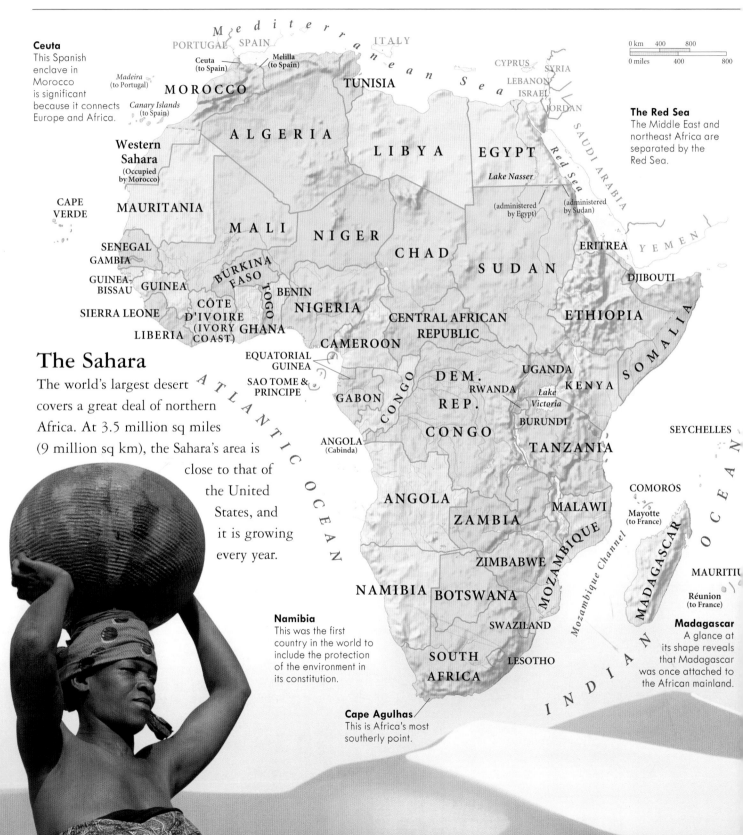

Ceuta
This Spanish enclave in Morocco is significant because it connects Europe and Africa.

The Red Sea
The Middle East and northeast Africa are separated by the Red Sea.

The Sahara

The world's largest desert covers a great deal of northern Africa. At 3.5 million sq miles (9 million sq km), the Sahara's area is close to that of the United States, and it is growing every year.

Namibia
This was the first country in the world to include the protection of the environment in its constitution.

Cape Agulhas
This is Africa's most southerly point.

Madagascar
A glance at its shape reveals that Madagascar was once attached to the African mainland.

0 km   400   800
0 miles   400   800

Mediterranean Sea

PORTUGAL   SPAIN   ITALY
Madeira (to Portugal)
Ceuta (to Spain)   Melilla (to Spain)
MOROCCO   TUNISIA   CYPRUS   SYRIA
Canary Islands (to Spain)   LEBANON   ISRAEL
JORDAN
Western Sahara (Occupied by Morocco)   ALGERIA   LIBYA   EGYPT   Red Sea   SAUDI ARABIA
CAPE VERDE   MAURITANIA   Lake Nasser
MALI   NIGER   (administered by Egypt)   (administered by Sudan)   YEMEN
SENEGAL   CHAD   ERITREA
GAMBIA   SUDAN   DJIBOUTI
GUINEA-BISSAU   GUINEA   BURKINA FASO   BENIN
SIERRA LEONE   CÔTE D'IVOIRE (IVORY COAST)   TOGO   NIGERIA   ETHIOPIA
LIBERIA   GHANA   CENTRAL AFRICAN REPUBLIC   SOMALIA
CAMEROON
EQUATORIAL GUINEA   UGANDA
SAO TOME & PRINCIPE   DEM.   RWANDA   KENYA
GABON   REP.   Lake Victoria
CONGO   BURUNDI
ATLANTIC OCEAN   ANGOLA (Cabinda)   CONGO   TANZANIA   SEYCHELLES
COMOROS
ANGOLA   MALAWI   Mayotte (to France)
ZAMBIA   MOZAMBIQUE   MADAGASCAR   MAURITIU
ZIMBABWE   Mozambique Channel   Réunion (to France)
NAMIBIA   BOTSWANA
SWAZILAND   INDIAN OCEAN
SOUTH AFRICA   LESOTHO

dominates the northern part of the continent. Despite its natural resources, Africa has had more than its fair share of problems. For years, Europeans colonized it, plundering the continent for their own gain. Since then, Africa has had to contend with wars, natural disasters, crippling debt, and AIDS. It is home to many of the poorest countries in the world. Despite its troubles, Africans are determinedly working toward a better future.

African statistics

LANGUAGES
Arabic and its dialects are Africa's most popular language. Lots of other languages are spoken by just a few thousand people each.

Arabic	112 million
Yoruba	20 million
Amharic	17.4 million
Igbo	17 million

RELIGIONS
In Africa it is very common for people to follow both a major world religion and to practice a local African religion.

Christian	373 million
Muslim	319 million
African religions	585 million
Other	8 million

URBAN POPULATION
Only 30 percent of Africans live in cities. Urban areas and their shanty town areas are growing rapidly due to migration.

Cairo	16 million
Lagos	13.5 million
Nairobi	6 million
Kinshasa	5 million

POPULATION BY COUNTRY
Nigeria has the greatest population in Africa. However, the tiny island of Mauritius is the most densely populated country.

Nigeria	127 million
Egypt	70 million
Ethiopia	66 million
D.R.Congo	54 million

AFRICAN FACTS

PLACES
Number of countries	53 +dependencies
Highest point	Kilimanjaro, Tanzania 19,340 ft (5,895 m)
Longest river	Nile River 4,145 miles (6,671 km)
Biggest lake	Lake Victoria 26,293 sq miles (68,100 sq km)
Biggest country	Sudan
Smallest country on Africa mainland	Gambia

PEOPLE
Population of continent	778 million
Male life expectancy	51 years
Female life expectancy	54 years

LITERACY RATE
Male	65%
Female	42%

POPULATION

Africa's population is growing fast. The densest populations are round the edges of the continent away from the parched, scorching Sahara desert that cuts across the continent, and the Kalahari and Namib deserts in the south.

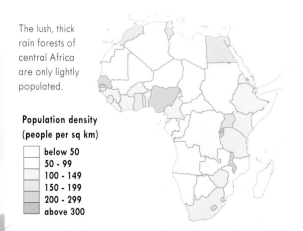

The lush, thick rain forests of central Africa are only lightly populated.

Population density (people per sq km)
- below 50
- 50 - 99
- 100 - 149
- 150 - 199
- 200 - 299
- above 300

The People of Africa FROM THE DESERT

merchants in the north to the Pygmy peoples in the central rain forests, and the nomadic herdsmen of the south, people have always moved around this enormous continent with little regard to national borders. In recent times there have also been very large migrations toward the cities.

A young Kenyan girl with the Nairobi skyline behind her.

BIG CITY

With the rapid growth of cities comes a host of problems. Kenya's capital, Nairobi, is the biggest city in east Africa, and also the site of possibly the continent's biggest slum. Almost one million people live here with no sanitation facilities.

Teenage boys reading about AIDS prevention.

INDEPENDENCE

Much of Africa was colonized by European powers, particularly the English and French, in the 18th, 19th, and early 20th centuries. Some countries retain strong links with their former colonial rulers. Here, the president of Ivory Coast greets the Prime Minister of France, who is making a diplomatic visit.

A DEVASTATING PLAGUE

AIDS, a sexually transmitted disease, has been ravaging the African continent. There is no cure for the disease, and the drugs used to treat it are very expensive. Tragically, so many adults have died that in some areas there are no parents or schoolteachers, and children are having to be brought up by their grandparents.

A rich culture

Beautiful African artifacts including fabrics, sculptures, masks, baskets, and jewelry have long been the envy of visitors to the continent. African myths and religious beliefs are less accessible to foreigners, but are no less powerful and compelling.

CRAFTWORK

Somali women weave baskets, which are both functional and beautiful. These qualities are the hallmarks of African craftwork traditions.

MASKS AND RITUALS

In some religious ceremonies, participants don fantastic masks or costumes and allow themselves to be possessed by a spirit or god.

MUSIC AND DANCING

African music and dance often serves a ceremonial purpose. Here, South African women celebrate Nelson Mandela's presidential campaign.

ORAL TRADITION

Writing is rare in African cultures. Important ritual and cultural information is communicated through art or songs, sometimes by spiritual leaders entrusted with this task.

COUNTRY LIFE

Many Africans live by cultivating land or raising animals. Some farmers produce enough food for themselves and maybe a little to sell locally; others work for big farms producing large amounts of cash crops like cocoa, coffee, or bananas for sale abroad.

Many rural Africans today live in huts something like this one.

MOORS

CIRCLING THE SAHARA

SAHARAN MAURITANIA HAS ONE OF THE LOWEST population densities in the world, with eight persons per square mile (three per square km). Less than 50 years ago nomadism was practiced by almost all Mauritanians, but today the Moors are one of the

The nomadic year

The Moors spend October to December in the north of their territory where there are few wells, but excellent grazing. As winter ends they move south through dunes and dusty plains. There is little movement between June and September, but after the fall rains the Moors trek every day to return to the northern pastures.

THE RHAL

Every family owns a *rhal*, a wooden platform with carved legs. When the family is on the move the *rhal* is placed upside down on a camel. Cooking pots and containers are hung from its sides, and the women and children sit on it, like a saddle. The *rhal* is the woman's responsibility and, like all her possessions, is kept on the northern side of the tent.

Curved wooden tent poles.

Head coverings protect people from the sun, wind, and sand.

PACKING UP THE CAMP

It only takes the women an hour or two to dismantle the tents for loading onto the camels. Once the tent components and other possessions are piled on board, the women are helped up and the children handed to them. Men walk behind the camels with the cattle. There is no definite destination for the next camp—the men stop when they see an appropriate spot.

few groups still leading a traditional life. Their movements are determined largely by their animals' need for water and pasture. But, like all nomads, the Moors do not live in total isolation or survive by their animals alone. Their travels invariably bring them into contact with their settled neighbors from whom they buy other essentials such as grain, vegetables, weapons, and even wives.

FAMILY GROUPS
Camps usually consist of close family members—in the local language the same word, *khayme,* refers to both camp and family. The camp varies in size from five to 20 tents, depending on how much pasture is available.

ANIMAL HIDES
Hammunat Moors use locally available materials. The women make water containers out of goatskin. The skin is dried, tanned, and then sewn up before the finished container is finally tested to make sure it is watertight.

A TENT OF HER OWN
A bride continues to live with her parents for a year after her marriage. During this time, her mother makes the new couple a tent out of heavy cotton strips sewn together. It will remain the bride's property in the event of a divorce.

HOME FURNISHINGS
The tents contain blankets, cooking utensils, the *rhal,* and a metal trunk holding clothes, perfumes, and mirrors. The floor is bare or covered with palm mats woven by the women.

MOROCCANS

DUSK FALLS ON MARRAKESH'S CENTRAL SQUARE

By day, Marrakesh's Djma el Fna is an enormous empty space close to the souks. As dusk falls is it magically transformed. Booths selling nuts and dried fruit open; squadrons of orange-juice stalls appear; a dozen or more barbecues roasting enormous quantities of meat are lit, sending plumes of smoke into the air; and entertainers of all kinds start to arrive. There are troupes of brightly clad but ragged child acrobats; storytellers; musicians; snake charmers; and belly-dancing female impersonators. Crowds amble around, eating and being entertained, while cars skim the perimeter of the square— giving the enchanted fairground the surreal air of a giant traffic island.

EGYPTIANS

AT THE ENTRANCE TO AFRICA

THE LIFEBLOOD OF EGYPT IS THE NILE RIVER, which passes through the center of the country. It has enabled many civilizations to flourish, among them the Ancient Egyptians, Nubians, Greeks, and

Bustling metropolis

Egypt's capital, Cairo, is the city with the largest population in all of Africa—over 16 million people live here. There has been a city on this site by the Nile delta since Babylonian times, so ancient monuments jostle with the sprawling modern metropolis. Cairo and its environs are home to the Great Pyramid at Giza and to many ancient churches, mosques, and synagogues.

CAR CITY

Over two million cars travel the streets of Greater Cairo daily, resulting in an almost continual rush hour with traffic so densely packed it barely moves. Parked cars contribute to the chaos: there are only 15,000 parking spaces though at least 45,000 are needed.

FRESH BREAD

This pitta-bread seller is carrying the most simple and basic type of bread. Flour and water are mixed together and baked rapidly in a clay oven. Because it is pocket shaped, the bread can be stuffed with meat and vegetables to form a handy sandwich.

Romans, as well as Muslim, Turkish, and European colonial powers in more recent times. Today, 69 million people live in Egypt, making it the most populous Arab country by a long stretch. Most are Muslims and Arabic is the national language. The country has been run as a republic since 1952. Tourism and tolls from the Suez Canal are Egypt's biggest industries.

A MIXED POPULATION

Most of Egypt's population is Egyptian, but Alexandria and Cairo particularly are also home to Bedouins, Berbers, Lebanese, Nubians, Syrians, and Sudanese from elsewhere in Africa and the Middle East, and also to many Europeans.

ABU SIMBEL

This temple in the south of Egypt was built by Pharaoh Rameses II around 1200 BC. In 1968 it was moved so its original site could be flooded to make room for the Aswan Dam, which provides water and electricity for all Egypt.

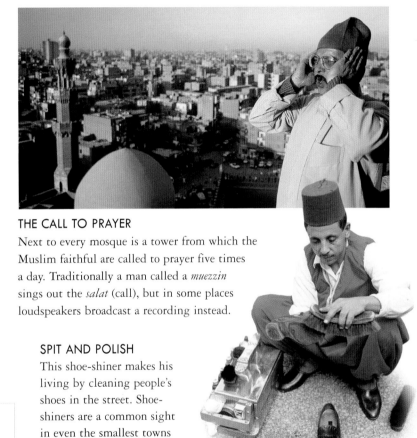

THE CALL TO PRAYER

Next to every mosque is a tower from which the Muslim faithful are called to prayer five times a day. Traditionally a man called a *muezzin* sings out the *salat* (call), but in some places loudspeakers broadcast a recording instead.

SPIT AND POLISH

This shoe-shiner makes his living by cleaning people's shoes in the street. Shoe-shiners are a common sight in even the smallest towns and villages in Egypt.

GIFTS OF THE NILE

This farmer is using donkey power to raise water for irrigating his crops. For centuries though, Egyptian farmers relied on the annual flooding of the Nile River to water their fields. Since the Aswan Dam was built the floods no longer occur. Instead, rain water is captured and stored in a reservoir until it is needed.

TUAREG

CROSSING THE SAHARA DESERT

FACES SWATHED IN INDIGO-DYED SCARVES that are only ever removed in private, the Tuareg are a romantic symbol of the harsh, nomadic desert life. Until the mid-20th century, many still traversed the desert as they had done for centuries, though now most have settled down to work the land. Descended from Arabs and Berbers, the Tuareg were the earliest inhabitants of the Sahara region. They served an important function in the global economy by transporting small, luxury items such as jewelry and weapons from Africa to the markets of the Middle East and Europe. These days, the nomadic lifestyle is dying. Droughts, civil unrest, and the people's minority status in their own countries have compelled many Tuareg to settle, but inevitably it is progress that has dealt nomadism the cruelest blow. The reason the Tuareg no longer command the desert is simply because their camels are no match for the trucks that effortlessly zip back and forth across the Sahara.

ASHANTI

A ROYAL TRADITION OF CRAFTWORK

EVEN TODAY WITH AN ELECTED GOVERNMENT, the Ashanti people of southern Ghana continue to place great importance on their king, who is known as the *asantehene*. Royal patronage enabled the arts to flourish

The cloth of kings

Graphically patterned *Kente* cloth has been worn by Ashanti royalty since the 12th century. Because every pattern has a name, often inspired by a famous person, event, or proverb, *kente* cloth is much more than fabric. It is the bearer of Ashanti history, culture, and beliefs.

1 Dyeing yarn
The yarn is boiled together with starch and dye in a large kettle heated over a fire pit. Then it is hung out to dry under the hot Ghanaian sun.

2 Big bobbins
Bobbo, a master weaver, winds the dry yarn onto enormous bobbins. He chooses a design and selects his colors before he sets up the loom and starts weaving.

3 Little bobbins
After school, Bobbo's son winds yarn and learns to weave by helping his father, as Bobbo did before him.

AT THE LOOM

Kente cloth is woven out of doors. A loom with very long warp threads is used so that long, thin strips of fabric are produced. The weaver opens and closes these using a lever controlled by his feet. At the same time, he throws the shuttle holding the weft threads rapidly back and forth between the warp threads.

The wooden loom is built and maintained by the weaver.

CORONATION PROCESSION

A spectacular procession takes place when a new *asantehene* (king) comes to power. It features the Golden Stool, which is believed to have descended from heaven in the 17th century. The *asantehene* may not actually sit on it but he is is lowered and raised three times over this symbol of Ashanti power. At his enstoolment, as on all state occasions, he wears gold jewelry and a type of *kente* cloth that is reserved only for kings.

THE FINAL STAGE

The long strips of fabric are sewn together to make the actual cloth. A man's robe requires 24 strips on average, while a woman's skirt needs far fewer.

and also gave rise to both power struggles and many ceremonies. There is still a strong and innovative tradition of craftwork among the Ashanti. A new tradition was born in the 1960s when a talented sculptor created the first fantasy coffin in the shape of a fish for his dying uncle who was a fisherman. In keeping with the lavish and lengthy funerals customary in Ghana, the idea was an immediate and lasting hit.

THE SEAT OF POWER

During the early days of the Ashanti Kingdom, a Golden Stool summoned by the high priest descended from heaven and came to rest on the knees of the first *asantehene*, Osei Tutu. This stool, still used in enstoolment ceremonies today, came to symbolize the soul and power of the Ashanti people and their king.

A SINGLE PIECE OF WOOD

Stools are a typically Ashanti item and are often made of soft sese or cedar wood. Craftsmen are exceptionally skilled and do not measure the wood; they simply begin carving it with a tool called an adze.

FANTASY COFFINS

Specially commissioned coffins in the form of airplanes, chickens, guitars, or even giant Bibles celebrate the achievements of the person who has died and enable them to go on their final journey in style.

Craftsmen sometimes incorporate images into the design that reflect the personnality of the owner.

DOGON

ASTRONOMERS AND MYTH-MAKERS

SOUTHEASTERN MALI is home to around 100,000 Dogon people. The majority live in small villages clustered around the foot of the 90 mile (145 km) Bandiagara Cliffs.

All dressed up

Many different Dogon ceremonies are celebrated, but the most important is the *sigui* ceremony which is held once every 60 years. Its exact date is calculated to coincide with the moment when Sirius appears between two mountains peaks. At this event power is symbolically handed over from one generation to the next and a new *toguna*, or meeting house, is built.

IN THE SHADOW OF THE CLIFFS

A group called the Tellem lived in homes carved out of the cliffs until 500 years ago. The Dogon live in the plains below but hoist their dead up to the ancient site.

DOGON RELIGIOUS SOCIETIES

All-male religious societies are an important part of Dogon life. The role of the *Wagem* cult is to keep dead ancestors involved in village affairs, while the *Binu* cult has a similar role with regard to members of the spirit world. The *Lebe* cult perform the *bulu*—an agricultural rite. It takes place just before the rains begin and its purpose is to ensure a sucessful harvest.

THE AWA SOCIETY

During a funeral, members of the *Awa* society lead the souls of the dead to their rightful place in the supernatural world. They wear masks indicating that they have been taken over by the souls of supernatural beings and speak a mysterious language called *sigi so*. Every 60 years the Awa society perform the most important rite of all, the *sigui*, a celebration of renewal.

The Dogon have a profound knowledge of astronomy. They determine the time of one of their ceremonies by the position of the distant star, Sirius. Dogon priests have long maintained that Sirius had a companion star— invisible to the naked eye—which Western astronomers finally managed to locate in 1995. Dogon stories about the creation and workings of the universe are some of the most complex known to anthropologists.

The toguna or "House of Words" is the spiritual center of Dogon life. It has a low roof so that no one can stand up and start fighting if there is a disagreement.

THE ONION CROP

The Dogon grow onions as a cash crop. These are pounded, shaped into balls, and dried in the sun. They will be taken by truck as far away as the Ivory Coast to be sold as ingredients for sauces. The pots used to water the crop are made out of clay by Dogon women.

The "chess-board" pattern symbolizes the relationship between the spirit world and the world of the living.

PROBLEMS WITH TOURISTS

Decorative gate posts were a feature of Dogon buildings but many were stolen by art collectors and tourists. These days few are made, and the Dogon have resorted to defacing the remainder so that no one will be tempted to steal them.

WODAABE

DRESSING TO IMPRESS

AT A WEEK LONG FESTIVAL celebrating the end of the dry season among the Wodaabe of Nigeria and Niger, makeup and jewelry are used to great effect in the quest for a marriage partner. Unusually though, it is the men doing the primping and preening. They spend hours applying makeup for the *yaake*, a contest in which they charm the female judges by making silly faces. In another contest, called the *geerewol*, men parade and dance in their finest clothes and jewelry for hours. If a man impresses one of the judges she may consent to marry him.

THE DINKA OF SOUTHERN SUDAN, like their neighbors the Nuer, are a seminomadic people. Although they grow crops and keep various animals, the Dinka particularly treasure their cattle. During the short rainy season

DINKA

LIFE IN THE CATTLE CAMP

Cattle wealth

The Dinka people are very proud of the long-horned cows that represent their wealth. Such is the importance of cattle that the Dinka write songs about their animals and perform dances to honor them. When a Dinka boy wants to marry he offers cattle to the girl's family. And when there is a dispute, cattle are given to the wronged party by a court of Dinka elders.

Dinka select cattle for the size of their horns.

A HOME FOR EACH SEASON

During the dry season the Dinka and their cattle move to camps by a river, leaving only the old and infirm in the villages. But when the rains come and the riverside grasslands become swampy they return to their villages once more. There they live in small groups of grass-roofed, mud houses and cultivate crops such as sorghum and millet.

the Dinka live in villages built on sandbanks emerging out of the swamps and cultivate crops. However, in the dry season, which runs from September to May, all able-bodied Dinka leave the village in search of pasture and water for their animals. Since 1983, southern Sudan has been blighted by civil war. Many people have been killed and vast numbers of cattle have died, gotten lost, or been abandoned in the course of the fighting.

MILK AND BUTTER

Women and children are responsible for milking the cattle and distributing dairy products. The milk is collected in gourds. Some of it is drunk right away, some is soured for storing, and if there is any extra, some is churned to make butter.

A NATURAL INSECT REPELLENT

Keeping flies and mosquitoes at bay is a priority in the cattle camp. Not only do they irritate both people and animals, but they are also capable of spreading diseases.

1 Dung repellent
A young girl collects cow dung at the Wunbel cattle camp in southern Sudan. There is plenty of it available for use as a natural insect repellent.

2 Bonfires
At dusk the dung is burned. People and animals gather around the fires fueled by burning dung. The smoke covers everything and keeps insects away.

3 Using the ash
The Dinka cover themselves with the insect-repelling ash. With typical Dinka concern for their animals, they also rub the ash into the skin of their cows.

A USE FOR EVERYTHING

Of course, milk and butter are valuable as food, but the Dinka find a way to use everything that the cattle produce. Cow urine, which is sterile and antiseptic, is collected and used for cleaning wounds, washing, and tanning hides. The ash from burned cow dung has many uses too, including insect repellent (see below), makeup, and toothpaste! Although cows are not generally slaughtered, when an animal dies its hide is used to make mats, drums, belts, and ropes. Nothing is wasted, not even horns and bones.

Calling the cattle

A Dinka child beats his drum to a specific rhythm to call his family's cows to his *khat*, a specific area in the middle of the camp where they will be tethered for the night. The cows have been trained to recognize and respond to this particular rhythm. The smooth management of thousands of animals in the cattle camp is possible because every family has its own rhythm.

Large drum made out of cow hide.

GAMO

HIGHLAND VILLAGERS OF ETHIOPIA

THERE ARE AROUND 700,000 GAMO PEOPLE in the highlands of southwestern Ethiopia. Their villages are dotted around the lush, green hills, and many are above 9,800 ft (3,000 m). Heavy rains fall from June

AN EXTRA ROOM

Frequently, simple round huts are built alongside the main family home. These are lower than the main hut and either house the family's son and his wife, or are used for cooking or storing grain.

1 Making the walls
Making a hut is a lot like making a basket. Vertical lengths of bamboo are planted in the ground and then horizontal lengths woven through them to form walls.

2 The roof
A small round base, similar to the kind that forms the bottom of a basket, is woven, placed on top of the walls, and then connected to the wall struts.

3 Layers of thatch
Dense thatch is placed over the roof to form a thick covering that will prevent the rain from entering the hut. A hut like this one can last for several years.

Family and friends

In the Gamo highlands, families live in compounds containing a number of huts. The main hut has a high, pointed roof so that rain can drain off the outside. Smoke from cooking escapes through the weave in the thatch. It can take five or six hours to cook dinner on the hearth at the back of the hut, so while women cook, men congregate to while away the time smoking and discussing local politics.

THE MAIN FAMILY HOME

The tall family houses are often 20 ft (6 m) or more, and feature a "nose," or little porch at the front. The enormous bamboo poles planted outside this home signify that the man of the house is undergoing initiation as a *halaka*, or elder. Bamboo grows abundantly and is important both for building homes and for rituals.

to September, and lighter rains in February and March. People rely on these to grow crops such as barley, wheat, corn, and sorghum. They also cultivate *enset*. Although it bears no fruit, this plant is related to the banana.

It has many uses and is virtually indestructible. Not only does it provide food, but its stems can also be made into rope, and its waterproof leaves used to keep off the rain.

Festivals and rituals

New year is celebrated after the heavy rains in September. Sheep are sacrificed, those who have been married or initiated in the previous year participate in special rituals, and everybody greets each other with the exclamation "Yo!". This is the main festival but there are others throughout the year, as well as particular Gamo practices relating to death and marriage.

Men performing a ritual to celebrate the new year.

AFTER A FUNERAL
Only close relatives attend a burial, but the entire community participates in the mourning ritual. Male relatives of the person who has died dress in their war outfits and carry their spears. At a special mourning field they, together with the rest of the community, run around in their battle gear chanting war songs, expressing the warriorlike strength it takes to confront death.

BRIDAL JOURNEY
On marriage, young women move from their parents' home to the home of their husband and his family. This bride makes the journey to her new family in style—riding on a donkey and proudly wearing a leopard skin. Leopards used to roam the lowland areas, where they were hunted and traded. There are not many left these days, but families who own leopard skins wear them at celebrations and weddings to signify power.

SHARING THE WORK
The men who own plots of land rarely tend them alone. Work groups of 10-15 people spend a day or two on each individual's plot. These men are preparing to plant barley or wheat by hoeing the ground. Lower down the slopes people plant corn or sorghum. Even if the rains fail and the crops do not grow there is no risk of famine because there are hardy *enset* plants—whose roots and stems are edible—to fall back on.

MBENDJELE

PYGMY PEOPLE OF THE RAIN FOREST

AS MANY AS 200,000 DIFFERENT GROUPS live in the forests of central Africa in countries such as Zaire, Gabon, Cameroon, Central African Republic, and Uganda. They are sometimes known collectively as

Women's work

Mbendjele women gather fruit, nuts, mushrooms, tubers, and caterpillars. They are not permitted to kill animals by drawing blood so rather than shoot, they fish or catch and kill small animals by clubbing them. At harvesttime women help gather in the crops for their settled neighbors in return for a share of the harvest.

MAKING MONGOLÉ

A woman prepares a red paste called *mongolé*, which is said to have protective and magical powers. It is made by adding nut oil to the powder produced when two sticks of dead wood are ground together with a little sand and water. *Mongolé* is rubbed onto babies to make them grow strong, and onto young adults during their most vulnerable time—initiation.

RAIN FOREST KITCHEN

Mbendjele groups move camp around 30 times a year. Fortunately, it only takes minutes to set up a new kitchen. Elderly women carry smoking embers wrapped in leaves to the new camp so it is easy to start a fire on arrival. The family machete and cooking pot are carried in the basket belonging to the woman of the family. The heavy mortar and pestle are either left at the site for next time the group returns or made anew. Chopping boards and plates are are simply readily available wood and leaves.

A CURE FOR ILLNESS

Mokodis are strings woven from tree bark, vines, and other forest materials. They are made by both women and men, and are worn on the affected part of the body to cure illness. Special *mokodis* are tied around the wrists and waists of newborn babies to protect them.

Hunters must be absolutely silent so as not to alarm the animals. They communicate using signs like this one which means "elephant."

Pygmies. All share a small stature and a profound knowledge of the rain forest—the most diverse habitat on Earth—from which they derive almost everything they need to live including food, building materials, and medicine. Mbendjele are one such people. They hunt and gather, moving frequently from place to place within the forest so as not to exhaust it. There are also settled farmers living near their trading partners.

PREPARING FOR THE HUNT

A clan elder takes the gunpowder from a few bird-shot pellets and combines it to make a bullet big enough to kill a pig. Mbendjele people do not own guns, but they sometimes make deals with local people who do, borrowing a gun in return for a share of the kill. Pygmy people do not want to deplete the forest so they only kill large animals such as elephants or buffalos if there is an unusually big crowd of people to feed because of a funeral or celebration.

1 A successful hunt
The Mbendjele are excellent hunters. This hunter returning to the camp is carrying two monkeys and a duiker (a kind of antelope) that he has killed.

2 Sharing the kill
A big feast follows a successful hunt. The animals are quickly cut up and cooked so that everyone in the group can benefit from the nutritious meat.

3 Cooking the meal
In the hot and steamy climate fresh meat, like this duiker head, soon spoils. One method of preservation is to smoke it over an open fire.

This sign means "gorilla." Mbendjele believe gorillas are reincarnated humans and never kill or eat them.

This sign means a hunter has spotted a chimpanzee.

THE MAASAI PEOPLE live along the Great Rift Valley in southern Kenya and northern Tanzania. Although they are seminomadic, and traditionally have not cultivated crops, they are tied to the land by their animals. Land

MAASAI

CATTLE HERDERS OF OF EAST AFRICA

JUMPING COMPETITIONS
Everyone sings and dances in Maasai ceremonies. *Moran* show their prowess by rhythmic vertical jumping—the higher the better. They can jump for hours, sustained by the singing and chanting of the rest of the group.

HELPING OUT
Maasai children spend most of their time playing, but they are allowed to look after sheep and goats, which are not as highly prized as cattle. They are encouraged to be respectful and to address all elders, not just their own parents, as "mother" or "father."

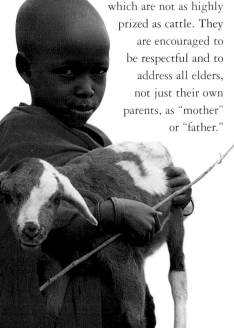

Men and cattle
The Maasai way of life revolves around keeping animals, particularly cattle. Maasai men are grouped with their contemporaries into age-sets in which they remain for their entire lives. Particular types of work are allocated to each age-set. Every few years, the entire age-set participates in a ceremony at which they move up a stage. Young men between their late teens and early twenties are *moran*, or warriors. During this period of their lives they live with and look after the cattle.

During their time as *moran* the young men learn to recognize every single animal in their care.

ownership was once foreign to the Maasai, yet they now find themselves struggling to gain access to their traditional grazing lands. This is due to the tourist industry, catering to the growing Western appetite for safaris.

Many Maasai have responded to this by opening their villages to tourists. Selling craftwork and performing for tourists brings in money, but some Maasai feel it is undignified to sell their culture in this way.

CATTLE BLOOD
High in protein, cattle blood is given to the sick, to women after childbirth, and to men recovering from circumcision. To extract the blood, a vein is opened up in the animal's neck. It is sealed after the blood has been extracted, doing no permanent damage to the animal.

Women and girls

Maasai women build and maintain the home, collect water and firewood, look after children and animals, and do skilled beadwork. More recently, some women have begun growing and selling vegetables. Maasai girls undergo initiation at puberty and are married soon after, often to much older men who have completed their time as *moran*.

BEAUTIFUL BEADWORK
Women buy bright plastic beads from non-Maasai and use them to make distinctive jewelry. Rules dictate which colors may be used and in what combinations. The women in the picture are in a tourist *manyatta* (village) on the edge of the Maasai Mara game reserve, where tourists can watch them as they work.

The end of an era

FROM WARRIOR TO JUNIOR ELDER

THE SOUND OF THE KUDU HORN awakens strong emotions among Maasai warriors, known as *moran*. The one occasion on which it is blown is to summon them to their *eunoto* ceremony where they cease to be *moran* and graduate to junior elders. Approximately every 10 years, *moran* from Kenya and Tanzania gather for the *eunoto*. As *moran*, the men lived and worked together tending cattle, hunting, and decorating themselves with red ochre. Now, the many restrictions on them will be lifted and they will be allowed to marry, but they will lose the excitement of their former lives. In their red robes and impressively painted, they take a final meal together and process back to the main camp. As the kudu horn is blown, hundreds of *moran* chant and present arms. Later, they will sit on the cowhides on which they were circumcised while their mothers shave off the long hair symbolizing their warriorhood. Many weep and tremble, believing that the best period of their lives has now ended.

CAPETONIANS

THE DIVERSE RESIDENTS OF CAPE TOWN

WHERE THE WARM WATERS OF THE INDIAN OCEAN collide with the cooler waters of the Atlantic lies picturesque Cape Town, huddled at the foot of Table Mountain. The first inhabitants of this region were the

Port city

Cape Town came into existence because merchant ships traveling between the Netherlands and the East Indies needed somewhere to take on food and drink. Members of the Dutch East India Company founded the settlement as a refreshment stop in 1652. Some of their employees left the company to become farmers, and so began the process of colonization.

Cape Town occupies an area of striking natural beauty.

WINELANDS
Stellenbosch, home to over 100 different wine estates, is only 30 miles (50 km) from Cape Town. Every year, thousands of tourists tour the region to enjoy the scenery and sample the wines.

nomadic San people, followed by Khoi herders. The Dutch began to arrive in 1652, bringing with them slaves from Indonesia, Madagascar, India, and Mozambique. The British came next. In the late 18th century the discovery of South African diamonds and gold caused a boom. Later immigrants included Jews escaping violence in Eastern Europe, Indian and African laborers, and more economic migrants from Europe.

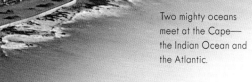

NATURAL BEAUTY

Capetonians appreciate their city's location and like nothing better than hiking in the surrounding countryside. The region has many national parks as well as Table Mountain which, at 3,563 ft (1,086 m), looks out onto stunning views over the city and the coast.

Two mighty oceans meet at the Cape— the Indian Ocean and the Atlantic.

CAPE MALAYS

The Bo-Kaap area is home to the Cape Malays, descendants of slaves from all over the Muslim world who were brought by the Dutch to South Africa in the 16th and 17th centuries. The first official mosque opened here in 1797.

EQUAL RIGHTS FOR ALL

Since the end of the apartheid era in 1994 full racial integration has been South Africa's goal, so mixed schools are becoming more common.

SHANTY TOWN

Many of Cape Town's black residents live in ghettos created during the apartheid era. Some of the poorest live in shanty towns, unofficial neighborhoods where people build shacks out of whatever is at hand.

ZULUS

MODERN LIVES, TRADITIONAL WISDOM

DURING THE REIGN OF KING SHAKA (1816-1823), Zulus became the mightiest military force in southern Africa. This small group conquered and absorbed many other tribes, resulting in a fifty-fold increase in the land they

Health and illness

Zulus believe bad luck, ill health, and death can often be attributed to sorcery or an offended spirit. The first step when a problem is suspected is to consult an *isangoma*. These healers, almost all of them women, feel called to their profession. They undergo intensive and lengthy training while apprenticed to an experienced practitioner.

UMUTI MARKET
While an *isangoma* diagnoses ill health and divines the reason for it, a specialist called an *inyanga* makes up and administers *umuti*—Zulu medicines. These are made of plant and animal products and many Zulus prefer them to Western medicines.

An *isangoma* carries an *ishoba*—a stick made with the tail of a wildebeest and decorated with beads—as an aid to diagnosis.

Isangomas wear distinctive beadwork in their hair.

controlled. Signs of their warrior past remain in their ritual costumes, which feature animal skins, spears, and shields. Some Zulus live in traditional homesteads known as *umuzis*, which are arranged in a circle.

Many *umuzis* are on land owned by white farmers, and at least one family member holds down a paying job. Other *umuzis* are open to the public and their inhabitants make a living from tourism.

GOING TO SCHOOL
Most of South Africa's three million Zulus live in the countryside of Kwa-Zulu Natal, herding cattle and growing crops. Like all South African children, Zulu children go to school until the age of 15.

Two *isangomas* participate in a healing ritual.

BASKETS AND BEADS
Beadwork is a well-developed Zulu craft. If a woman has, or would like, a relationship with a particular man she can send a subtle message to him through her jewelry. Zulu basketwork is much admired too. Baskets are even watertight enough to hold liquids, thanks to the tight weave and to the fact that the liquid in the baskets causes the fibers to swell.

MINING FOR COAL
Zulus do some of the hardest and most poorly paid jobs in South Africa. Many Zulu men live and work in South Africa's coal mines hundreds of miles from Kwa-Zulu Natal. The men usually live in basic dormitory accommodation, only returning to see their wives and families for a few days once or twice a year.

SAN

HUNTER-GATHERERS OF THE KALAHARI

OFTEN REFERRED TO AS "BUSHMEN," the many different groups now known as San are the original inhabitants of the Kalahari Desert in South Africa, Botswana, and Namibia. Their lifestyle resembles that of the

MONKEY ORANGES
The San are entirely self-sufficient and are skilled at getting every possible use from the little that is available in the bush. The fruit of the monkey orange tree is good for quenching thirst but also has a number of other uses. The fruit can be used as dye or soap, the bark as medicine, and the leaves to heal wounds.

A FLEXIBLE LIFESTYLE
A San community consists of a few extended families who are all related to each other. Everyone builds their homes close together inside a walled compound. The doors to each home face toward the central area where people meet, cook, and socialize. When water and food have become scarce, the group simply leaves the homes to fall apart naturally and moves to a new site where they build another camp.

The San way of life

Survival in the desert requires a number of different skills. Men make weapons and hunt for animals, while women fashion skin bags and use these to gather fruit and nuts. In San society everything is shared and everyone is treated equally. When an animal is killed the meat does not belong to the person who killed it but is shared with the entire group. Although there is no formal leadership, skilled and experienced individuals are highly respected.

ROOTS AND TUBERS
Roots and tubers provide moisture as well as food to the San. Women are expert at finding and digging these up, and are also knowledgeable about their medicinal properties and uses.

SAN CAVE ART

The oldest San cave paintings are thought to be 27,000 years old. The animals represented in the cave paintings may record the experiences of San spiritual leaders. These leaders, or shamans, would hold a trance dance to heal someone or ensure good hunting. The paintings show what the shaman may have seen while in a trance.

very earliest, preagricultural societies. The San, like the Pygmy peoples of central Africa, are hunter-gatherers who live in family groups of 10-30 people. The members of the group live as equals and share everything.

They are very skilled at hunting animals, and at finding food and water in the bush. They keep only minimal possessions so that they can move easily to a new site if their water source dries up.

Hunting and trapping

Although the San do much of their hunting with a bow and arrow, they also set traps like this one, which is designed to catch a guinea fowl. San men and women are extremely skilled at this and their traps very rarely fail to catch birds or small animals. The animals most commonly hunted are antelope, wildebeest, gemsbok, giraffe, reptiles, and birds.

PREPARING FOR THE HUNT

Because there are few animals in the bush, hunting is a skilled task and something of a ritual event, reinforcing the relationship between the men in the group.

1 Finding poison
A hunter digs for beetle larvae. They contain a poison which, when it enters an animal's bloodstream, can kill it. One arrow may require the poison of 10 larvae.

2 The mixing bowl
He extracts the poison and mixes it with plant juice and saliva in one of the ball sockets of an eland. The juice acts like glue, making the poison stick to the arrow.

3 Delicate work
The poison is placed on the arrow shaft, not the tip. This is to prevent the hunter from getting poisoned if he accidentally scratches himself with one of his arrows.

PATIENCE AND SKILL

The small poisoned arrows do not inflict much damage on a big animal. The hunter will have to follow the animal's tracks for four or five days until it succumbs to the poison.

MALAGASY

THE FIRST SETTLERS ON MADAGASCAR CAME, not from Africa, but from Southeast Asia, nearly 6,000 miles (10,000 km) away. They settled on the central highlands of the island. Later, Africans settled in the

AFRICAN AND INDONESIAN ROOTS

A miniature continent

Thousands of islands litter the Indian Ocean. The largest, Madagascar—which is the world's fourth largest island—lies 250 miles (400 km) off the east coast of Africa. Ecologically, it is one of the most diverse countries on Earth. Almost 98 percent of the land mammals and a high proportion of plants, reptiles, and birds live only here.

A woman taking a fish home from market by balancing it on her head.

MARKET DAY

Although their main crop is rice, which is consumed locally, farmers on Madagascar grow various crops including coffee, vanilla, cloves, and sugar for export. In order to produce decaffeinated coffee the beans must be treated. However, there is one exception to this rule—the Madagascar coffee species *mascarocoffea vianneyi* produces naturally decaffeinated beans.

A RICH SOURCE OF FOOD

Coastal Malagasy have always eaten fish, crab, and shrimp, but recently fishing has become more intensive in order to supply fish and shrimp for export. Although this generates much-needed income for Madagascar, there is concern that overfishing might seriously deplete the waters and cause a food shortage.

coastal regions and further immigrants came from the Muslim world. Today, 16 million Malagasy comprise almost 20 distinct ethnic groups, sharing a language, a nationality, and many similar beliefs and customs. The incredible diversity of Madagascar's human population is matched by the variety of its animals and plants, which evolved in the millions of years after the island broke off from the African mainland.

Some graves in the south of the island are decorated with carved figures and the horns of zebu cattle.

The importance of fady

Complex and varied *fady*, or taboos, exist in every group on Madagascar. For instance, the Mahafaly people in the south of the island consider it unlucky for children to sleep in the same house as their parents. Some *fady* are concerned with the proper way to treat the dead.

CARING FOR THE DEAD

Around half of the Malagasy people follow traditional religions, but even those who are Christian retain the traditional beliefs and practices concerning the *razana*, or dead ancestors. *Razana* must be kept happy or they will bring bad luck to the living.

1 Family reunion
Some years after the death and burial of a relative, the Merina and Betsileo people of the central highlands dig up the body and wrap the bones in a new shroud.

2 A new shroud
The *famadihana*, or "turning of the dead" allows relatives to show respect for a *razana* and ensure that he or she will continue to protect them in the future.

3 Homes for the dead
Not everyone performs the *famadihana*, but all Malagasy take good care of the dead. On Madagascar, tombs are often more lavish than the homes of the living.

VANILLA

Madagascar produces half of the world's vanilla—a complicated crop to produce. Each plant must be pollinated by hand, allowed to grow for six months, and then undergo a series of processes for a further three months.

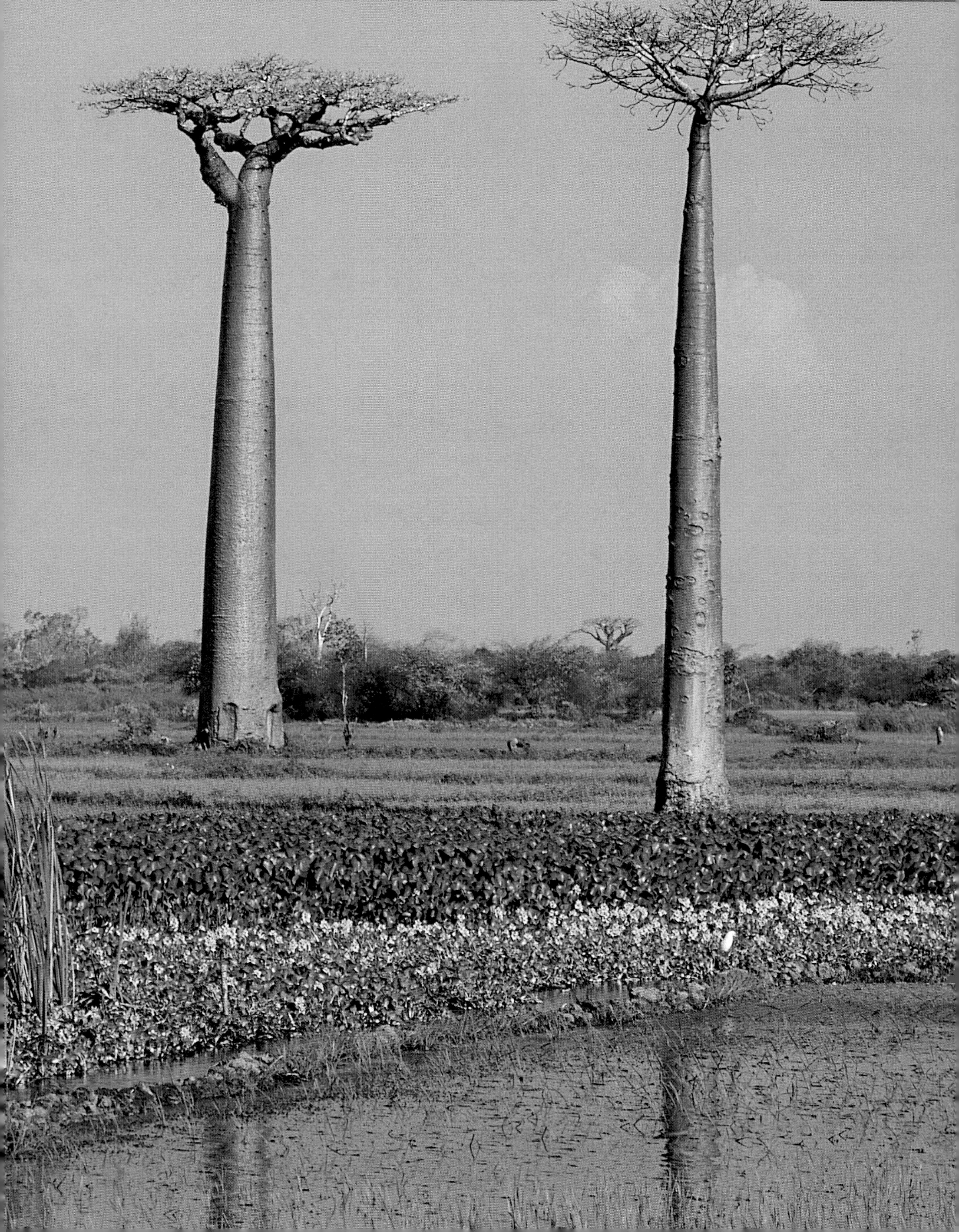

Africa's paddy fields

GROWING RICE IN MADAGASCAR

STRIKING BAOBAB TREES TOWER OVER PADDY FIELDS edged with water hyacinths on the west coast of Madagascar. Rice is the staple food of the island, and is grown on every available piece of land. Ironically, its very cultivation is contributing to a food shortage. Madagascar has always suffered from soil erosion, but the clearing of 80 percent of its forests to provide farmland has accelerated this process. Sadly, the exquisite water hyacinths make matters worse. Choking up rivers and lakes all over Africa, these weeds are responsible for killing fish and smothering crops. They are just another obstacle to Malagasy farmers trying to produce enough food for the islanders.

THE PEOPLE OF
Europe

EUROPE

A CENTER OF INDUSTRY AND COMMERCE

GOOD AGRICULTURAL LAND, RICH MINERAL RESOURCES, and a relatively compact size have enabled Europe to prosper. It is home to four of the world's five richest countries— Luxembourg, Switzerland, Norway, and

The borders of Europe

To the west, Europe is bordered by the Atlantic Ocean; to the north, by the Arctic; and to the south, by the Mediterranean Sea. The Ural Mountains and the Caspian Sea divide Europe from Asia. Russia and Turkey are included in both Asia and Europe.

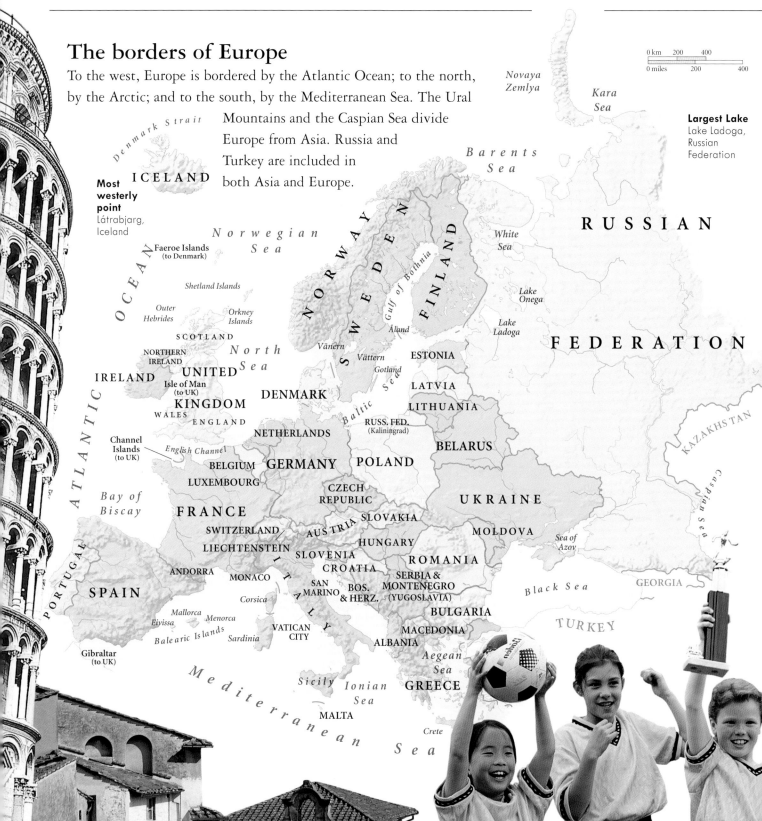

0 km 200 400
0 miles 200 400

Largest Lake
Lake Ladoga,
Russian
Federation

Novaya
Zemlya

Kara
Sea

Barents
Sea

White
Sea

Most westerly point
Látrabjarg, Iceland

Denmark Strait

ICELAND

Norwegian
Sea

Faeroe Islands
(to Denmark)

Shetland Islands

Outer
Hebrides

Orkney
Islands

SCOTLAND

NORTHERN
IRELAND

North
Sea

IRELAND

UNITED
Isle of Man
(to UK)

KINGDOM

WALES ENGLAND

Channel
Islands
(to UK)

English Channel

NETHERLANDS

BELGIUM GERMANY

LUXEMBOURG

Bay of
Biscay

FRANCE

SWITZERLAND
LIECHTENSTEIN

ANDORRA MONACO

PORTUGAL

ATLANTIC

OCEAN

SPAIN

Corsica

Mallorca Menorca
Eivissa

Balearic Islands Sardinia

Gibraltar
(to UK)

Mediterranean

Sea

NORWAY

SWEDEN

Vänern

Vättern

Gotland

Åland

Gulf of Bothnia

FINLAND

Lake
Onega

Lake
Ladoga

RUSSIAN

FEDERATION

ESTONIA

LATVIA

LITHUANIA

Baltic Sea

RUSS. FED.
(Kaliningrad)

BELARUS

POLAND

UKRAINE

CZECH
REPUBLIC

SLOVAKIA

AUSTRIA

HUNGARY

SLOVENIA

CROATIA

ITALY

SAN
MARINO

VATICAN
CITY

BOS.
& HERZ.

SERBIA &
MONTENEGRO
(YUGOSLAVIA)

ROMANIA

MOLDOVA

Sea of
Azov

Black Sea

KAZAKHSTAN

Caspian Sea

GEORGIA

TURKEY

BULGARIA

MACEDONIA

ALBANIA

Aegean
Sea

GREECE

Sicily

Ionian
Sea

MALTA

Crete

DENMARK

Liechtenstein, (the other being Japan). Access to education and standards of living are high compared to the rest of the world. The second smallest of the worlds continents, Europe contains 44 countries, including six "microstates." Most of Europe is Christian, and most European languages stem from Latin, German, or Slavic roots. Yet Europe is changing both ethnically and religiously due to migration from all corners of the globe.

European statistics

LANGUAGES
The relationship between most European languages can be traced; the exception is Euskara, which may predate the others.

Russian	170 million
German	98 million
English	63 million
French	60 million

RELIGIONS
The majority of Europeans are Christian. The influence of the religion on art, architecture, and culture can be seen everywhere.

Roman Catholic	185 million
E. Orthodox	105 million
Protestant	103 million
Muslim	20 million

URBAN POPULATION
Two of Europe's biggest cities are in Russia, its biggest country. None of these cities, though, is very large by world standards.

Moscow	8.4 million
London	7.4 million
St. Petersburg	4.6 million
Berlin	3.3 million

POPULATION BY COUNTRY
Europe's microstates have tiny populations. Only 25,000 live in San Marino, but Vatican City has far fewer residents—just 770!

Russian Fed.	145 million
Germany	82 million
France	59 million
United Kingdom	59 million

POPULATION

Europe's highest population density is in Monaco, the UK, and the Low Countries; its lowest is near the Arctic circle, where the climate is inhospitably cold, and in the vast Russian Federation, half of which belongs in Asia.

Population density (people per sq km)

	below 50
	50 - 99
	100 - 149
	150 -199
	200 - 300
	above 300

Around 73 percent of Europeans live in cities.

EUROPEAN FACTS

PLACES
Number of countries in Europe ...44 (incl Turkey and Russia)
Highest point ....Mount Elb'rus, Russia, 18,510 ft (5,642 m)
Lowest point.........................Volga Delta, Caspian Sea, Russia,
-92 ft (-28 m)
Longest river ....Volga River, Russia, 2,292 miles (3,688 km)
Biggest island ....Great Britain, UK
Biggest country ....Russian Federation
Smallest country ....Vatican City

PEOPLE
Population of continent ....728 million
Male life expectancy ....69 years
Female life expectancy ....78 years
Male literacy rate ....97 %
Female literacy rate ....97 %
People per doctor 294

The People of Europe

THE VAST MAJORITY of Europeans enjoy good health and material comfort in comparison to those in the non-Western world. Yet, in this largely urban, materialistic environment people suffer from loneliness in a way unthinkable in places where extended family groups and a more tightly knit community structure are the norm.

CITY LIVING

Around three-quarters of Europeans live in cities where they enjoy a high standard of living. Many are unfamiliar with the countryside, agriculture, or farming, instead buying everything they need from stores.

Compared to children in other parts of the world, European children are rarely allowed out unaccompanied by adults.

THE EUROPEAN UNION

EU Flag   **The euro**

A UNITED EUROPE?

The EU started in 1957 when Belgium, France, Italy, Germany, Luxembourg, and the Netherlands formed the European Economic Community (EEC) to improve trade and cooperation between their countries. In 1993 it became the European Union, and it currently has 15 members, 12 of which share a currency, the euro.

CULTURAL MIX

Europe's big cities are blessed with a tremendous mix of people. Migrants, particularly from Europe, Africa, and Asia, have had a major impact on the human face of the continent. As well as adding their numbers to the workforce, immigrants have also enriched Europe with their food, music, and religious customs.

Having a good time

Most Europeans work fixed and quite long hours, and all look forward to the holidays that dot their calendar. As well as major religious celebrations like Christmas, each country and region holds local festivals and events. Some holidays and events are ancient in origin, while others, such as sports tournaments, are more recent inventions but just as popular.

A NIGHT OUT

Most European cities have concert halls, opera houses, and theaters where formal, well-rehearsed performances of music, dance, or plays are put on. Spectators, like those at the ballet, must pay to watch; and unlike in other cultures, they do not participate.

SPLAT!

The tomato festival held near Valencia in Spain each year was only recently instituted. It owes its popularity to being so much fun.

FESTIVAL OF LIGHT

Celebrated in deepest midwinter in Sweden and Norway, St. Lucia's Day helps to cheer people up during the darkest part of the year.

CARNIVAL

The Venice Carnival is an old tradition that allows people to disguise themselves with masks and have a wild time.

FANTASTIC CONSTRUCTIONS

Europe has some wonderful buildings, the earliest of which are the castles and churches constructed by royalty. More recently, the emphasis has changed to buildings for government and business, and also to museums where a nation's treasures are displayed.

PASSION FOR SPORTS

Soccer matches and other sports events have, to some extent, replaced religion in arousing people's passionate involvement. Sports stadiums, especially when hosting soccer games, are one of the few public places where people cheer, laugh, and even cry.

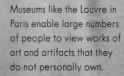

Museums like the Louvre in Paris enable large numbers of people to view works of art and artifacts that they do not personally own.

ICELANDERS

A MASS OF VOLCANIC ROCK in the middle of the north Atlantic Ocean,
Iceland's inaccessibility meant that for centuries contact with the rest of the world was infrequent. In its isolation the country developed its own

EUROPE'S REMOTE ISLAND NATION

Water, water everywhere

As well as being an island, Iceland has a lot of inland water, most famously hot springs, which are a major tourist attraction. The word *geyser* means a spurting, hot spring and comes from Geysir, the place in southwest Iceland where a spurt was first recorded in 1294. Geysers are caused by geothermal energy, the natural heat from the Earth that also causes volcanoes to erupt. In fact, geothermal energy formed this island in the first place.

CAPITAL CITY
The first settlers came to Iceland from Norway in the ninth century. They named the city they founded Reykjavik, or "Smoky Bay" because of the steam rising from the hot springs. Over 60 percent of Iceland's population live in or around Reykjavik, the world's most northerly capital.

GEOTHERMAL ENERGY
The Svartsengi power station takes in steam from naturally boiling seawater, heated by moten lava 6,000 ft (2,000 m) below the ground. The energy is used to heat freshwater for domestic use, or to drive turbines to create electricity. Using geothermal energy is clean and efficient, and, unlike resources such as natural gas, the water will never run out.

AN IMPORTANT SKILL
All children in Iceland learn how to swim, a skill that adults use frequently too. Iceland's outdoor swimming pools are open all year round. The weather might turn cold, but at 84°F (29°C), the naturally hot water keeps people warm.

language, and a unique and rich culture. Iceland does not need to use gas, coal, or oil because it is blessed with abundant geothermal energy. This means it has almost no pollution, air quality is excellent, and food is untainted by chemicals. The country's relationship with the sun is a strange one: for some months during the winter it is entirely absent, while during the summer weeks go by without it ever setting!

THE FISHING INDUSTRY

Iceland has the highest ratio of fishermen of any population. They catch 2.2 million tons (two million tonnes) of fish every year. Cod is the most common saltwater fish but shrimp, redfish, and herring are plentiful too. Freshwater trout and salmon are caught as much for sport and personal consumption as for industry.

HANGING OUT TO DRY

Fish is one of Iceland's staple foods. It is served baked, stewed, or sometimes simply dried and salted. Icelanders are proud of their fish, which swim in uncontaminated waters, and of the purity of their food, which is grown without artificial fertilizers.

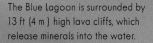

The Blue Lagoon is surrounded by 13 ft (4 m) high lava cliffs, which release minerals into the water.

STILL HOT AFTER 30 YEARS

Heimaey island is home to a volcano that erupted very violently in 1973. Today it is still possible to bake bread by burying an unbaked loaf in the volcano's ashes and leaving it for some hours.

THE BLUE LAGOON

A by-product of the Svartsengi geothermal power station is an artificial spa known as the Blue Lagoon. After the hot sea water has been used by the station, it enters a pool where it is mixed with freshwater and cooled to a comfortable 100-110°F (37-39°C). The slightly sulfurous water is only 4 ft (1.2 m) deep, but it is brimming with blue-green algae and white silica mud, which are said to be good for the skin.

CELTIC PEOPLE

CHILDREN OF ANCIENT INVADERS

Irish castles

Irish nobles from the 12th century onward protected themselves from invasion by living in castles with deep moats, thick walls, and fortified battlements. These were so well-built that many are still in good condition today and have been converted into hotels.

THE HIGHLAND GAMES

With Scottish clans separated by miles of craggy hillsides, the Highland Games were a way for people to get together. Today, Highland Games are held in Scotland and elsewhere. Traditional competitions, such as caber tossing and throwing the hammer, lie at the heart of these events, but Scottish dancers, bagpipers, and drummers may feature too.

Throwing the hammer.

IRISH DANCING

Today, Irish dancing is extremely popular among people of Irish origin living outside of Ireland. Its popularity is partly due to the *Conradh na Gaeilge* (Gaelic League), which was founded in 1839 to revive Irish folk culture. The organization standardized Irish dances and still issues rules governing how they are taught and judged in competitions.

SCOTTISH TARTAN

The distinctive mark of a tartan check is the square formed where threads of two different colors cross. Although tartan cloth had existed in Scotland for hundreds of years, its popularity grew enormously at the end of the 18th century when clans began to identify strongly their own particular pattern.

throughout the British Isles, particularly in Scotland, Ireland, and Wales, and many take great pride in their heritage and regional differences. There are scarcely any native speakers of Celtic languages such as Irish, Scottish, Cornish, and Manx, though their study and use are actively promoted. Welsh too is in decline, although 20 percent of Welsh people speak it, and it is taught at many schools in Wales.

TOSSING THE CABER
The caber is long pole up to 18 ft (5.5 m) long and 150 lbs (70 kg) in weight. Competitors lift the caber and try to throw it in a straight line.

Tartan kilts (skirts) are the traditional costume of Scottish men.

The caber is lifted at the thinner end, and flipped during the toss.

PIPING IN THE HAGGIS
The Scots celebrate the birth of their greatest poet, Robert Burns, on January 25. Haggis, a traditional food made out of stuffed sheeps's stomach is served at the meal. A great fuss is made over the haggis—it is brought in to the sound of a bagpipe, and speeches are made in its honor.

The haggis is stuffed with the heart and liver of a sheep and mixed with oatmeal and seasoning.

WHAT THE WELSH WORE
Welsh national costume is based on the clothes of Welsh peasants 200 years ago. For women and girls it consists of a striped petticoat worn under an open-fronted dress, called a bedgown, with an apron, shawl, and a tall hat. It is sometimes worn on Saint David's Day (March 1), Wales's national day.

SHEEP SHOW
Wales is the most important sheep farming region in Europe. There are 11 million sheep here alongside a human population of just three million. Sheep shows like this one allow farmers to come together to share news and information about sheep farming.

ENGLISH

A PATCHWORK NATION

THE ENGLISH PEOPLE THEMSELVES often feel uncertain about the the difference between the United Kingdom, Great Britain, and England. The United Kingdom is the name of the country that consists of Great

Englishness today

Unlike Americans, English people tend not to describe themselves as English. Perhaps this is because English people are descended from a mixture of so many groups: Romans, Normans, Danes, Vikings, and Celts. More recently, waves of immigration in the 19th and 20th century have brought substantial numbers of people from almost every corner of the globe to England.

A plush lawn, a slightly overcast sky, and a cathedral form the perfect backdrop for a cricket match.

MOST POPULAR DISH

There are more traditional contenders for the English national dish, (among them roast beef, or fish and chips) but "curry"—referring to almost any Indian dish—is without doubt England's most popular meal. Indian restuarants and carry outs exist in every English city, town, and perhaps, village.

SPORTING PASSION

The game of cricket traveled around the globe with English colonial administors in the 19th and 20th centuries. The English are still passionate about it, playing games on village greens in the summer.

MULTICULTURAL MARKET

English cities are home to immigrants from all corners of the Earth. The British Empire forged a bond between England and many African, Asian, and Caribbean countries. Migrants, especially those from former colonies, have helped to keep England vibrant.

Britain and Northern Ireland. Great Britain, then, refers to the island consisting of three somewhat independent regions: Scotland, Wales, and England. While the Irish, Scottish, and Welsh have distinctive national customs, it is harder to pick out the elements of a specifically English identity. It may be fairest to say that the English people form a patchwork of identities, samples of which are explored below.

MORRIS DANCERS
Historically an important part of annual springtime festivities, Morris dancers wear bells on their feet and leap athletically to lively folk music while waving sticks or handkerchiefs.

CARNIVAL!
London's Notting Hill Carnival has it origins in the West Indies. Trinidadian immigrants organized the first Carnival in 1964. Gradually it evolved from a celebration of black culture to a mainstream, multiracial event, a highlight of London's calendar. With one million participants, it has outgrown its route and may soon relocate.

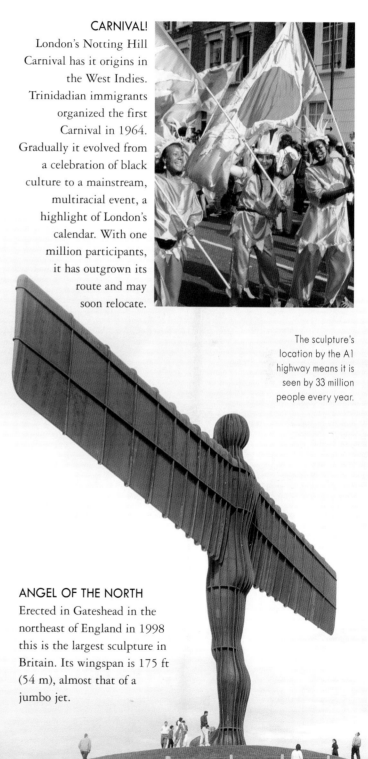

The sculpture's location by the A1 highway means it is seen by 33 million people every year.

TRADITIONAL PUBS
English pubs are a national institution and a mainstay of English social life. They vary greatly in style ranging from quaint, low-ceilinged timbered networks of rooms, to chic wallpapered and chandeliered Victorian pubs, to beer gardens popular with families. English law insists they close at 11pm, shortly after calling for "last orders."

UNIVERSITY TOWN
World-famous (along with Oxford) for its university founded in 1209, Cambridge is still dominated by student life. There are 31 colleges where students live and under whose care they are while at the university. Here, a punt (a flat bottomed boat) travels along the Cam River past St. John's College.

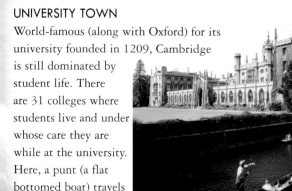

ANGEL OF THE NORTH
Erected in Gateshead in the northeast of England in 1998 this is the largest sculpture in Britain. Its wingspan is 175 ft (54 m), almost that of a jumbo jet.

SHETLAND ISLANDERS

A VIKING FIRE FESTIVAL RECALLS A SCANDINAVIAN INVASION

ON THE LAST TUESDAY OF JANUARY, nearly 1,000 men in Lerwick, the capital of the Shetland Islands, march in a torchlight procession behind a Viking longship carried through the streets. A relatively modern festival, *Up-Helly-Aa* only came into being in 1870 when a group of local men dreamed up the name and injected Viking disguises and a formal procession into a local post-Christmas celebration. They are led by an elected leader, *Guizer Jarl*, and his squad of Vikings. Following him, go 40 separate squads, each with its own theme and matching costume. The march ends with the spectacular blaze as the longship is set alight, but the revelry goes on all night with every squad visiting each of the 11 local halls in turn to perform funny sketches for the benefit of the townspeople.

THE NORTHERN REACHES OF EUROPE are famous for their long, cold, dark winters, and contrastingly brief summers in which the sun barely, or never, sets. People living in these regions owe their

SCANDINAVIANS

EUROPE'S NORTHERNERS

The Holmenkollen Ski Jump is a Norwegian insitution and home to an annual competition that first took place in 1892.

What's in a name?

The term "Scandinavia" does not have a strict definition. Geographically speaking, the Scandinavian peninsula consists of Norway, Sweden, and a bit of Finland, though the term is more commonly used to refer to Norway, Sweden, and Denmark. The broadest definition, however, also includes Iceland and Finland.

CHURCHBOAT RACES

Church services in the Swedish village of Rattvik attracted people from across the bay, some of whom traveled by boat. A custom evolved with the villages building longboats and racing one another. Today, the races are staged for the benefit of tourists.

SANTA LUCIA

December 13 is Santa Lucia Day. Traditionally, in Sweden and Norway, the youngest daughter in each family brings breakfast to her parents dressed in a white dress, red sash, and candle headdress. The name Lucia means "light," a welcome sight in the long, dark winters.

GETTING AROUND

Cross-country skiing was invented centuries ago in Scandinavia as a practical means of getting around in a snowy climate. It is still a popular sport today, particularly in Norway.

ICE FISHING

Even when the ice is solid enough to sit on, life continues beneath the surface. This warmly dressed Norwegian woman lying on a bearskin has drilled a hole into the thick ice covering a lake and is waiting patiently for the fish to bite.

height, blue eyes, and blonde hair to their Viking ancestors. Today, the Scandinavian countries tend to be industrialized with a good standard of living. Most of the population is concentrated in the south, though plenty live within the Arctic circle. Officially Scandinavian countries have Christianity as their national religion, but religious practice is weak and beliefs are often blended with pre-Christian elements.

WELFARE STATES

Taxes in Scandinavia are set high, but in return people benefit from excellent welfare services. Denmark provides the best state child support in Europe. A parent may take an entire year off work to care for a baby while still, in most cases, being paid in full.

GRADUATION DAY

At their graduation ceremony students wear a distinctive white cap with a red or blue band. After the ceremony, students, still wearing their hats, drive around the streets in decorated open-topped cars and vans with music blaring, tooting their horns.

CONNECTING COUNTRIES

The idea for a bridge uniting Sweden and Denmark is not a new one. Suggestions date back to the 19th century. The plans finally came to fruition in 2000 with the opening of the Øresund Bridge linking Malmö in Sweden with Copenhagen in Denmark. At 10 miles (16 km), it is the longest single bridge in the world to carry both road and railroad traffic.

CITY OF BIKES

Bicycle travel is common in Denmark, where the government encourages people to cycle rather than drive. Copenhagen is even known as the City of Bikes. On average, every Dane cycles two miles (3 km) per day, and even the Prime Minister is often seen out and about on his bike.

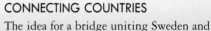

SAMI

A NOMADIC LIFE IN THE CHILL

THE SAMI PEOPLE OF NORTHERN EUROPE live in the Arctic area popularly known as Lapland. Originally the Sami hunted reindeer, but by the 17th century, hunting was replaced by herding. These days few

Life in the freezer

In a land where the vital activities of getting food and keeping warm are the difference between life and death— temperatures can plummet to a chilly -49°F (-45°C)—the Norwegian Sami herders live remarkably in tune with the land. For centuries the Sami have formed work teams called *Sii'das*—groups of families that herd their reindeer together and share the work. Each reindeer is marked, according to the *Sii'da,* when it is born, usually by a small nick cut out of one ear.

CLOTHING

Some Sami still wear the traditional bright red and blue costumes. Women wear dresses belted at the waist and men wear belted tunics. In the winter they wear reindeer skins with their clothes. The women use looms made of wood and antler to weave the belts and ribbons that decorate clothes.

Tall hats are sometimes stuffed with grass to help keep the head warm.

A traditional lifestyle does not stop the Sami from enjoying modern conveniences.

ZT 24285

BELIEFS

Originally the Sami followed an animistic religion, believing that all objects in nature have a soul that must be respected. This has long been replaced by the Lutheran faith, and marriages take place in churches. However, they still believe that spirits inhabit the natural world and those who do not respect nature will have trouble living off the land.

The Sami people started converting to the Christian faith in the 17th century.

Sami herd and only those in the north of Norway are still seminomadic. These people migrate each spring, with their reindeer, from the tundra to the coast and islands, where the calves are born. They then return to the tundra in the fall. The Sami live in towns on the tundra and enjoy a modern standard of living much like other Norwegians. The Sami who migrate are some of Europe's last nomads.

Annual migration

In the spring instinct prompts the reindeer to start moving north on their migration to the coast or to islands off the coast where their calves will be born. A Sami group member on skis leads the herd, and teams of men with dogsleds bring up the rear to stop any of the animals from wandering off. Their long and arduous journey can sometimes take them over highlands and across rivers.

COUNTING THE HERD
Before the spring migration, the herd of up to 3,000 reindeer needs to be gathered and counted. Huge lengths of burlap are swished around the reindeer to round them up, and dogs (pointed-eared pomeranians) are used to drive the reindeer to enter into a corral. The pregnant females are sometimes taken to the coast in trucks before calving time.

KEEPING WARM
On the migration, it is essential to keep warm. The Sami wear thermal underwear and a thick overgarment called a *peske* made out of reindeer skin. They often stuff their boots and hats with dried sedge grass for extra insulation. At night teepee-style tents are set up and fires are lit inside for warmth.

Curly-toed boots are strapped beneath ski straps to hold the skis in place.

Exhausted reindeer.

As well as snowmobiles, the Sami people also use walkie-talkies and sometimes even helicopters to aid herding.

MODERN MIGRATION
These days modern ski wear combines with traditional Sami clothing, and snowmobiles are commonly used. It is however essential to let the animals walk at their own pace. If a reindeer gets tired, someone will often give it a free ride on the back of the snowmobile!

FINNS

OLD TRADITIONS AND NEW INVENTIONS

SITUATED IN THE NORTH OF EUROPE, Finland shares some unusual features with its neighbors. The most noticeable is the long, dark winter, when temperatures can drop to -49°F (-45°C). Living in the cold

An independent country

Finland belonged to Sweden from the 12th to the 19th century, and after that to Russia. It became independent in 1917 and successfully resisted invasions from both the Soviet Union and Nazi Germany. In recent times Finland's telecommunications industry has grown rapidly, to the extent that Finns use more mobile phones per person than anyone else in the world.

WINTER SPORTS
Naturally, the climate means that sports like cross-country skiing and snowboarding are popular in Finland, but so is *pesäpallo,* the national sport, which is somewhat like baseball. People also keep in shape by cycling instead of driving cars.

HOLIDAY ON ICE
Ski holiday week, or *hiihtolomaviikko,* takes place around March and always boosts morale. Officially this is a students' holiday, but adults also take the opportunity to go cross-country skiing or snowmobiling. In the evening, people stop for a barbeque supper and set up camp overnight in the forests.

WOOD IS GOOD
Three-quarters of Finland is forest, providing hunting, fishing, land for grazing animals, and, most importantly, wood. In the past, wood was needed for fuel, furniture, and other everyday items. Today it is used to a lesser extent, but exporting wood is still vital to the Finnish economy.

LIGHTING THE WAY
This family is making a beacon that will help their children to find their way home from school in the dark. During the winter months some days will only have two hours of sunlight.

Even very young children are used to playing in the snow with sleds or skis.

and dark has created an emphasis on saunas and exercise, which help to keep people feeling fit and happy. From June 21 until December 22, four minutes of daylight are lost every day. The sun might not be seen at all during midwinter, but when it appears in the summer, it is celebrated. Forests cover much of Finland and up until recently, many people held jobs in forestry. Finns today still respect nature and enjoy the scenery.

MIDSUMMER BONFIRES

Midsummer, or *Juhannus*, marks the summer solstice. It became a Christian feast although it was marked even before Christianity came to Finland. Today it is a celebration of nature. People go to the countryside, or decorate their towns with lilac and birch. At night they light *kokkos* (bonfires), which symbolize purity and ward off evil spirits. *Juhannus* also provides an occasion for people to fly the national flag.

A HEALTHY SWEAT

Although not a Finnish invention, the word "sauna" is Finnish, and steam baths have been a part of Finnish culture for over 1,000 years. There are 1.7 million saunas in Finland—that's one for every three people.

1 Hot house
Almost every house has its own sauna, and minisaunas are even built inside apartments! Saunas are a great way to relax and socialize during the dark winters.

2 Heating up
In the steam room rocks are heated on a stove and then splashed with water to create steam. The point of a sauna is to induce sweat, and thereby open the skin's pores.

3 Cooling down
From the steam room, bathers plunge into a pool of icy water or else roll in the snow. The sudden contrast is invigorating and refreshes both body and mind.

LAST DAY OF SCHOOL

Graduating from school in Finland calls for a big celebration. Those graduating are presented with their diplomas, red roses, and a distinctive white cap. After the formal ceremony at the school, families host parties for their graduating son or daughter.

DUTCH

TULIP FIELDS IN FULL BLOOM

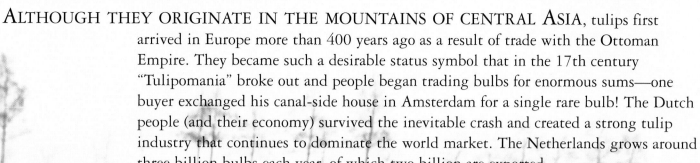

ALTHOUGH THEY ORIGINATE IN THE MOUNTAINS OF CENTRAL ASIA, tulips first arrived in Europe more than 400 years ago as a result of trade with the Ottoman Empire. They became such a desirable status symbol that in the 17th century "Tulipomania" broke out and people began trading bulbs for enormous sums—one buyer exchanged his canal-side house in Amsterdam for a single rare bulb! The Dutch people (and their economy) survived the inevitable crash and created a strong tulip industry that continues to dominate the world market. The Netherlands grows around three billion bulbs each year, of which two billion are exported.

THE KINGDOM OF SPAIN was formed in 1492, when King Ferdinand and Queen Isabella united the kingdoms of Castilla and Aragón and made Roman Catholicism the national religion. Today, Spain has 17 regions

SPANISH

A NATION ON THE IBERIAN PENINSULA

Old traditions, current passions

Many aspects of Spanish culture have evolved out of traditional folk customs, yet it is Roman Catholicism that has had the greatest impact on Spanish culture. Over 3,000 religious festivals—ancient and modern, local and national—are celebrated throughout the country.

CAPITAL CITY
Madrid sits in the very center of the country. One of its major landmarks, the Plaza Mayor, was the scene of many coronations and executions.

FERIA DE ABRIL
Men dressed as Andalucian peasants ride horses and carts through the streets during Seville's annual fair. Hundreds of tents house temporary dance halls during the week-long festival that attracts one million people.

SPANISH SNACKS
Every bar in Spain serves *tapas*, small plates of snacks to go with drinks. Originally free, these days they must be paid for. Typical *tapas* might be sausages, meatballs, squid, prawns, olives, potatoes, or mushrooms. Spanish people sometimes spend an evening going from bar to bar and sampling each one's speciality dish.

and four official ethnic groups with their own languages—Castilian, Catalan, Galician, and Basque. Regions are self-governing and have their own definite flavor, so there is great diversity among the Spanish people. For much of its history, Spain was ruled by other civilizations ranging from the Romans to the Moors. Each has left its influence on the culture, arts, and landscape of today.

CASTELLS IN THE SKY

These men making a human castle (castell, in Catalan) at a festival in Tarragona, are called castellers. Castellers attend every festival in the region and are also a popular sight on television. Tradition says that the castell must be at least eight tiers tall.

BAGPIPES

The music of Galicia in northwest Spain is nothing like the flamenco music of Andalucia in the south. Gaita (bagpipes) feature strongly because Galicia was once occupied by Celtic people like those who settled in Scotland and Ireland.

BASQUE PEOPLE

Inhabiting a region that straddles both France and Spain, the Basque people have a strong sense of their own identity. Their language, Euskara, intrigues scholars because it appears unrelated to any other European language.

TOMATO PASTE

An unusual festival takes place on the last Wednesday of August in the Spanish town of Buñol, near Valencia on the east coast. Around 30,000 Spanish and foreign revelers squish 265,000 lbs (120,000 kg) of tomatoes and then pelt one another with them. The festival is said to have been started by schoolchildren in the 1940s.

THE SARDANA

The sardana is the traditional dance of the Catalan people in the northeast of Spain. Dancers link hands and hold their arms up, while taking graceful and precise steps. New dancers can join in at any point by entering the circle. When it gets too big, dancers form more circles.

PORTUGUESE

HOPING FOR A GOOD CATCH

PUSHING THEIR COLORFUL *DÓRI* (FISHING BOAT) OUT TO SEA these fishermen hope they won't need to travel too far from the coastal village of Praia de Mira to find fish such as sardines, anchovies, and tuna. Their ancestors were a hardy breed, many of whom were prepared to venture a great deal farther. From the 15th to the mid-20th century, Portuguese fishermen spent long months from April to September in the hazardous, freezing waters of the North Atlantic. They traveled as far as the coasts of Norway, Iceland, and Labrador in search of cod. Sometimes fog or storms would suddenly descend and a boat would disappear, making widows and orphans of entire communities back home.

FRENCH

AN APPRECIATION OF THE GOOD LIFE

FRANCE BORDERS SEVEN OTHER COUNTRIES—Spain, Andorra, Italy, Switzerland, Luxembourg, Belgium, and Germany—and is only separated from the United Kingdom by the English Channel. The French people

THE ROLE OF RELIGION

France has been a secular country since the time of the French Revolution, so there is no national religion, nor is religion taught in schools. Many people belong to the Roman Catholic church, and France is also home to many Muslims who have emigrated from North Africa.

WINE PRODUCTION

The French have been producing wine since at least Roman times. Wines from each region taste different thanks to a variety of factors including the type of grape, climate, soil, and the way the wine is fermented.

Free time

Quality of life and leisure time are very important to the people of France. All French workers are entitled to five weeks of paid vacation annually, and many take the entire month of August off. They decamp to the countryside to vacation homes or hotels, leaving the cities virtual ghost towns.

TRADITIONAL PASTIME

Boules, or *pétanque*, is a popular French game played with metal balls. The goal of the game is to get your ball as close as possible to the target ball known as the *cochonnet*. Players are also allowed to thrown their balls at the *cochonnet* so as to nudge it farther from their opponents' balls and closer to their own.

are very proud of their country, believing it to be highly cultured, and in possession of the best food and wine. They value a chic personal appearance, and the pleasant presentation of even the most basic foods and commodities is taken for granted. Intellectual and cultural life are important too, and there is a strong movement to protect French language and culture from being overwhelmed by foreign influences.

BASTILLE DAY

On July 14, 1789, the French people stormed the Bastille Prison, beginning the revolution that freed them from the monarchy and made the country a republic. The day is celebrated every year as a national holiday.

ENDURANCE TEST

The *Tour de France* is a world-famous bicycle race which lasts for three weeks. Its 2,100 miles (3,400 km) are broken into 20 stages which cover many of the different terrains that make up the French countryside. 2003 marks the 100th year of the *Tour*.

The Eiffel Tower.

BRETONS

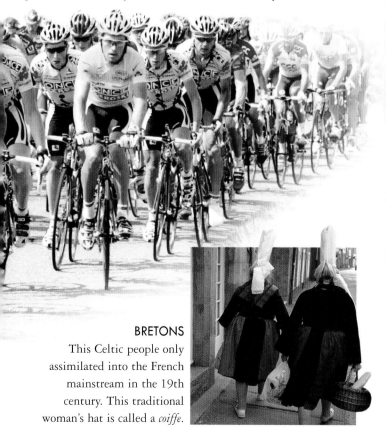

This Celtic people only assimilated into the French mainstream in the 19th century. This traditional woman's hat is called a *coiffe*.

CAFÉ CULTURE

The Champs Elysées is the most famous street in Paris. Wide, tree-lined sidewalks mean people can sit outdoors at its cafés and restaurants and watch the world go by. Dining, or just drinking a coffee at an outdoor cafe, is an everyday pleasure greatly valued by the French people.

Big country

FRANCE IS THE LARGEST COUNTRY in Western Europe. It mostly consists of flat plains but there are some mountainous areas including the Pyrenees in the south, the Massif Central in the center, and the Alps in the east. France also administers some overseas territories left over from colonial times.

MODERN MONUMENT

The *Grand Arche* is a striking 35-story office block. It was one of a number of buildings commissioned at the end of the 20th century to symbolize France's role in art, politics, and the world economy. It is situated in Paris's La Defense district, home to 14 of France's top 20 corporations.

APPRECIATING THE ARTS

France has a long tradition of distinguished artists and an appreciation for the arts is instilled in French children from an early age. Art education is a compulsory part of the French school curriculum for children aged 5-15. They are taught both how to enjoy and understand art, and how to produce artworks of their own.

At the top of the building is a public gallery, which looks out onto spectacular views of Paris.

FILM FESTIVAL

Cannes' population is just under 70,000 but swells to almost three times this number during the annual international film festival every May. The town is situated on the French Riviera in the south of France and is also a popular destination during the summer months for both French and foreign tourists drawn to its mild climate and beautiful beaches.

Away from the cities

France enjoys great geographical diversity and each region has its own distinct character and food. Particular areas of natural beauty include Brittany with its rugged coast, the mountain ranges of the Alps and the Pyrenees, the Mediterranean coast around the Cote d'Azur, and the glorious vineyards and lavender fields of Provence.

SKIING

There is plenty of choice when it comes to winter sports in France. There are many well-established ski resorts in the mountains of the Alps and the Pyrenees, and cross-country skiing is becoming more popular in the Jura and Massif Central.

WEEKLY MARKETS

Many French towns host weekly markets where farmers sell their own produce ranging from fruit and vegetables to wine, sausages, and cheeses. The foods vary according to the region and season.

FRAGRANT FIELDS

The lavender plant needs little water and grows wells in the dry, hot climate of southern France. Its sweet fragrance makes it a popular ingredient in soaps and perfumes. It has one additional quality—it is a strong natural insect repellant.

Provence is well-known for its acres of lavender fields, which are harvested at the height of the summer.

GERMANS

TODAY, GERMANY HAS THE THIRD LARGEST ECONOMY in the world, perhaps because Germans tend to be so organized and thorough in their affairs. Yet until recently there were actually two Germanys. The

NO LONGER DIVIDED INTO TWO NATIONS

A unified country

Germany's 16 states each have their own capital and regional government. Prior to reunification, East Germany was one of the richest of the communist countries, yet its citizens experienced a considerable degree of material hardship and cultural repression compared to the people of West Germany. Today, the gap in prosperity between these two groups still persists, though it is slowly closing.

FRIESIAN FOLK
Both the Netherlands and Germany have Friesian populations who traditionally live a rural life and keep animals. Windmills and cottages (often thatched) dot the region.

THE FIFTH SEASON
During the carnival in the village of Bad Waldsee, revelers wear costumes or traditional hand-crafted wooden masks to parade through the streets. It only lasts a few days but the carnival is so important that it is referred to as the "fifth season" of the year.

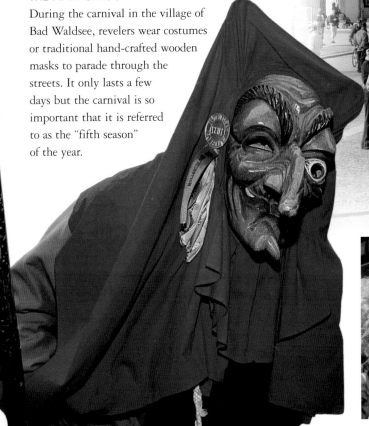

CARNIVAL IN COLOGNE
The highlight of Cologne's carnival is the *Rosenmontag* (Rose Monday) procession. Dozens of floats decorated with huge figures relating to topical events move through the streets, and candies and flowers are thrown into the crowd.

country was divided in the aftermath of World War II—the western part became the Federal Republic while the eastern zone, dominated by the communist Soviet Union, became the German Democratic Republic. The GDR was the poor relation, so much so that a wall was erected to prevent East Germans from defecting to the West. The Berlin Wall came down in 1989 amid great rejoicing and emotional reunions.

THE BRANDENBURG GATE

Berlin's Brandenburg Gate is an important landmark. It was modeled on the entrance to Athen's Acropolis and was completed in 1791. Ironically, though intended to symbolize peace, the gate was incorporated into the Berlin Wall and its meaning only restored in 1989 when the wall came down.

The Gate is a major tourist attraction. Only taxis, buses, and officials are allowed to drive through it now.

GERMAN SAUSAGES

There are thousands of different types of *wurst* (German sausages); some are cooked and eaten hot while others are sliced or spread. The meat—mostly pork, sometimes beef or veal—is combined with peppercorns, spices, and other ingredients.

WOOD CARVING WORKSHOP

A clockmaker carves the face for a cuckoo clock in his Black Forest workshop. Cuckoo clocks were first made in the 18th century when peddling "clock carriers" found customers for them by literally carrying the clocks around in backpacks to prospective buyers. Demand still remains high for the handmade clocks today.

CAR INDUSTRY

Germany was producing 900 cars a year in 1901. Today, the number is closer to 10 million, and firms such as Audi, Daimler, Mercedes, BMW, Volkswagen, and Porsche employ 1.26 million people.

Bavarians

THE LARGEST REGION IN GERMANY is called Bavaria, but Bavarian dialects and architecture can be found in parts of Germany, the Austrian Tyrol, and even South Tyrol in Italy. The folk customs of this area are particularly rich – yodelling, the alpenhorn, many different kinds of dance, and a variety of national costumes all originate in this region.

A rich heritage

Local governments support cultural organizations in their efforts to keep Bavarian traditions alive. No subsidies are necessary, however, to promote Bavarian foods: beer, meatballs, and sausages are still as popular as ever.

OKTOBERFEST

The Oktoberfest has been held in Munich every year since 1810 when it was instituted to celebrate a royal wedding. It is an enormous festival with over six million visitors annually. The mayor opens the event by tapping a keg of beer and declaring "O'zapft is" which means "it's been tapped".

TOWN SQUARE
The town of Lindau nestles on an island on the shores of Lake Constance, Germany's biggest lake. During the Middle Ages prosperous merchants lived here. Their brightly painted, half-timbered houses overlooking picturesque town squares are very popular with tourists.

BRASS BAND
Jolly Bavarian "oom-pah" music is traditionally played outdoors by a brass band. It features at celebrations, – most famously at Munich's boisterous Oktoberfest.

SCHUHPLATTLING

The *Schuhplattling* (shoe-slapping) dance which goes back to the 11th-14th centuries is the most well-known Bavarian dance. The man's slapping movement is said to mimic a species of bird which flaps its wings to attract a mate.

SANTA CLAUS IN BERGHOFEN

On the 5th of December at 8pm black hooded figures with long straw beards and bells attached to their stomachs meet in Berghofen. Until midnight they run through the town, bells clanging deafeningly, visiting the local farms to banish evil spirits.

CHURCH IN THE HILLS

The town of Berchtesgaden nestles among valleys and lakes with the magnificent Bavarian Alps as its backdrop. This region was once a separate little country, one of the smallest states in the Holy Roman Empire.

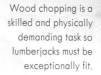
Wood chopping is a skilled and physically demanding task so lumberjacks must be exceptionally fit.

WOOD PULLING

During the autumn lumberjacks chop wood in the forests of the Allgau. The logs are stored high in the mountains and brought down to the valley when needed. The wood is transported by helicopter or by horse-drawn carriage, which is cheap, efficient, and much better for the environment!

SORBS

EUROPEAN RESIDENTS FROM BEFORE THE ROMAN CONQUEST

IN BRANDENBURG AND SAXONY, not far from the German borders with Poland and the Czech Republic, live 150,000 people who regard themselves not as German, but as Sorbian. Descendants of the Slavic tribes that dominated central Europe before the arrival of the Romans, they are not related to the Serbs of today. The Sorbs have their own Slavonic language, and around 60,000 people not only speak it, but also perform plays, broadcast on television and radio, publish newspapers, magazines, and books, and teach it in schools, too. The traditions of the 15,000 Sorbian Catholics are particularly strong. One of the best preserved is the Easter Riding in which processions of mounted locals visit nearby villages in traditional costumes to announce the resurrection of Jesus in song.

ALPINE PEOPLE

EUROPE'S MOUNTAIN PEOPLE

RUNNING ACROSS SEVEN DIFFERENT COUNTRIES and approximately 750 miles (1,200 km), the Alps divide the northern and southern parts of mainland Europe. This mountain range

Outnumbered by skiiers

What was once the quiet season is now the busiest and most profitable time of year for many Alpine towns and villages. In some towns, during the skiing season, tourists outnumber locals by 40 to one. Hotels, restaurants, cable cars, and ski lifts as well as many new roads have all been built to support the booming tourist industry.

Tourists also visit the Alps during the summer to hike and enjoy the warmer weather.

DELICIOUS CHEESE

The fresh, sweet grass and wild flowers eaten by Alpine cows result in wonderfully tasty milk and cheese. The best cheeses are made by hand and then left to mature for weeks or months in a special cheese cave where they must be turned over and rubbed with salt on alternate days.

Cheese is made by mixing fresh milk with rennet, an enzyme found in the stomach lining of calves reared solely on milk.

POTATO FARMING

Some Alpine regions provide the right conditions for growing potatoes. Seeds are planted between February and April and the crop is harvested between May and September. Potatoes were brought to Europe by explorers returning from travels in the New World in the late 1500s.

stretches from southeastern France through Italy, Switzerland, Liechtenstein, Austria, and into Slovenia. The Alps can be divided into four main climatic regions, although virtually every valley has a slightly different climate. Until recently, the mountains were considerable barriers to travel, so people in these areas developed in separate clusters resulting in different traditions, languages, and dialects.

HEADING FOR THE HILLS
During the winter, the cows must be kept away from the snowy slopes and eat hay in the valley. In the middle of June, they are herded back up the mountains. A whole day is dedicated to the task. People armed with sticks keep the cows moving if they get distracted by the juicy grass.

Most Swiss are Christian, with the numbers divided almost equally between Catholics and Protestants.

MAKING HAY
June and July are a particularly busy time for Alpine farmers. While their cows are enjoying the grass high above the treeline, the farmers gather the grass growing on the lower slopes to make hay. It is heaped into nets and hauled away to be stored in haylofts. This hay will provide the cattle with food during the long winter to come.

Seasonal fun

LIFE IN THE ALPS is exceptionally healthy. The water is clean, the air is clear, and the steep slopes and out-of-doors life provide ample excercise. Although many tourists visit the Alps to experience these benefits, local people too live in every peak and valley. Each group has its own history, customs, and even language.

A ROMANTIC SLEIGH RIDE
On a Sunday in January or February, young people in the Engadine traditionally participate in the *Schlitteda*, a procession of horse-drawn sleighs. It is a picturesque event, as the sleighs are beautifully decorated and their riders dressed in old-fashioned costumes. After the ride there is a celebratory ball. The *Schlitteda* was originally held in order to provide an opportunity for young men and women to meet and fall in love, though nowadays married people participate too.

A winter wonderland

Though for the most part Swiss-German is spoken in the Engadine area of the Swiss Alps, which is very popular with tourists, some 70,000 people here speak *Romansh*, the fourth-largest language in Switzerland. Actually, *Romansh* consists of a number of distinct but related dialects. Just as the language persists, so do some of the traditional customs, such as the *Schlitteda* and the *Chalandamarz* (see below.)

The "herdsman" who heads the procession also leads the singing.

CHALANDAMARZ
On the first of March, local boys carrying cow bells form a procession. The boy with the biggest bell leads. He represents a herdsman and those behind him are his "calves." Their job is to make as much noise as possible so as to drive winter away.

WRESTLING CONTEST

Schwingen is a style of wrestling that originated with Swiss farmers in the Alps. Today, *schwingen* is a popular sport in Switzerland, and the national championships that take place every three years are watched by more than 40,000 people.

Sunny days

Summers in the Alps are short but bright. There is a lot to do because while the cattle are on the high mountains enough hay must be prepared for the winter. Locals enjoy the good weather, as do tourists who visit at this time when the hills are green and perfect for hiking.

Information about every single cow in Switzerland is kept on a central computer.

Traditionally, only boys took part in the *Chalandamarz*, but now girls join in too.

COW BEAUTY CONTEST

In April, independent experts spend a day in each village judging the cows and establishing the value of each one. This day is critical so farmers spend a lot of time preparing for it. Each cow is scrubbed with warm, soapy water, its hooves are clipped, and it is made to parade in front of the judges.

RUSSIANS

EUROPE'S LARGEST ETHNIC GROUP

RUSSIANS ARE DESCENDED FROM THE SLAVIC PEOPLE living north of the Black Sea. Most Russians were rural peasants working for aristocratic landlords until the Communist Revolution. From 1917-1991,

City life

About three-quarters of Russians live in cities. A shortage of housing means that most families have small apartments inside enormous housing blocks. During the communist era, apartments were owned and allocated by the government. Today, families must buy their own homes. The high cost means that it is very common for grandparents, parents, and children to live together.

This Moscow housing block is home to hundreds of families.

CONSUMER CULTURE

Until communism ended in Russia in 1991, the state looked after many aspects of peoples' lives. Food, clothing, and various other items were rationed. These days, big Russian cities boast boutiques, chic restaurants, and well-stocked department stores, but the goods are too costly for many people.

Fast-food restaurants have opened in Russia.

TEMPERING

Russians traditionally believe that the body should be "tempered" in order to enable it to withstand diseases in the cold climate. This process, which is still performed on children today, is called *zakalivanie*. It involves briefly plunging all or part of the body into snow or freezing cold water.

under communism, the central government managed land in large state farms and was responsible for allocating housing. During the 20th century, some European and central Asian countries subscribed to communism, joined the Soviet Union and submitted, to a greater or lesser degree, to Russian control.

St. Basil's Cathedral in Moscow features striking onion-shaped domes and spires.

ICE SCULPTURES
Every February, Moscow's Gorky Park hosts an ice-sculpture festival featuring the work of both local and international artists. It takes hours of work in the freezing cold to create a sculpture like this cat.

TIME FOR TEA
The *samovar* symbolizes home for Russians. Its function is to keep tea—drunk at all times of day—and the water used to dilute it hot. A central cylinder containing smoldering charcoal keeps the brew hot in a traditional *samovar*. Newer models sit on the gas stove or use electricity instead.

A PLACE IN THE COUNTRY
Many urban Russians own a home in the country, called a *dacha,* where they spend the weekends and summer vacation. Under communism, food came from collective farms, which were controlled by the government. People would supplement this food with vegetables that they grew on plots of land next to their *dachas*. These small gardens are still an important part of the *dacha* experience.

Maslenitsa

RUSSIA OFFICIALLY JOINED the Eastern Orthodox Church in 988 AD. Under communism, however, religion was condemned and many churches closed. Newly created holidays and pre-Christian celebrations like Maslenitsa replaced traditional Christian observance. Nevertheless, the Church, though suppressed, survived and is now enjoying renewed popularity.

An ancient tradition

Maslenitsa dates back to pre-Christian times. Its counterparts exist in the many festivals in the northern hemisphere that commemorate the rebirth of nature at the end of a long, dark winter. Different activities are assigned to each day of the week-long celebration including parties, sleigh rides, and even a day to visit grandparents.

LADY MASLENITSA
A straw dummy dressed as Lady Maslenitsa is made to accompany the festivities. She symbolizes the hope for a good spring and a successful harvest later in the year.

GOODBYE TO WINTER

On the last day of *Maslenitsa*, the Lady Maslenitsa dummy is burned together with any leftover *blinis*. This gesture is a farewell to winter and marks the start of Lent. The day is also called Forgiveness Day because people beg pardon of one another before the 40 days of Lent begin.

A carnival atmosphere during Maslenitsa means lots of eating, drinking, and snowball fights in the city's parks.

EASTER CELEBRATIONS

The 40 days of Lent end with *Paskha*, or Easter. In Russian Orthodox churches on Easter Sunday the priest blesses the breakfast meal. This traditionally consists of a sweet cylindrical bread, *kulich*, eaten with a cheese mixture in the form of a pyramid also called *paskha*.

Snow covers the ground for many months of the year so Muscovites are used to dressing for the cold.

PANCAKES GALORE

Stuffed with delicious fillings, pancakes called *blinis* are round, warm, and golden to symbolize the sun. The tradition of eating *blinis* during Maslenitsa originated because rich foods were not eaten during Lent. *Blinis* made for Maslenitsa provided an opportunity to use up eggs, sugar, milk, and butter before the great fast began. In fact, *masla* is the Russian word for butter.

POLES

LIKE OTHER COUNTRIES IN EASTERN EUROPE, Poland was badly damaged by World War II (1939–1945), and shortly afterward adopted communism. Unfortunately, the country also suffered for many years under communist rule. The Polish

A DEVOUTLY RELIGIOUS PEOPLE

Ethnically and religiously unified

The borders of the country that is modern Poland have changed in significant ways since the 10th century. Despite this, nearly all of its population is ethnically Polish, which makes Poland the most racially uniform country in Europe. Almost the entire population is also Roman Catholic, with three-quarters actively practicing their religion. Polish people are extremely proud that the current Pope, John Paul II, is a Pole and former Archbishop of Krakow.

SOCIALIST HOUSING
During the communist era enormous, identical apartment blocks were built in Poland and other communist countries. It was believed that identical homes would make people feel equal.

FIRST COMMUNION
By the time they are eight or nine, Polish children will have experienced their First Communion. On this day girls in white dresses and veils, and boys in dark suits participate fully in the Catholic Mass for the first time.

MUSHROOM PICKING
Historically, mushrooms were the great equalizer in the Polish diet; growing wild they were available to rich and poor alike. To this day, mushroom picking is a favored Polish pastime.

solidarity movement led the way throughout Eastern Europe for the rapid, yet peaceful decline of communism in the late 1980s and early 1990s. Poland enjoys fertile farmland, and even though the country has recently transformed itself into a capitalist democracy, nearly a third of its citizens maintain a rural lifestyle, living and working on small, family-run farms.

Small-scale Polish farmers seldom use machinery, and instead rely on human and animal power.

FARM LIFE

Unlike in other communist countries, Polish farms were never taken over by the state but remained the property of their owners. As a result, Poland is home to almost two million farms. Most are small, family-run affairs which exist in order to feed those who work on them, and not to produce food for sale.

COLORFUL COSTUMES

About 60 distinct ethnic regions exist in Poland. In some highland areas, traditional dress is still made and worn on holidays and at festivals. In other areas, folk costumes are made mostly for dance groups or choirs.

FOLK ART

For centuries, traditional art has thrived in rural Poland. The paintings on the walls of this cottage are a good example of folk art—the creation and decoration of functional objects.

ROMA

A TRADITION OF TRAVELING

COMMONLY CALLED GYPSIES, Roma were persecuted because their nomadic lifestyle meant they were perceived as outsiders with foreign customs and their own language. There are more than 12 million Roma

Mobile home

Roma living in mobile homes value their freedom, but they also live this way because many European peoples have refused to let them set up permanent homes. Roma like to do many household activities, such as eating and cooking, out of doors. This is true even of those who today live in houses.

A TRAVELING HOME

Throughout Europe, Roma were well-known for their beautifully decorated *vardos* or caravans. This one belongs to a Roma family visiting the French village of St. Maries de la Mer. Roma gather there every May to celebrate Sarah, their patron saint. *Vardos* used to be drawn by horses, which not only provided a means of transportation, but were also at one stage a commodity that Roma bought and sold.

MARIMÉ LAWS

Roma have complex laws so they do not come into contact with anything *marimé*, or impure. Food cooked by non-Roma is *marimé*. Cooking and eating utensils must be washed in a basin used only for this purpose. It would become *marimé* if anyone were to wash their hands or launder clothes in it. Roma would prefer to eat with their hands rather than use *marimé* implements.

FUNERAL CUSTOMS

Roma funerals are big events. Dead people are buried in their best clothes and tools, food, jewelry, and money may be buried with them. After the funeral, their remaining belongings are destroyed.

worldwide today. The largest communities are in Romania, Bulgaria, and Hungary, but there are Roma throughout Europe as well as North America and Australia. The Roma people originated in northern India. They left India in the 11th century in search of a better life, reaching Europe a couple of centuries later. Prejudice against them persists, although most are now settled.

A ROMA CELEBRATION
An international Gypsy Festival is held every May in the Czech Republic. Roma dancers and musicians from as far as Brazil, Russia, and Egypt attend the festival, which features concerts, performances, discussions, and a parade through the city's streets. The festival shows how Roma performers have contributed to the cultural life of the countries they live in.

A LOVE OF MUSIC
Because they valued the freedom to travel, Roma chose professions that they could practice wherever they found themselves. They became famous for their music. Roma musicians have contributed to Hungarian and Spanish music, particularly the Spanish *flamenco* style.

Most of the would-be brides are still in their teens.

LOOKING FOR LOVE
The groom traditionally pays the bride's family for the right to marry her. Every year, a fair is held in the Bulgarian town of Stara Zagora at which families decide who their daughters will marry. The girls wear their finest clothes for the occasion.

THERE ARE ABOUT SEVEN MILLION ALBANIANS living around the Adriatic Sea, less than half of whom live in Albania itself. Albanians form the majority in Kosovo, and large numbers also live in Macedonia,

ALBANIANS

PREPARING FOR A BRIGHT FUTURE

Many religions, one nationality

Religion never divided the Albanian people. In fact, Albania was the only country during World War II that managed not only to save their own Jews from the Nazis, but also to save the Jews from neighboring countries who fled to Albania. Since communist rule ended, Albania has been trying to find a way to accommodate religious practices within a secular state.

YOUNG PEOPLE

Education in Albania is compulsory between the ages of six and 14. Albania is still a very poor country, so conditions in schools are often very basic, with many even lacking adequate toilets. Polls suggest that many young Albanians would like to emigrate, but confidence in the future of the country is growing as conditions get better.

MUSLIM MAJORITY

Seventy percent of Albanians are Muslim, 20 percent are Orthodox Christian, and 10 percent are Roman Catholic. All mosques and churches were closed and religious observances forbidden under communism from 1967 to 1990. They are undergoing a cautious revival now.

ANCIENT ROOTS

Christianity came early to Albania. Saint Paul, one of the religion's founders, came to preach in the area in the first century AD.

THE ADRIATIC COAST

At their closest point, Albania and Italy are separated by less than 30 m (50 km) of sea. Apart from its coastline, Albania is largely a rocky and mountainous place. This may explain why 19th century European explorers always regarded it as a mysterious, impenetrable country.

Montenegro, and Greece. The Albanian language contains many Latin and Greek words but it does not really resemble any of the Slavonic languages. Albanians are proud that for centuries their shared ethnicity has united them above their religious differences. Albania was isolated and relatively poor under communist rule, but with communism's demise in the 1990s, its standard of living started steadily improving.

TRADITIONAL MUSIC

Albanian folk music shows Persian and Turkish influences. One popular instrument is the *çifteli*, the long-necked two-stringed mandolin shown here.

GETTING AROUND

Horses and carts are still a common means of transportation in Albania, which is quite poor by European standards. About two-thirds of Albanians live in rural areas and the rest in cities. Hundreds of villages have no access to telephones either, because after the communist regime ended many phone wires were cut and used to build fences instead.

RURAL LIFE

Agriculture is responsible for bringing in half of the money made in Albania, yet most Albanian farms consist of small, family-owned plots of land where traditional methods are used and people and animals do the work that, elsewhere in Europe, would be done by machine.

THE COUNTRY WE KNOW AS ITALY only came into existence in 1861, around the same time as a widespread knowledge of the national language, Tuscan Italian, began to take root. Even today people still feel a strong

ITALIANS

CUSTODIANS OF AN ANCIENT LEGACY

Rome wasn't built in a day

Italy's capital, Rome, is known as the Eternal City due to its long history. Legend has it that Rome was founded by twin brothers named Romulus and Remus around 753 BC. Many civilizations have left their mark on the city, which is said to have more spectacular buildings than any other in the world.

CITY WITHIN A CITY

Vatican City has the status of a country, but it lies entirely within Rome. It is officially governed by the Pope, who is also the religious leader of one billion Catholics worldwide.

The Spanish Steps lead down to the Spanish Embassy.

BUZZING AROUND

Mopeds became popular in Italy after World War II with the creation of the curvy yet robust *vespa* ("wasp"). They were easier to ride than cars on bomb-damaged roads.

Mopeds are slower and less powerful than motorcycles.

CHIC TAILORING

Stylish clothes are a matter of honor for almost all Italians. Italy's fashion industry is among the most famous in the world. It is an important part of the economy and employs one million people.

CAR INDUSTRY

Turin is the center of the Italian motor industry. Giovani Agnelli founded a car factory here in 1899, which later became the Fiat factory. Other companies have sprung up alongside it that design and manufacture car components.

loyalty to their region, its customs, and language. Nevertheless, there is much that Italians share despite their regional variations—among these are strong family ties, the Roman Catholic faith, and an utter obsession with soccer. Traditional features of the daily routine, though less common now, include a midday nap, and the *passeggiata*—an evening stroll instituted more to satisfy the need to see and be seen than for exercise.

CHESS GAME

Every two years a lifesize game of chess is played on an enormous board in the public square of Marostica. Over 500 performers in old-fashioned costumes take part while an audience of 4,000 watch the game.

Eating well

Italians are proud of their healthy Mediterranean diet of pasta, beans, fruit, vegetables, and small amounts of meat, fish, and seafood. A leisurely lunch of three or more courses used to be the main meal of the day but this is changing as more women work outside the home.

As with wine, many factors influence the taste of olive oil—the type of olives used, when they are harvested and pressed, the climate, and the soil where they are grown.

PASTA CHEFS

The Italians did not invent pasta, their national food. However, Italy is the leading producer of durum wheat, which, in the form of semolina, is its main ingredient. On average, every Italian consumes 65 lbs (30 kg) of pasta annually.

STREET FESTIVAL

Italians love their festivals. As well as national holidays, every town and village has its own holidays, often involving communal eating and drinking. Here, tables and chairs have been laid out in the town of San Casciano in Tuscany so that all the locals can join in the feasting.

SICILIANS

LIFE NEAR EUROPE'S BIGGEST VOLCANO

THE ISLAND OF SICILY lies just by the southern tip of Italy. It is the largest island in the Mediterranean and the one with the richest historial and artistic heritage. Its location has been responsible for a culture that contains

Fruits of the land and the sea

Sicily's mild climate is perfect for farming. In fact, centuries ago, the island was one of the main suppliers of food to the entire Roman Empire. Fishing is important too, and enormous tuna, which can be 10 ft (3 m) in length and weigh up to 1,400 lbs (650 kg), are still caught in the traditional way.

TUNA FISHING

Mass catches called *Mattanzas* occur every year when the tuna return to the Mediterranean to mate. These are necessary because at around 45 days, the fishing season is a relatively short one. A series of nets are used, and the catch starts with a prayer led by the head fisherman, or *rais*.

SALT FROM THE SEA

Salt marshes lie between Trapani and Marsala on the west coast of the island. Salt extraction for human use here dates back to Roman times. In the 19th century salt was obtained from the water with the help of windmills.

CITRUS ORCHARDS

Oranges and lemons were first planted in Italy during the Arab conquest of neighboring Spain. Today, orchards of citrus trees are a common sight and Sicily is famous for its oranges, particularly the ruby-red blood orange with its sour taste.

Arabic, Greek, and Spanish, as well as Italian influences. The soil of Sicily's coastal regions and the Mediterranean climate lend themselves to farming, and the region is famous for its grapes and citrus fruits.

Fishing is also extremely important to the local economy, though overfishing is a problem. The Mafia still operates in Sicily, but organized crime is no worse here than in some other parts of Europe.

Every day is a festa

Sicilians love their festivals and many are held in the course of a year. As well as Christian holidays such as Christmas and Easter, many people celebrate St. Joseph's Day in March, which commemorates the time when the saint saved people from famine. Every town and village holds celebrations to honor the local patron saint.

PALERMO'S SAINT

The festival of St. Rosalia is the occasion for a spectacular parade every July in Palermo. Rosalia was born in Palermo and became a hermit. Nearly 450 years after her death, the discovery of her remains was said to have halted a plague devastating the city.

VILLAGE LIFE

Life on Sicily and the tiny islands associated with it runs at a peaceful pace. Shops open early and shut late, but they close for a rest during the hottest part of the afternoons, from 1 to 4 o'clock.

DEVIL MASKS

San Fratello hosts a Parade of Devils during the Good Friday Festival just before Easter. The parade began life as a religious ritual, but bright costumes and large crowds have given it the air of a carnival.

LIVING NEAR A VOLCANO

Mount Etna, Europe's most active volcano, is still erupting regularly today. The town of Catania, which lies at the foot of the mountain, is used to the disruption, and local farmers even use ash from the volcano as fertilizer.

BELONGING TO GREECE, the island of Crete is home to about 600,000

CRETANS

A HIGH REGARD FOR TRADITION

people. Five times that number visit Crete annually on vacation, making tourism the island's biggest industry. The Mediterranean climate is perfect

Christian calendar

Almost all Cretans are Greek Orthodox but their religious allegiance is not to the Greek mainland church but to Constantinople. Some Cretans still celebrate saints days according to the Julian calendar, which was dropped by most of Europe in the 16th century in favor of the Gregorian calendar. They are known as "Old Calendrists."

A RELIGIOUS ISLAND

Religion is part of everyday life for Cretans, although it is mainly the older generations who attend Sunday church services. Easter is the the biggest festival, with almost the entire island observing the various fasts and feasts.

MINISTERING TO THE COMMUNITY

The village *papas* or priest with his distinctive flowing robes and stovepipe hat is a familiar figure. As well as presiding over baptisms, weddings, and funerals, priests may sometimes find themselves blessing a flock of sheep, or traveling to a church or monastery in some out-of-the-way location to conduct a service.

ROADSIDE SHRINES

There are thousands of small shrines by the roadside in Crete. Some commemorate traffic accidents, but many are simply dedicated to a particular saint. When people pass by they light a candle and say a short prayer.

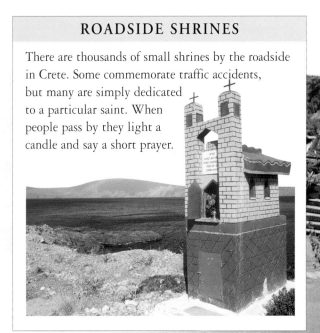

for cultivating olives, grapes, and other fruit. Cretan olive trees represent more than 30 percent of the Greek crop. Farmers keep flocks of sheep and goats for their milk, wool, and meat. From 1699 to 1898 Crete was under the control of the Ottoman Empire but prior to that it was ruled by the Venetians. The Greek spoken on the island differs slightly from that of the mainland and retains traces of these conquests.

PLACE OF WORSHIP
This modern church can be found in Neapoli, eastern Crete. Its tiled dome looks very plain, but belies its more ornate interior. Cretan churches are famous for their medieval frescoes (wall-paintings) which depict Biblical scenes.

Churches are among the top Cretan tourist attractions.

COFFEE AND COMPANIONSHIP
The local *kafenion* is the center of village life in rural Crete. Men, particularly, spend hours drinking coffee or *raki*, snacking, gossiping, discussing politics, and playing *tavli* (backgammon) at the local coffee-house.

THE LOCAL BREW
Cretan *tsikoudia* or *raki* is an alcoholic drink made from the residue left after grapes have been crushed to make wine. The traditional time for making the drink is October.

ISLAND FOOD
Because Crete is an island, seafood features largely on its menu, with octopus a common appetizer. Fish, beef, and rabbit are also staple foods, and salads are served at every meal.

THE PEOPLE OF
Asia

AS WELL AS BEING THE LARGEST and most populous continent, Asia is remarkable for the enormous range of climates and geographic terrains it encompasses. North to south it extends from the Arctic Sea to the

ASIA

ONE-THIRD OF THE WORLD'S SURFACE

Big countries

The world's biggest continent is home to some very large countries. The vast Russian Federation, which straddles both Europe and Asia, is the biggest country in the world; China, India, and Kazakhstan also feature in the top 10.

Japan is prone to earthquakes because it lies on the overlap between a number of the plates that form the Earth's surface.

Indonesia The largest archipelago in the world consists of almost 14,000 islands.

Indian subcontinent India takes up three-quarters of this land mass. The rest is made up of Pakistan, Nepal, Bhutan, and Bangladesh.

ARCTIC OCEAN

PACIFIC OCEAN

Bering Sea
East Siberian Sea
Laptev Sea
Kara Sea
Sea of Okhotsk
Kurile Islands
Sakhalin

RUSSIAN FEDERATION

EUROPE

Lake Baikal
Hokkaido

Black Sea
TURKEY
GEORGIA
CYPRUS
ARMENIA
AZERB.
LEBANON
ISRAEL
SYRIA
JORDAN
IRAQ
KUWAIT
SAUDI
BAHRAIN
QATAR
ARABIA
UAE
YEMEN
OMAN

KAZAKHSTAN
Caspian Sea
AZERBAIJAN
Aral Sea
UZBEKISTAN
TURKMENISTAN
Lake Balkhash
KYRGYZSTAN
TAJIKISTAN
AFGHANISTAN
(claimed by India)
(line of control)
(administered by China, claimed by India)

MONGOLIA

NORTH KOREA
SOUTH KOREA
Sea of Japan
JAPAN
Honshu

IRAN
PAKISTAN

CHINA

(Much of Arunāchal Pradesh is claimed by China)

Yellow Sea
East China Sea
Ryukyu Islands

AFRICA
Red Sea
The Gulf
Gulf of Oman
Gulf of Aden
Socotra (to Yemen)

Himalayas
NEPAL
BHUTAN
BANGLADESH
INDIA
MYANMAR (BURMA)

TAIWAN

Arabian Sea

INDIAN OCEAN

Bay of Bengal

LAOS
VIETNAM
THAILAND
CAMBODIA

Hainan Dao
South China Sea

Luzon
Philippine Sea
PHILIPPINES
Mindanao

Andaman Islands (to India)
Andaman Sea
SRI LANKA
Nicobar Islands (to India)

Gulf of Thailand
BRUNEI
MALAYSIA
SINGAPORE
Sumatra
Borneo
Celebes
Java Sea
Java
Flores Sea

INDONESIA

New Guinea
Papua (Irian Jaya)
Moluccas

EAST TIMOR

0 km 400 800
0 miles 400 800

tropical islands of the East Indies; while east to west it ranges through the desert countries of the Middle East—a distinct region bordering both Europe and Africa—across the majestic Himalayan mountain range, and along to the volcanic islands of Japan and Philippines. The area south of the Himlayas is referred to as the Indian subcontinent because it is a distinct landmass jutting out of the body of the continent.

Asian statistics

LANGUAGES

Almost three times as many people use Mandarin Chinese as use English, the next most popular of the world's languages.

Mandarin Chinese	874 million
Bengali	189 million
Hindi	182 million
Russian	130 million

RELIGIONS

The majority of Asians do not subscribe to a major world faith, but to another religion which has a smaller and more local range.

Muslim	822 million
Hindu	815 million
Buddhist	338 million
Christian	315 million

URBAN POPULATION

Mumbai (formerly Bombay) has the largest urban population in Asia. The city struggles to provide facilities for so many people.

Mumbai	12.2 million
Karachi	11.2 million
Seoul	11.3 million
Manila	10.1 million

POPULATION BY COUNTRY

Around half of the world's 6.2 billion people live in Asia. China and India have the most people, not just in Asia, but in the world.

China	1,290 million
India	1,000 million
Indonesia	236 million
Russia	144 million

POPULATION

The Indian subcontinent and the many islands that make up Indonesia in the south of the continent are the most densely populated parts of Asia.

Few people live in Asia's mountainous northerly reaches.

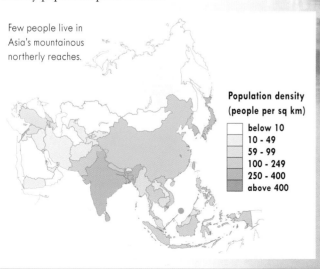

Population density
(people per sq km)

- below 10
- 10 - 49
- 59 - 99
- 100 - 249
- 250 - 400
- above 400

ASIAN FACTS

PLACES

Number of countries 48
Highest point ....Mount Everest, China-Nepal, 29,035 ft (8,850 m)
Lowest point ....Dead Sea, Israel-Jordan, -1,293 ft (-394 m)
Longest river ....Chang Jiang, (Yangtze), China 3,965 m (6,380 km)
Biggest island ....Borneo
Biggest country ....Russian Federation
Smallest country ....Maldives

PEOPLE

Population of continent ....3,674 million
Male life expectancy ....,,,,,,...............65 years
Female life expectancy ....,,,,,,.....................68 years
Male literacy rate 82%
Female literacy rate 71%

The People of West Asia

RELIGION HAS ALWAYS exerted an enormous influence on this part of the world. Islam—which originated in the Middle East and spread rapidly to both north Africa and western and central Asia—is an important force. Hinduism, and to a lesser extent, Buddhism, both of which developed farther south, are also very much alive here.

MECCA

One of the Five Pillars of Islam is the *hajj* (pilgrimage to Mecca). Devout Muslims, like the people on these buses, dream of making this journey at least once in their lives. Mecca was the birthplace of Islam's founding prophet, Mohammed, and the place where he first preached his faith.

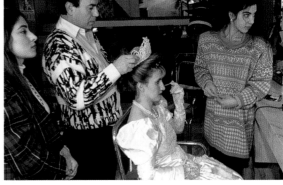

TRADITION AND MODERNITY

This bride preparing for her wedding wears a white bridal gown similar to those worn in the West. People worldwide are being exposed to foreign practices, some of which they take on, adapt, and even incorporate into their own traditions.

Most Muslim girls and women cover their hair.

DUBAI

One of the Gulf States, the United Arab Emirates has enjoyed great prosperity thanks to its precious natural resource—oil. Dubai, one of its main cities, is a wonder of both traditional Arab and ultramodern architecture.

Art and culture

Where people have lived nomadic lives, their arts tend to be portable, so textiles, jewelry, music, and dance are the most notable art forms in the more mountainous reaches of central Asia. Wonderful examples of literature and architecture have been and continue to be produced in the region too.

Cricket came to India with the British in the 19th century and became an absolute and lasting passion.

A MONUMENT TO LOVE

India's most famous building, and perhaps one of the most beautiful in the world, is the Taj Mahal. It was built by Emperor Shah Jahan in memory of his second wife. The structure was finally completed in 1653, having taken 20,000 craftsmen and builders over 20 years to build.

ARABIC ARTS

Islam forbids the depiction of God or of the human form, but Arabic buildings and artefacts are far from plain. They are decorated, instead, with geometric shapes or with curvacious Arabic script—an exquisite art form in itself.

MAGIC CARPETS

Wonderful rugs and carpets are produced, often by hand, throughout central Asia. Beautiful as well as durable, they often function as family heirlooms or substitute for savings accounts, in the way that jewelry sometimes does in the West.

BOLLYWOOD

The Bollywood film industry, based in Mumbai (Bombay), is the biggest in the world, producing over 800 films a year.

MIND AND BODY

The discipline of yoga, which consists of excercises good for both physical and mental well-being, originated in India centuries ago.

THESE MYSTERIOUS PEOPLE TRACE THEIR ORIGINS to 11th century

DRUZE

GUARDIANS OF A SECRET RELIGION

Cairo where they began as a reform movement within Islam. Because they do not adhere to the Five Pillars of Islam they are not recognized by

The wise and the ignorant

Druze society is comprised of two groups. While everyone attends the *khalwa* (place of worship) on Thursdays, the majority—the *juhaall*—leave after the first part of the service, while a select few—the *uqqal*—remain for the recitation of religious texts.

THE STATUS OF WOMEN

Women are considered to be more spiritual than men because it is assumed that they have less contact with secular society. While women may be initiated alongside men, it is rare to find a woman who has been permitted to get her driving license.

Druze women work mostly in the home and sometimes in fields nearby.

THE *UQQAL*

Only the most pious and wise men and women belong to the *uqqal*, and even then only after a lengthy period of candidacy. Within the *uqqal,* the most honored group are the *ajaweed* (the good), who possess religious and legal authority.

WHAT THE WISE WEAR

Uqqal men wear a distinctive white hat and a long dark robe. Weaving is an important craft in Druze villages because some very devout Druze only wear clothes made out of handwoven fabric. One Druze sect is known as "the blues" because they wear only hand-dyed and handwoven blue garments.

Muslims. They believe strictly in one God and in reincarnation, and do not accept converts into their religion. Men are forbidden from having more than one wife. There may be as many as one million Druze people alive today but it is difficult to know the exact number since many practice their faith privately while outwardly conforming to the local religion. Most live in the mountain regions of Syria, Lebanon, Israel, and Jordan.

A PLACE OF PILGRIMAGE

Druze believe in seven prophets—Adam, Noah, Abraham, Moses, Jesus, Mohammed, and Mohammed ibn Ismail al-Darazi. They also revere Jethro, Moses' father-in-law. He is said to be buried at Nebe Shu'eib in northern Israel. Every April Druze make a pilgrimage to this site.

ALL DRESSED UP

Druze children in Israel attend schools where they are taught in both Arabic and Hebrew. Many also belong to the Druze wing of the Israeli Scout Organization. Here, Druze schoolgirls wear their best dresses to attend a dance party.

MOUNT HERMON

The Druze town of Majdal Shams is built on the lower slopes of Mount Hermon, Israel's highest mountain. There are four other Druze villages in the area, which was captured by Israel from Syria during a war in 1967. Many Druze have relatives living just across the border in Syria.

ARMENIA, ALONG WITH AZERBAIJAN AND GEORGIA, lies close

ARMENIANS

to the Caucasus Mountains. Armenians are proud to be one of the world's ancient civilizations. They call themselves Hayer because they

THE FIRST CHRISTIAN NATION

A new republic

Armenia is the smallest of the independent states of the former Soviet Union. It became independent in 1991 with the demise of communism, and since then the culture has changed. Many people work in the agricultural sector, religion is thriving again, and folk dancing and other traditions have been revived.

An elderly Armenian with his worry beads. Men gather with their beads in the evening to chat.

This Armenian is preparing for the cold weather by collecting firewood on his cart.

IN THE COUNTRYSIDE

There are over 900 small, rural communities in Armenia. After independence, previously state-owned farms became private. These provide work for the people, but farming depends on good weather. Recent droughts have led to crop failure, meaning poverty for many.

GROWING ECONOMY

Armenia's economy relies on agriculture, with nearly half the population working on small, family-run farms. Stalls of homegrown produce, such as apples, grapes, and apricots, are a common sight in markets and along the roadside.

THE ARMENIAN CHURCH

In 301 AD, Armenia became the first nation to accept Christianity as its state religion. The Armenian Church (along with the Russian and Greek Orthodox Churches) is part of the Eastern Church. These worshippers are lighting candles during a morning service in a cathedral.

believe they are descended from Haik, great-grandson of the Biblical Noah, whose Ark came to rest on Mount Ararat in the Caucasus Mountains. Yerevan, Armenia's capital city, is one of the oldest continuously inhabited places on Earth. Archeological evidence demonstrates that a city existed in this region as long as 5,000 years ago. Today, 1.25 million people live in Yerevan, and it is the focus of Armenian life.

CITY LIFE

Two-thirds of Armenians live in cities or towns, with half of them in Yerevan. This makes it a crowded city where space is limited. Many homes are in high-rise apartment blocks. Most of these are privately owned, not government owned.

MOUNT ARARAT

In the past, this mountain was part of Armenia, but today it lies inside Turkey's borders. However, it is still a symbol of Armenian national identity and a religious site. Many Armenians live near Mount Ararat, and for those living far away, it represents their homeland.

LOVE OF DANCE

Armenia has a strong tradition of both folk dance and ballet. As part of the Soviet Union, the arts were heavily subsidized, but less money is available for music and dance today.

VOSKI ASHUN

Every October in the town of Hrazdan, people from all over Armenia gather in traditional dress to celebrate the changing seasons in the festival of *Voski Ashun*, or "Golden Fall."

VARDAVAR

The whole of Armenia takes part in this water festival, held in the height of summer. Water is precious, but on this day it is thrown around generously. People believe that watering someone makes them pure—but most children just like an excuse for soaking adults!

There's nowhere to hide *Vardava*—even drivers keep their windows shut to avoid a drenching.

MARSH ARABS

MAKING THE MOST OF THE ENVIRONMENT

IN A REGION KNOWN FOR its deserts, artificial islands scattered throughout the marshlands of Iraq are home to the Ma'dan, or Marsh Arabs. The Ma'dan are accomplished canoeists and experts at utilizing this environment, which they have inhabited for over 5,000 years. They build islands and homes from marsh reeds, grow rice in the marsh water, and catch fish for food and trade. Perhaps most importantly, the marsh provides ideal grazing for the buffalo, a family's most prized possession. A buffalo supplies dung for fuel and milk for dairy produce, which is eaten or traded for wheat to make bread. Buffalos are rarely eaten, and are so cherished that an owner will even sing to soothe a sick animal.

PERSIANS

AN ANCIENT RELIGION AND CULTURE

THE ORIGINAL RELIGION OF THE PERSIAN EMPIRE and perhaps the oldest monotheistic religion still alive today is Zoroastrianism, which flourished until it was overtaken

Celebration of spring

Millions of people from Asia to the Middle East celebrate the main Zoroastrian festival, *Nowruz*. In recent years *Nowruz* has enjoyed renewed popularity in some Central Asian republics that were previously part of the Soviet Union, where religion was not encouraged, and also in Afghanistan, where non-Muslim traditions used to be forbidden.

THE AVESTA

The Zoroastrian holy book is called the *Avesta*. It contains a range of different writings, but the oldest sections are thought to be written by Zoroaster (also known as Zarathustra), the prophet who founded the religion sometime between 1500 and 1000 BC.

Man dancing to celebrate *Nowruz* in Afghanistan.

OUT WITH THE OLD

Chaharshanbeh Souri is the first day of *Nowruz*, the holiday that celebrates the new solar year in March. It is believed to date back to 1725 BC. Bonfires are lit and people jump over them to bring good luck for the coming year.

PERSIAN RUGS

Persians regard their rugs as some other cultures regard jewelry—a luxurious display of wealth and skill and a thing of beauty. They also function as a form of savings account, which can be sold off at any time for cash if needed.

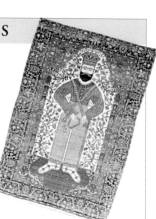

by Islam in the seventh century. Although most of the people who identify themsleves as Persians today are Muslim, a small number in Iran and elsewhere still observe this religion. They believe in one God, *Ahura Mazda*, who created the world and whose sacred symbol is fire, representing the triumph of light over darkness. *Ahura Mazda* is in perpetual conflict with the force of evil, who is known as *Angra Mainyu*.

ENJOYING THE SPRING WEATHER
On *Sizdah Bedar*—the 13th and final day of *Nowruz*—it is considered bad luck to stay indoors so people go for a festive picnic in the countryside. Some people take a small pot of sprouting grain, planted some weeks earlier, and toss it into running water or plant it to signify the start of a new agricultural year.

A HOLY PLACE
More than half of the world's 200,000 Zoroastrians live in Iran. Every year, pilgrims gather for a five-day pilgrimage to one of Zoroastrianism's most sacred sites, the mountain temple at Chakchak in southern Iran. The entrance to the temple displays the cardinal principles of their faith—"Good Thoughts, Good Words, Good Deeds."

GOLDFISH FOR THE NEW YEAR
Seven items—the *haft sin* (see below)—are displayed in honor of *Nowruz* in Persian homes. Other objects such as candles, a mirror, a copy of the *Avesta,* and goldfish in a bowl may also be laid out.

THE SEVEN Ss
A festive table of items called the *haft sin* might consist of *seer* (garlic), *seeb* (apple), *serkeh* (vinegar), *samanu* (a sweet made of wheat shoots), *sombol* (hyacinth), *sekeh* (a gold coin), and *somagh* (sumac).

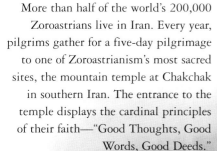

ORIGINALLY THERE WERE TWO DISTINCT ARABIC CULTURES—

BEDOUINS

ARAB WANDERERS OF THE MIDDLE EAST

settled and nomadic. Settled Arabs found fertile land and cultivated it, while nomadic herdsmen—Bedouins—traveled between oases, extracting

The Bedouin way

The detailed knowledge the Bedouins have of the deserts meant that in the past they controlled trade routes, acting as guides and charging taxes to those who wanted to cross the desert. Although many Arab countries romanticize the Bedouin lifestyle, they are frequently less enthusiastic about actual Bedouin groups who make use of the desert's precious resources despite not owning the land. Some have tried to make the Bedouin abandon their nomadic ways and settle in one place.

HOSPITALITY

In the vast, inhospitable deserts, meeting a stranger is an unusual event and a welcome surprise. *Diyafa*—or honoring guests—is part of the Bedouin code of behavior, so guests will always be welcomed and plied generously with sweet tea, strong coffee, and the best food available.

AT THE BACK OF THE TENT

These women are spinning wool and milling grain. Bedouin women tend the flocks, do the housework and cooking, and are also responsible for pitching and dismantling the tents. They are protected by a strict code of honor and many live less restricted lives than their non-Bedouin counterparts. Bedouin tents are divided into two sections. The front is reserved for men, and the back for women.

DESERT CLOTHING

Women wear long dresses that are often dyed or beautifully embroidered. All women cover their heads and some also wear a veil. The coins on this woman's veil show how wealthy her family is. The traditional dress for a man is a roomy robe worn with a checked or plain headscarf. The scarf is secured with a doubled black cord called the *agal*.

what they could from the harsh environment before moving on. Bedouins originated in Saudi Arabia and other countries of the Arabian Peninsula. Today they also live in Jordan, Egypt, and Israel. They travel in family groups and trace their descent through the male line back to a particular clan, and beyond that to a tribe. They have a strict code of honor and even those who are no longer nomads are proud of their heritage.

Bedouins belong to the Muslim religion, though they sometimes maintain pre-Islamic beliefs and customs too.

GOD'S GIFT
Camel breeding is traditionally the most noble Bedouin profession. Camels are known as "God's gift" because they are so well adapted for the desert. Camel breeders travel huge distances in large groups, sometimes surviving for months on camel milk alone.

AN ORAL TRADITION
Bedouin are excellent poets and record their history through poems that are passed down from one generation to the next. These may be accompanied by instruments such as a drum or a harp like the one shown here.

KAZAKHS

THE SECOND LARGEST MUSLIM GROUP in Central Asia, the Kazakhs
live not only in Kazakhstan but also in China, Uzbekistan, Russia, and Mongolia. Like others in the region, their traditional occupation used

ROAMING THE STEPPES OF CENTRAL ASIA

A round house

A domed wooden frame covered with felt forms the basis for a *yurt*. At the entrance to the *yurt* is a carved wooden door of birch or pine, often decorated with traditional motifs. Inside there is a gap in the *yurt's* roof where smoke from cooking can escape. Scattered everywhere are brightly colored rugs made of wool and felt.

TRAVELING LIGHT

Yurts vary in size, but they are all built to the same basic design that uses about 60 interlocking poles and one or two layers of waterproof felt. They are quick and easy to dismantle and transport by horse or camel.

Yurt-dwellers love having guests. A Kazakh saying claims "Kazaks' hearts are like the steppes—wide, kind, and generous."

to be herding animals. Few Kazakhs these days live as nomadic shepherds, traveling with their animals around the grasslands of the steppes. Around half of the population live in crowded cities, while the other half live settled lives in rural areas where there is plenty of space but often no electricity or running water. Modern Kazakhs recall their former lives fondly, even building *yurts* (traditional huts) for use on special occasions.

COOKING AND EATING

At the very centre of the *yurt* is the hearth, with a cauldron called a *kazan* suspended above it. On the steppes, Kazakhs rely on meat such as mutton or horse, dairy products, and bread. Vegetables are very rarely available. Meals traditionally start with *chai* (tea), which may be accompanied by bread, nuts, and sweets as appetizers.

Bundled up snugly, this baby will be warm and comfortable even while the family is traveling.

FELT

The *yurt* is covered in one or two layers of felt. Kazakh women are famous for their felt, which they make by pounding wool in hot water, then rolling and compressing it until durable and waterproof.

A LOVE OF HORSES

Some archaeologists believe that human beings first learned to ride horses on the steppes of Central Asia as long as 6,000 years ago. Nomadic Kazakhs—heirs to this tradition—are accomplished riders and some are capable of shooting arrows accurately from the back of a moving horse. In the past, it is said, children often learned to ride before they could walk.

THE BIG MATCH

The people of the steppes invented a number of games that were played on horseback. *Kokpar* is a little like polo and is played with a headless sheep's or goat's carcass. Two teams line up at either end of a large meadow and charge forward. In this exciting game the players have to grab the goat and drop it into their goal.

NENETS

WESTERN SIBERIA IS A COLD, WILD PLACE with few habitable areas.
One group of people who live there and survive the harsh conditions are the Nenets. Certain Nenets groups are entirely nomadic, traveling with

LIFE AT THE END OF THE EARTH

The reindeer

The Nenets people's lives revolve around reindeer. They could not live without the animal—the fur is used for clothing and houses, ropes are made from the hide, the reindeer are used as transportation and, of course, as food. For this reason they take great care of these hardy animals, watching over them each night and looking after the ill ones. They maintain a close relationship with one another.

MODERN LIVING
Some Nenets are completely nomadic, setting up their camp where the reindeer migrate. For this reason, modern children are sent to boarding schools in order to gain an education. The Nenets are eager that they return to continue the traditional way of life.

CROSSING RIVERS
To help them walk over snow, reindeer have large, splayed feet, which make very efficient paddles as well. They can swim at 10 mph (15 kmph) and at this speed the sleds they pull through the water remain dry and above the waterline.

STAPLE DIET
The Nenets eat mainly meat, fish, and some bread but reindeer meat is the staple diet. The meat is sometimes cooked, but often eaten raw. When a reindeer is killed, everyone gathers around to drink the warm blood, which is rich in vitamins and minerals.

ARCTIC CLOTHING
Everything that the Nenets wear is made from reindeer skin – from coats to boots. *Yagushka* are women's double-layered reindeer coats that have the fur facing inside and out. The skins are incredibly warm and windproof. Baby reindeer skins are used for baby clothes, and wood shavings are used as baby nappies.

the reindeer on their migrations twice a year, with not one permanent living area. The Yamal Peninsula, (Yamal means "the end of the Earth") is home to some groups of Nenets who travel across it seasonally. This peninsula stretches into the Arctic Ocean and in the winter temperatures can sink to -58°F (-50°C). It is a difficult place to live but these Nenets have been living there for over 1,000 years.

Ancient beliefs

The Nenets practice an animistic religion and worship their own god *Num*. A lot of Arctic people converted to Christianity as missionaries spread their word, but in Siberia, when it was part of the Soviet Union, it was impossible for missionaries to reach the Nenets people. This means that in most instances their ways of life and beliefs are as they were hundreds of years ago.

THE SACRED SLEIGH

At times of sacrifice or on special occasions, the sacred sleigh will be unpacked by a respected elder. The sleigh carries religious idols, bear skins, coins, and anything special that has been collected in a lifetime. A sacred drum is sometimes carried, which is given in difficult times to a shamen (a religious man) who uses it to appeal to the god.

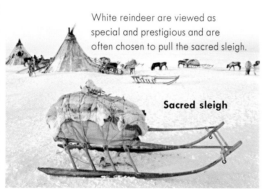

White reindeer are viewed as special and prestigious and are often chosen to pull the sacred sleigh.

Sacred sleigh

MAMMOTH IVORY

Between 5,000 and 25,000 years ago, large mammoths roamed the Yamal Peninsula in great numbers. For thousands of years the Nenets have found their ancient skeletons and used the ivory tusks to make buttons, boxes, harnesses, etc.

THE HOUSE IDOL

If a respected member of a family dies, a doll, or *yaminga,* is made with reindeer skin to represent them. The person's artifacts, such as jewelry, are attached. They are kept to protect the family and ward off evil.

SUPERSTITION

The Nenets are superstitious people. For example, women can never step over a lasso, and household contents have to be laid out in such a way so as not to bring bad luck. They have a number of religious artifacts that are carried on the sacred sleigh, which is very rarely unpacked.

As Arctic people evolved they had less facial hair since it is not practical in cold climates.

The reindeer trek
THE THREE MONTH JOURNEY TO THE END OF THE EARTH

STRETCHING INTO A SNOWY HORIZON, thousands of reindeer trek toward the Yamal Peninsula. It is early spring but the temperatures can drop to below -22°F (-30°C), and the winds are chilling. The Nenets and their reindeer are traveling the 600 miles (1,000 km) from their winter camp, farther south in the Boreal forest, to the summer pastures of the tundra. The journey takes about three months. They travel in a long and spectacular line stretching back miles along the landscape, which consists of 4,000–5,000 reindeer pulling endless rows of wooden sleds covered by thick, furry reindeer pelts. The reindeer walk naturally in lines when the snow is soft, following the prints of the animal in front; otherwise they walk in groups. The women and children in their hooded coats travel on sleds with every belonging they own. They are heading toward the lush, green grass of the tundra, where they can rest and the reindeer can fatten up for three months before embarking on the same three-month route back again in the fall.

SHERPAS

PEOPLE OF THE EAST

THE NAME "SHERPA" COMES FROM THE TIBETAN WORDS for people (*shar*) and east (*wa*). The Sherpas are a distinct group of people who come from Tibet. There are 18 Sherpa

The high life

Sherpas are famous for guiding mountaineers up Mount Everest. Living at high altitudes between 8,500 and 14,000 ft (2,600 and 4,300 m), Sherpas are used to the mountainous terrain and thin air. Only certain animals and plants, such as yaks and potatoes, survive in this environment. Sherpas use them as much as possible, as everything else has to be brought in, even essentials like food and paper.

By law, no load should weigh more than 65 lb (30 kg).

A LOAD TO BEAR

Portering is a common occupation for men and women. Seventy percent of Nepal is so mountainous, it has no roads. All goods must be carried in, including cooking pots and oil.

POTATO HARVEST

Sherpa women and men have equal status. They share the work, from raising children to heavy farming. These women are hoeing potatoes, a staple food that is able to grow at high altitudes.

MORE THAN A PET

Looking after the yaks in the highlands is an important job. They provide almost everything the Sherpas need. Wool is turned into clothes, and leather into shoes. Dung is used as fuel and fertilizer. Yaks also transport heavy goods over long distances.

MAKING CHEESE

Yak's milk is an important commodity. It can be drunk in tea, or turned into butter or cheese. This boy is stirring cheese curds for his family. Cheese making is a growing industry, with cheese sold mainly to tourists.

clans, and each person takes the name of their clan as their last name. Over 35,000 Sherpas live in West Asia. Set high in the Himalayas, eastern Nepal has the largest Sherpa population, with over 10,000 people.

Sherpas also live in Tibet, Bhutan, and India. Within Nepal, the biggest community is in the Khumbu valley—"the gateway to Mount Everest"—where there is plenty of work in the tourist industry.

SERVING THE TOURISTS

This village shop caters to tourists, many of whom come to Nepal to see the Himalayas. The shop sells souvenirs such as Sherpa-style teapots, and practical goods like backpacks used in mountaineering. Sherpas also act as guides for mountaineers, especially on major expeditions up Mount Everest. Before climbing Everest, Sherpas perform *puja*, a ceremony honoring the mountain deities, asking for a safe return.

BUDDHISM

Sherpas are Buddhists. A small minority become monks and dedicate themselves entirely to their faith. They live in the monastery all year round, studying scriptures and praying.

These houses are built into the mountainside at a height of around 13,000 ft (4,000 m) above sea level.

UZBEKS

MERCHANTS OF THE SILK ROAD

AMONG THE ANCESTORS OF TODAY'S UZBEKS were merchants who traded along the Silk Road centuries ago. Arab conquerors in the seventh century ushered in a golden age in which Bukhara became one

The importance of Islam

The vast majority of Uzbeks are Muslims. Islamic religion and culture have been a major influence in central Asia since the arrival of the Arab conquerors in the seventh century. After the official atheism of the communist era, Islam has enjoyed renewed support, but for many Uzbeks this is more cultural than religious.

ARABIC INFLUENCE
Bukhara was once the capital city of the Persian Empire. Among its magnificent buildings is the Mir-i-Arab Madrassah, still a functioning *madrassah* (school for Islamic religious studies). Nearby is the Kalyan Mosque; its 150 ft (45 m) high minaret is visible from almost everywhere in the city.

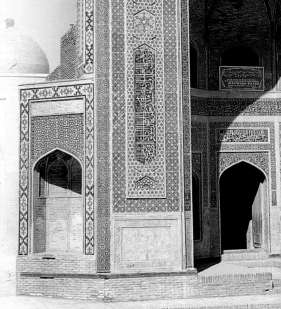

MUSLIM PRAYER
An *imam* (prayer leader) and his assistant pray at central mosque in the city of Margilan. Since independence Uzbeks officially enjoy freedom of religion, but mosques and religious leaders are nevertheless closely monitored by the state.

BEAUTIFUL BREAD
Round Uzbek loaves known as *nan* (as in India) are subject to many traditions. It is considered disrespectful to place bread upside down on the table; and bread is never cut with a knife but torn into pieces and given to those present.

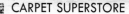

CARPET SUPERSTORE
Merchants and traders have plied their wares along the cities of the Silk Road for hundreds of years. Even today Tashkent, the capital of Uzbekistan, is famed for its lively bazaars. This is the carpet department of the main market.

of the world's great cities. Various Turkic tribes then settled in the region, but a national Uzbek identity only emerged in the 20th century with the creation of Uzbekistan by the Soviet Union. The country became independent in 1991. Its population of 25 million, of whom 70 percent are ethnically Uzbek, is the largest in Central Asia, though significant Uzbek communities also exist in Afghanistan, China, and Kazakhstan.

TEA GARDENS

Uzbeks drink green tea, served with *nan* (bread). Men gather at a *chai khana* (tea house) or tea garden where they sit on flat wooden beds covered with a thin mattress of colorful fabric. A plastic tablecloth is spread in the middle on which the tea and food is served.

SILK WEAVING

Silk thread is produced from the cocoons spun by a type of moth larva. Each cocoon is made of one continuous thread 1,000–3,000 ft (300–900 m) long that is unraveled, dyed, and then woven in a labor-intensive process. Uzbek silk production is particularly centered around the city of Margilan.

Islam forbids the depiction of God or the human form, so buildings are decorated with geometric patterns and verses from the Koran.

GUESTS OF THE GROOM

The traditional Uzbek wedding consists of three parts: the *erkak ash*, a morning ceremony open only to men (pictured below); the afternoon ceremony known as *khotin ash*, which is just for women; and the *toy*, an evening celebration for all the guests. Professional musicians and dancers often perform at these lively events, which are always attended by hundreds of guests.

THREADS OF GOLD

Embroidery is one of the most popular of the applied arts in Uzbekistan. State-sponsored handicraft schools make sure that the skills are taught to a new generation of artisans. Here a student at one school models a wedding gown richly encrusted with gold thread.

KALASH

DESCENDANTS OF THE ANCIENT GREEKS

AROUND 4,000 KALASH PEOPLE LIVE IN CHITRAL, northwest Pakistan. They maintain that they are descended from Alexander the Great, who passed through the area around 400 BC, and that this is why

Valley people

As well as cultivating corn, wheat, and millet on the mountain terraces, and tending to their fruit trees, the Kalash also keep sheep and goats. While the milk is a valuable part of their diet, goats are important for another reason—they are sacrificed, sometimes in large numbers, on many of the festivals that punctuate the Kalash year.

HOME SWEET HOME
Houses are built out of local wood and stone and normally have two floors and a balcony. The ground floor is used to store grain or to shelter cattle, while people live on the upper floor. A fireplace in this room provides heat and somewhere to cook but also creates a lot of soot. During the summer, people cook and sleep on the balcony.

GOING TO SCHOOL
Kalash children in the remote valleys travel very far to get to school. Because government schools are Muslim, they are taught about Islam in an attempt to convert them.

they do not look like other Pakistani people. Unlike most of Pakistan's population, they are not Muslims, but follow their own nature-based religion which bears some similarities to the ancient Greek religion.

The Kalash are not permitted to worship their main god directly but only via lesser gods. They believe in demons and witches—who must be avoided—and in fairies, who inhabit certain mountains.

SACRIFICIAL ALTAR

The most important Kalash festival is *Chaumos*, which lasts for two weeks around the time of the winter solstice. On the final day of *Chaumos* large numbers of male goats are ritually slaughtered in front of an altar dedicated to the god *Balimain*. The altar is decorated with four horse heads carved in wood because the god is said to appear on a horse.

OPEN GRAVE

When someone dies people sing, dance, and mourn for two days and nights before the burial. Until 30 years ago the Kalash did not bury their dead at all but left them in open wooden coffins. They stopped doing this because the graves were raided by dogs.

Unlike elsewhere in Pakistan, Kalash women do not wear veils or cover their hair.

WOMEN'S CLOTHING

A plain black dress, called a *piran*, provides the basis of the clothing worn by Kalash women. It is decorated with an embroidered sash and elaborate embroidery on the chest and cuffs. Strands of colored beads and a headdress complete the outfit. On special occasions a different headdress is worn which features an enormous pom-pom on the top.

CROWNING GLORY

Kalash women wear their hair divided into five braided strands, with the middle strand emerging from the front of the head. Over this sits a headband thickly decorated with shells and beads running down the back of the head to the waist. They comb their hair outside near a river because they believe it brings bad luck to do this indoors.

Headdresses are studded with buttons and cowrie shells.

RAJASTHANIS

THE NAME OF THE INDIAN STATE OF RAJASTHAN derives from the *rajputs*, a high-caste people who commonly married Mughal royalty and nobility. But Rajasthanis are descended from other tribes too. The

INDIA'S MOST COLORFUL RESIDENTS

Holy place

Among hundreds of temples in the city of Pushkar is the only one in India dedicated to the god Brahma, the creator of the universe. Though less popular than Vishnu, the preserver, and Shiva, the destroyer, the cult of Brahma nevertheless attracts pilgrims who visit the temple and bathe in its sacred lake.

HENNA

Women through much of Asia use henna or *mehndi* to decorate their skin on special occasions. The custom originated in Rajasthan, which is still a center for the manufacture of henna.

SALVATION
Devout Hindus believe that bathing in the lake can put an end to further reincarnation and guarantee instead that they will go straight to heaven after they die.

DECORATION
The Rajasthani love of color and ornamentation can be seen not only in their own clothes but also in their animals. This cart is pulled by a donkey whose body is covered with bright splashes of paint.

desert state is renowned for its temples, forts, and mosques, and also for the arts and crafts produced here, with each principality having its own specialization. Most striking, however, are the colors of Rajasthan. Women wear dazzlingly bright fabrics studded with embroidery or mirror work and accessorized with quantities of silver jewelry. Men wear colorful turbans, and even working animals and their carts are often vibrantly painted.

POPULATION EXPLOSION
Only 13,000 people live in Pushkar, but during the fair a further 200,000 descend on the town, bringing with them 50,000 camels, horses, and cattle. Most stay in tents, turning the sand dunes just outside this tiny town into an enormous campsite.

SWIRLING SKIRTS
Rajasthani women are famous for their vibrant clothes. During the *ghoomer* dance they twirl gracefully, allowing their skirts to flare out. Most folk dances are performed by groups of men or women, but rarely by both together.

Pushkar fair
During the annual five-day festival every November thousands of people, including both Indian and foreign tourists, visit the city. Another tradition has grown up around this event—cattle and camel trading. At least 25,000 camels are brought here to be groomed, admired, raced, and, with luck, sold.

CAMEL FESTIVAL
Camel races and competitions are organized in vast arenas before thousands of spectators. Camel beauty contests also take place, and a version of musical chairs is played in which the winning camel is the one that can support the largest number of people.

THE PEOPLE OF BANGLADESH—which got its independence in 1971—

BENGALIS

PEOPLE OF THE GANGES RIVER DELTA

and those of the Indian province of West Bengal speak the same language, share a rich literary heritage, and come from the same ethnic stock. However,

Calcutta

Calcutta—or Kolkata, as it has been renamed—is one of India's main cities and home to 14 million people. The city's resources have been stretched to their limits. The air is polluted with traffic fumes and the water contaminated with disease, especially during the flooding of the monsoon season.

Garlands of flowers for Hindu worship on sale at Howrah flower market.

HINDU WORSHIP

Having ritually bathed in the Ganges River these women offer gifts of flowers, incense, and holy water to the god Shiva. Shiva represents destruction and is identified with the Ganges, whose waters bring both prosperity and death. There are many gods in the Hindu religion, each representing a different aspect of the one ultimate God, Brahman, and the workings of the universe.

GETTING AROUND

Calcutta has buses, trams, taxis, a subway system, and car, cycle, and human-drawn rickshaws. The latter come into their own during the floods when water often reaches waist height.

ON THE STREETS

Many homeless people live on the streets of Calcutta. This small shelter is home to a family of seven. Their father can only afford to send one of his five children to school.

the majority of Bengalis in Bangladesh are Muslims, while most of those in West Bengal are Hindus. Some reside in densely populated cities such as Calcutta in India and Dhaka in Bangladesh, but millions more live in rural areas. Bengali fishermen and farmers rely on the annual flooding of the Ganges and Brahmaputra rivers for their livelihoods. Often though, these very same floods cause devastation and huge loss of life.

BRITISH LEGACY

During the 18th and 19th centuries, the British Raj (colonial rulers) built grand, European-style buildings in Calcutta. These include an imposing memorial to Queen Victoria and the gothic St. Paul's cathedral.

Farming in Bangladesh

Over 60 percent of Bangladeshis work in agriculture growing rice, jute, tea, and wheat as their main crops. Many live on and cultivate land that is prone to flooding—they have little choice when about a third of the country floods regularly during the monsoon season. The climate coupled with widespread poverty has resulted in numerous environmental problems.

AN IMPORTANT CROP

Jute, which is used to make sacks and carpet backing, is Bangladesh's biggest export. About 25 million people, almost a quarter of the population, make a living from growing or processing the crop.

1 Harvesting
Jute grows in hot, humid conditions. Plants are harvested when they are 8-12 ft (2.5-3.5 m) tall. The stalks are bundled up and soaked so the fiber can be extracted.

2 Processing
The fibers are passed through a series of machines to soften them and remove any bits of bark. Eventually they are turned into a strong yarn.

3 The end result
Jute fabric has a variety of uses. It is known as burlap, sacking, or canvas, depending on how fine or coarse it is.

Women extract the golden fibers from jute plants that have been left to soak.

HINDUS

BATHING IN THE HOLY RIVER

EVERY YEAR THOUSANDS OF HINDUS make the journey to Varanasi on the banks of the Ganges River. Many plan to live out their final days and die in this holy city. They believe that when, after death, they are cremated and their ashes scattered on the river they will finally escape the cycle of death and rebirth and attain eternal peace. At dawn, the faithful descend to the waterfront down flights of stone steps known as *ghats*. They practice meditation and yoga, make offerings, and bathe in the holy waters.

A PEARL-SHAPED ISLAND JUST TO THE SOUTH OF INDIA, Sri

SRI LANKANS

A NATION OF TWO PEOPLES

Lanka is home to two distinct ethnic groups. Sinhalese account for three-quarters of the population, while the remainder are mostly Tamil. The

The changing face of work

Almost half of Sri Lanka's population works in agriculture, although manufacturing industries such as clothing and textiles account for more of the country's earnings. Women, who tend to do poorly paid, unskilled jobs, make up one-third of the labor force.

TEA PLANTATIONS

Sri Lanka is the world's largest exporter of tea. The crop was brought to the island by the British in 1849. Tea is grown at 3,000-8,000 ft (900-2,400 m) and is handpicked, mostly by female workers.

KILLER ELEPHANTS

Cutouts of human figures are placed by the roadside to scare off wild elephants, which have been known to trample people to death in this area.

Puppets are used to enact stories from the Hindu epic, the *Ramayana*.

BUFFALO CART

This is still a common form of transportation in Sri Lanka. Traditional songs are sung by cart drivers to keep themselves awake during their long, solitary, nighttime journeys.

RUBBER TAPPING

Latex, the thick white sap of the rubber tree, is collected by cutting a spiral groove into the bark of the tree and suspending a metal cup below it. An expert tapper can handle as many as 400 rubber trees in a day.

ongoing friction between the two groups since the island became independent in 1948 has adversely affected its economy. The island is nevertheless blessed with an excellent climate for farming, seas teeming with fish, and mineral resources such as emeralds, rubies, and graphite. The main religion of the island is Buddhism heavily infused with Hindu beliefs and practices, and the national languages are Sinhala and Tamil.

Esala Perahera

The procession, or *perahera,* that takes place in the summer month of *Esala* is an annual highlight in Kandy, a former capital of Sri Lanka nestling in the hills at the center of the country. The celebration lasts 10 days, and features nightly parades.

TOOTH TEMPLE

When King Kit Siri Mevan brought one of the Buddha's teeth to his capital city, Kandy, from India in 313 AD he paraded it through the streets in a custom that continues annually to this day. The tooth is not only an object of great devotion, but also an important symbol of Buddhist Sinhalese identity.

MALIGAWA TUSKER

Heavily ornamented and flanked by two other elephants, the Maligawa Tusker is the highlight of the procession. This elephant carries a golden casket holding the sacred relic—the Buddha's tooth.

A Kandyan dancer holds a spectacular mask. It may have been made in Ambalangoda in the south of the island, a town famous for its mask makers.

TRADITIONAL DANCERS

Under the caste system dancers were born into their professions, which they learned from their parents. Royal patrons supplied them with land in return for dancing and performing other religious rituals. Now that dancers are hired only for special occasions, their numbers are diminishing.

Guarding the family seat

A TRADITIONAL SRI LANKAN FISHING TECHNIQUE

THE INDIAN OCEAN AND THE NEARBY SEAS have the largest number of active fishermen in the world. International agreements determine how far into the Palk Straits—the body of water that separates Sri Lanka from India—fishermen from the respective countries may fish. There are disputes and violent, sometimes tragic, misunderstandings between fishermen out at sea in small boats from both countries. Meanwhile, closer to the shore, other fishermen simply wade out to their wooden perches and wait for the fish to come to them in the shallows. Nobody knows where this peculiar technique originated, but the spots are handed down from father to son and jealously guarded.

The People of East Asia

EAST ASIA CONTAINS the most populous and the least populous regions in the world. China has the highest population of any one country, whereas parts of Siberia and the Tibetan plateau are virtually uninhabited. The people of East Asia practice a wide range of religions and have a rich tapestry of ancient cultures, as well as thriving industrial economies.

TECHNOLOGY

Within the last 50 years countries such as Japan, China, and the Republic of Korea have taken off in terms of technology and industry. Seoul, the capital of the Republic of Korea, is now a sprawling, industrialized city.

MARTIAL ARTS

These famous fighting disciplines from Asia have become popular all over the world as forms of self-defense and self-discipline. Among many others, Tae kwon do comes from Korea, Judo comes from Japan, and Kung fu comes from China.

FESTIVAL

The people of East Asia are renowned for their large, colorful festivals which can last for weeks on end—in China, the Lunar New Year can last up to 15 days. The majority of festivities are religious. Below, towering fruit and flowers are carried at Mengwi Festival, Bali.

Tai Chi is a slow martial art that many Chinese people practice for exercise.

RICE FARMING

Although wheat and tea are widely grown in northern Asia, rice is the chief food of the continent, with more than one-fifth of the world's rice grown in Southeast Asia. Numerous farming villages and shimmering rice paddy fields are scattered across the landscape.

The arts

East and Southeast Asia have a rich tradition of performing arts, from music to drama and dance, or a combination of all three. Shadow puppets are a popular form of entertainment in Indonesia and Malaysia; silhouette puppets behind a sheet perform everything from love stories to battle scenes.

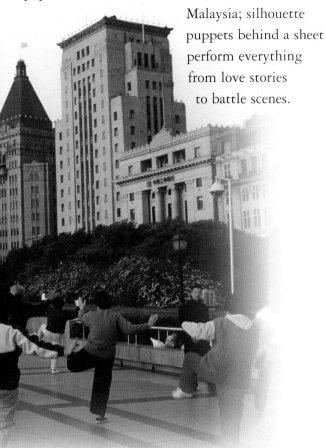

CRAFTS

The people of East Asia are renowned worldwide for their beautiful crafts. These include richly colored silks from Thailand and batik designs from Bali. The Chinese are skilled at kite making, jade carving, and papermaking, and products such as these beautiful parasols are popular all over the world.

RELIGION

Although Buddhism was founded in Nepal and India, it quickly spread across East Asia and has become one of the main religions in China, Japan, and Southeast Asia. Indonesia is predominently Islamic with the exception of Bali, which is Hindu, and Philippines and Timor, which are Roman Catholic. The Asiatic part of Russia is also Christian. Other minority religions include Shinto in Japan and a Korean religion called Chondogyo.

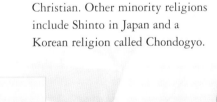

Buddhist monks are allowed few possessions and spend much of their time meditating.

HINDUISM ON BALI

The majority of Balinese practice a unique form of Hinduism called *Agama Tirtha*. It is predominently Hindu, with Buddhist elements that were added to preexisting, religious customs.

FOR THOUSANDS OF YEARS TIBETAN PEOPLE have been living in

TIBETANS

AN ANCIENT BUDDHIST PEOPLE

Tibet and areas that are now part of China, India, Nepal, and Bhutan. The Tibetan culture, in particular their written language

Tibetan nomads

The Tibetan Plateau lies north of the Himalayas and is a huge, rugged plain where an estimated one million nomads live. The land cannot be farmed so the nomads are the only inhabitants. Some nomads have a winter home and travel with livestock at various times during the year.

The storms are sometimes so bad on the Tibetan plateau that they can blow a man off the back of a yak.

THE ESSENTIAL ANIMAL

For centuries the nomads have been leading sheep, goats, and yak from pasture to pasture. The animals are used for food, transportation, clothes, and wool products. Cashmere wool from the goats has recently been lucrative because of the demand for cashmere in the West.

One group of Tibetan nomads are the highest resident population known in the world.

THE CAMPS

There is little or no wood on the plains of Tibet, so when the nomads move their herds around they set up tents made of black yak hair. Wood for the winter cabins is brought up from the lowlands. Lake water is too salty to drink so they camp by springs.

YAK MILK

Tibetan nomads live mainly on the foods derived from their animals, such as milk products. They use yak milk to make their butter tea, which consists of yak butter and salted black tea mixed together into a kind of broth.

and shared faith in Buddhism, unite the people living in these countries. Since Tibet's incorporation into the People's Republic of China many people have been influenced by modern Chinese culture, however, most still practice Buddhism and retain many of their traditions. Ngari and U Tsang make up the Tibetan Autonomous Region where two-thirds of Tibetans live.

Tibetan Buddhism

By the eighth century Buddhism had already been introduced from India and it grew into a unique branch of the religion in Tibet over the following centuries. Tibetan monks have spiritual leaders called Lamas who belong to groups of monasteries.

EDUCATION
A typical course of study in the Tibetan monastery lasts between 18 and 25 years and children begin as young as eight years old. During these years trainee monks study Buddhist philosophies as well as poetry, medicine, and art.

PRAYER WHEELS
The practice of spinning prayer wheels and hanging prayer flags is common in Tibetan Buddhism. Prayer wheels are cylindrical wheels filled with rolls of paper that are printed with mantras (sacred texts) and prayers. Devotees spin the wheel clockwise while reciting the mantras and prayers.

TIBETAN MONASTERIES
More than 6,000 monasteries were destroyed in the 1950s–1970s. Since then many have been reconstructed and other schools reestablished in Southern India. The monks here are debating—a popular part of their education.

DUNG-CHENS
Dung-chens are 10 ft- (3 m-) long horn trumpets used in Buddhist rituals. The bass tones are said to resemble the sound of elephants calling.

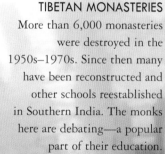

MONGOLIANS

MONGOLIA IS ONE OF THE HIGHEST countries in the world. The permanently snow-capped Altai mountains are to the west, and the Gobi Desert—an area of land that is in places almost completely uninhabitable—is to

THE NOMADIC HORSE PEOPLE

Mongolian horses

It is impossible to imagine the Mongolians without the horse. It is the most beloved animal of the Mongolian people and the symbol of the Mongolian nation. Their small horses are stocky and spirited, with powerful necks, dense coats, and thick legs. They are very hardy animals and can run for hours without tiring. They stay outside on open pastures all year.

THE DEEL

Mongolia has seen some Westernization but traditional clothes, such as the *deel*, (a long textile gown with a sash) are still worn. The *deel* is heavy and very warm, protecting against cold temperatures and bitter winds.

MONGOLIAN SCRIPT

Neglected for more than half a century, the beautiful Mongolian script has resurfaced and is now recognized as an important aspect of national culture.

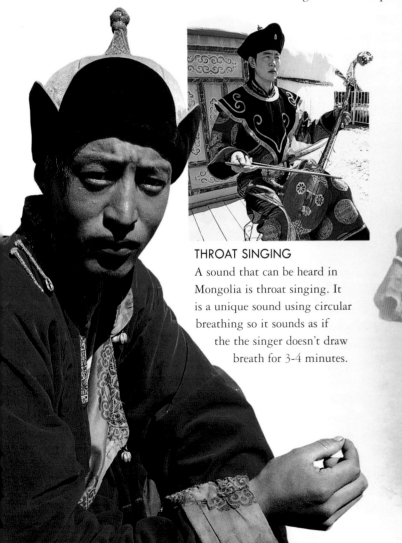

THROAT SINGING

A sound that can be heard in Mongolia is throat singing. It is a unique sound using circular breathing so it sounds as if the the singer doesn't draw breath for 3-4 minutes.

Both good riders and horses are held in high esteem, but the prestige largely goes to the horse.

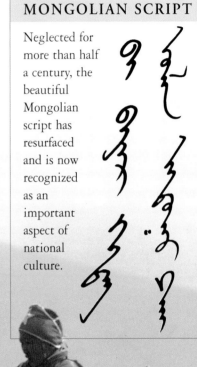

the south. In between lie the breathtaking grasslands, or steppes. Roughly two-thirds of the 2.4 million people in Mongolia live in cities and towns. The rest live as nomads always moving their herds to different seasonal pastures. Cursed with bitterly cold winters and a short growing season, the steppes have attracted few new people and much of the grasslands have changed little over hundreds of years.

LIVESTOCK

As well as horses, the Mongolians breed yaks, sheep, cattle, goats, and the hardy, two-humped camel, for milk, meat, wool, leather, and transportation. The nomads live mainly on flour, meat, and milk products; anything green or leafy is considered to be animal food. The horses are kept for riding and milk.

NAADAM FESTIVAL

The biggest festival in the Mongolian calendar is the *Naadam* festival held in July. For three days the nation enjoys a spectacle of horse racing, archery, and wrestling. People feast, tell legends, and sing ancient melodies.

The jockeys who race at the festival are normally between the ages of four and 10.

THE HOME

The Mongolian home is a large, white tent called a *ger*, which can be moved easily and quickly and erected in half an hour. Even the city Mongolians often live in *gers*. The door of a *ger* always faces south.

1 Building the frame
The frame is made up of supporting poles and wooden latice work, standing in a ring. They are fastened with leather thongs and studs.

2 Covering the ger
The frame is then covered with thick, white felt and fastened with ropes. Every *ger* has an opening at the top for light and ventilation.

3 Inside the ger
The insides of the finest *gers* are spectacular. The furniture is painted in bright colors and intricate patterns.

WOLF HUNTERS

There are strict hunting rules that prohibit the shooting of she-wolves or cubs in the winter when wolf's fur is at its thickest. The Mongolians ride motorcycles when they are hunting wolves.

A land that time forgot

THE MODERN WORLD CREEPS IN

SOME MONGOLIANS STILL BELIEVE THAT GENGHIS KHAN will return and lead Mongolia to greatness once again. The steppes of Mongolia today have changed little since the days when Genghis Khan founded his dynasty in 1206. It is thought that the nomadic population may not have even risen significantly since that time. The land is not easy to live on, most of it is unsuitable for agriculture, and almost all of the steppe land continues to be used for grazing livestock. Westernization, however, is never far away and, although electricity is available mainly in the cities, occasionally the lure of a good television program can reach even the steppes!

YAKUT

IMAGINE THE COLDEST WEATHER you have ever known, then triple it, and you are somewhere near the kinds of temperatures the people in Siberia have to endure. The town of Verkhoyansk lies in the area of the

LIFE IN THE WORLD'S COLDEST TOWN

Verkhoyansk

Traditionally, the Yakut way of life revolves around reindeer herding, and also, more unusually in the Arctic, horse and cattle raising. Most Yakut people today are urban dwellers and live in towns like Verkhoyansk. Farming in this area is difficult due to the freezing conditions, however, because of the continental climate, the temperatures do rise in the summer so grass can be made into hay and vegetables can be grown.

HORSE RAISING

The horses that the Yakut use are extremely hardy animals. They have a thick layer of fat and thick fur. They survive the winter on natural pastures without being fed by humans. As well as reindeer fur, the Yakut people also wear horse skins to keep them warm.

TOWN

The area around Verkhoyansk is rich in natural resources, including diamonds, gold, silver, coal, natural gas, tin, and much more. These are a major source of income for the Russian economy, so there is a lot of industry and mining in the area. A lot of the Yakut people have given up their traditional ways to work in industry.

THE BOREAL FOREST

In order for a town to function in such bitterly cold temperatures, enormous amounts of wood have to be burned. Verkhoyansk lies in the vast Boreal forest region of Siberia. Filled with larch and pine trees the forest provides plenty of wood.

Republic of Sakha, Siberia, and is considered the chilliest region in the northern hemisphere. The town is the coldest in the world and has been described as the most uninhabitable place on Earth. The lowest temperature ever recorded was a staggering -90°F (-68°C). One group of indigenous people who choose to live and survive in this chilly town are the Yakut people, who are one of the only Arctic peoples to keep horses.

Everyday survival

The temperatures in this part of Siberia can get so cold that the moisture in a person's breath can freeze in the air and fall to the ground. Parts of the body can freeze incredibly quickly if they are not wrapped up warmly. The Yakut make clothes from a mixture of animal furs.

A COZY HOME

Keeping a house warm is difficult if every time a door is opened, the cold air rushes in. For this reason some of the houses have three doors. Once you are through the first door you close it and go through the second, close it, and the third door takes you in. Warm rooms are essential.

MILK STORAGE

In a town where everything is frozen, often the best way to keep food fresh is to leave it outside. Cows are milked inside sheds and the milk is then poured into any available pot. The milk freezes in minutes; it is then taken out of the pot and stored as round chunks.

Simply melt the milk block to drink it.

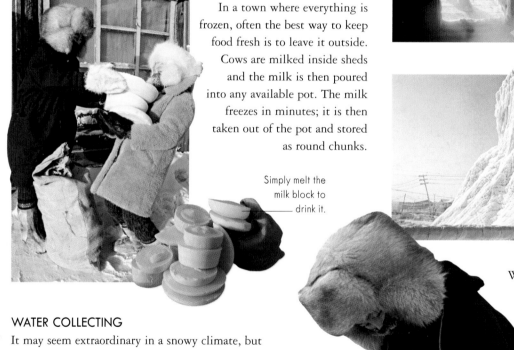

BURSTING PIPES

Water pipes are susceptible to freezing in cold climates like that in Verkhoyansk. This pipe has burst and forced water up into the air. Because of the incredibly low temperatures it has frozen in midair, the water creating a huge ice sculpture.

WATER COLLECTING

It may seem extraordinary in a snowy climate, but collecting water is more difficult than you might imagine. Snow does not provide a large volume of water so ice is generally collected. The people take a horse and sled to a frozen river and chisel off huge chunks of ice. The ice is then kept outside and used when needed.

The ice never melts when left outside in the winter.

CHUKCHI

LIVING ON THE EASTERN TIP OF SIBERIA

THE CHUKCHI PEOPLE LIVE ON THE FURTHEST northeastern part of Siberia both on the coast and inland. The administrative language of the area is Russian but the Chukchi language still exists. Only about five percent of

Divided people

The Chukchi are divided into two groups: the coastal Chukchi, who have permanent homes on the coast, and the inland Chukchi, who breed reindeer and migrate with them between summer and winter pastures in the Boreal forest. There has always been a friendly alliance between the two, which comes in handy when trading items, such as fish and reindeer skin.

THE PEOPLE ON THE COAST

The coastal Chukchi live in settlements along the coast on the very northeastern part of Siberia. They survive by fishing and hunting marine animals, such as seal and walrus. They still use traditional walrus skin boats, called *umiak*, that are made of wooden frames. In the winter it is sometimes necessary to drag the *umiak* miles over the ice to the water.

These boats can vary from 9-30 ft (3 – 9 m) long and be up to 8 ft (2.5 m) wide.

HOME OR AWAY

Most Chukchi live in small towns scattered along the coast and inland, such as this town of Uelen, which is famous for carvings. Some of the inland Chukchi, however, are seminomadic, moving with herds of reindeer biannually from the tundra to the taiga and back.

The Chukchi use hessian-filled bags as saddles when riding reindeer.

CHUKCHI SEASONS

The Chukchi divide the year into five seasons according to natural phenomena such as the rising and setting of the sun, numbers of mosquitoes, and the state of the snow. *Leleng* is their winter, which they then subdivide into three. So it could be said that the Chukchi have seven seasons.

the people, however, still speak the Chukchi language in their own home and it is now classified as an endangered language. It was originally just a spoken language but in 1932 it was written down for the first time.

Although the area that they live in is now inhabited by other peoples, some Chukchi have remained very traditional in their lifestyle. The word "Chukchi" means "rich in reindeer."

Spiritual belief

Like many Arctic peoples, the Chukchi have an animistic religion—they believe that every object, whether animate or not, possesses a spirit or life force that may be beneficial or harmful. They believe that these spirits roam the Earth, and everyday tasks, such as hunting and fishing, include certain customs intended to make the hunt successful and all the spirits happy.

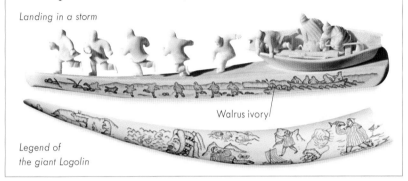
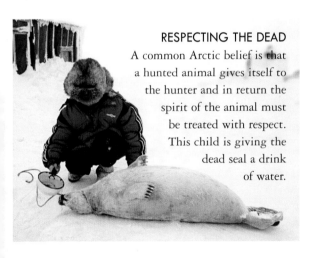

RESPECTING THE DEAD
A common Arctic belief is that a hunted animal gives itself to the hunter and in return the spirit of the animal must be treated with respect. This child is giving the dead seal a drink of water.

SHAMANISM
Traditional Chukchi people believe in shamans, figures who are capable of communicating directly with spiritual powers, often in ecstatic states. The drum is the only instrument that the Chukchi people have and it is always used in conjunction with a shaman.

Wooden idol

REINDEER PROTECTION
The Chukchi make reindeer idols out of deer skin and wood, and sometimes decorate them with beads. These idols are created to protect the reindeer and keep them from harm. If one of the herd gets lost, the Chukchi take out the idols and beat them in the belief that this encourages the spirits to send the reindeer back unhurt.

The drum is made out of reindeer skin.

CHINESE

THE WORLD'S OLDEST CIVILIZATION

WITH A POPULATION OF 1.28 BILLION, China has the largest population of any country on Earth. One person in five in the world is Chinese. The country also has the world's oldest continuous civilization,

FARMING

Even though there are a lot of cities in China, nearly three-quarters of the population live in the countryside and farm the land, of which only about 10 per cent is fertile. The main crops are rice, wheat, and millet.

City living

For many years the communist Chinese government had control of all industry. However, since the 1980s the government has given greater freedom to people starting businesses and encouraged international trade. As a result, the cities have gone through an economic boom, with the industry starting to draw in millions of workers from the countryside. Modern architecture stands alongside ancient buildings.

CHINESE NEW YEAR

Chinese New Year is the first day of the first month in the lunar calendar. Festivities go on every day until the 15th day, which is the Lantern Festival, when people decorate their homes with beautiful, richly colored lanterns.

TRADITIONAL CULTURE

Old ways of life are still very much evident in China, and some have even spread throughout the world. Chinese herbal medicine and the ancient art of acupuncture are now commonly used worldwide, and Chinese food is popular in many countries, brought in by immigrant Chinese communities.

TAI CHI

Many Chinese people practice Tai Chi, which is a martial art that can also be performed slowly and used to decrease stress and maintain physical health. Every morning, in parks all over China, people can be seen practicing Tai Chi forms.

with a recorded history beginning 4,000 years ago with the Shang dynasty. Over thousands of years China has developed a rich culture. Ninety-two percent of the country are Han Chinese; the rest of the population belong to other minority groups, each of which has varied traditions, languages or dialects, and religions. Most Chinese live in the eastern part of the country.

Chinese minority groups

There are 55 minority ethnic groups in China, in addition to the majority, Han. Fifty-three of these use spoken languages of their own and 23 have their own written languages. Most of the remaining eight percent live in the vast areas of the west, southwest, and northwest.

HAN

The Han Chinese are the largest ethnic group in the world. The Han culture is incredibly old and the language of the Han, commonly known as Mandarin Chinese, is not only the most widely spoken in the world, but is also the most ancient language in the world.

DAI

The Dai people live in the southern part of Yunnan Province and have a rich, colorful culture. They live in bamboo houses and have a history stretching back more than 1,000 years.

BAI

The Bai people have a population of around two million, 90 percent of whom live in the Bai Autonomous County in Yunnan Province. They are known for their worship of the color white.

The Uigur people have their own language and alphabet.

UIGUR

The Uigur people, with a total population of 7.21 million, have lived at the foot of Mt Tianshan, western China, for several centuries. The Uigurs rely heavily on agriculture as their main source of survival, planting cotton, wheat, corn, and rice. The Uigurs follow the Islamic faith, which influences family life, marriages, and food.

MIAO

AN ANCIENT CHINESE CULTURE

WITH A POPULATION OF OVER SEVEN MILLION, the Miao people form one of the largest ethnic minorities in southwest China. They also have one of the world's most ancient cultures and can trace their

The Long-Horned Miao

One clan of the group are the Long-Horned Miao, who are famous for their unique costumes and horned headpieces. They are from a village called Longga in southwest China, and it is only since the highway to the village was built in 1994 that these amazing people and their culture have been revealed to the world.

FABRIC DESIGN

The Miao people specialize in batik and embroidered fabrics, which are evident in their everyday dress. A girl learns to work with fabrics from the age of six or seven, and her skills greatly increase her value as a wife.

Houses on the hillsides are often built on stilts with the animals living beneath them.

HORN HEADPIECES

The women wear extraordinary headpieces that consist of hair wrapped around animal horns protruding from each side of their head. To keep the horns in place they wrap their own hair and an elongated bun made from linen, wool, and hair from ancient ancestors around them, and fix it all with white cord. The headpiece can be up to 10 ft (3 m) long and weigh up to 4 1/2 lb (2 kg).

ancestors back over 4,000 years. There are many different Miao clans living in this mountainous area, each with its own individual characteristics and dialects. All, however, share a basic culture that has

clearly developed from a common root. The Miao are known for their beautiful arts and crafts, particularly their fabric designs, and for their spectacular festivals and celebrations filled with song and dance.

THE SHENG

A popular instrument in the Miao culture is the *sheng*, a wind instrument made from a bundle of different lengths of bamboo. It can produce chords as well as single notes and is thought to have been used up to 3,000 years ago in China.

THE DRAGON

Many Miao still follow their traditional religion. They believe that spirits in the shape of dragons protect them, and often decorate fabrics with the beautiful, mythical creatures.

Farming

Much of the Miao area is hilly or mountainous, drained by several rivers. The weather is mild with plenty of rain so farming is a large part of the people's lives. The staple crop is rice, supplemented by corn, wheat, and all kinds of fruit and vegetables. Men mainly do the farming and hunting while women raise livestock and keep the home.

Traditionally the headdress was solid silver but these days only the smaller ornaments tend to be.

SILVER JEWELS

Women's headdresses have special importance in Miao culture. When a girl is born, her family starts to save money to buy silver head ornaments that are worn for special occasions. Each clan has a slightly different designs and at festivals the women dance in them, showing off their family's wealth.

KOREANS

A COUNTRY DIVIDED

KOREA TAKES THE FORM OF A PENINSULA stretching southward, like a thumb, from the center of the northeast coast of Asia. Since 1955, the country has been divided into North and South Korea, North

Education

One of the most important elements in Korean life is a good education—teachers are deeply respected and trusted. Children are expected to study hard and parents are encouraged to offer full support for their child's education. Schools are regarded as a kind of extended family.

INDUSTRY

In the 1960s, the Republic of Korea started to change from an agriculturally based country to an industrial one. The incredibly rapid success of their electronics, shipbuilding, communications, and car industries have turned Korea into a model for development worldwide.

PLANT A TREE

Each year, school children from all over the Republic of Korea take part in a relatively new annual event, Tree Planting Day. Every child must plant a tree in order to protect the environment.

The capital of the Republic of Korea is Seoul, which is very modern and industrialized, and full of skyscrapers.

Korea being communist, and South Korea, or the Republic of Korea, being an industrial nation. Despite the separation, however, the Koreans have many shared traditions and beliefs. The landscape ranges from high mountains to lowland forests and plains and the summers are warm, while the winters can be bitterly cold. The predominant religions in Korea are Buddhist or Confucian, with some Shamanism and Christianity.

A traditional life

Although Korea has changed dramatically in the last 50 years, the people still retain many aspects of their traditional life. Music is a large part of their culture and they claim to have 60 types of traditional instrument. They also have a long history of paper craft and make all kinds of objects with paper including mats, bowls, and even furniture.

TAE KWON DO

The national sport of Korea is Tae kwon do, which was invented in Korea and dates back 200 years. This self-defensive martial art uses the whole body and not only strengthens it but also cultivates a good mental attitude.

KIMINCHI

For thousands of years Koreans have been eating pickled vegetables, such as *kiminchi*, or fermented cabbage. It is rare in Korea to eat a meal without it.

A farm woman carries a large bundle balanced on her head.

KOREAN DRESS

On the streets of Korea, Westernized clothing is the most common style of dress seen. However, during traditional holidays and celebrations women may wear the traditional *hanbok*, which is a simple wrap-around skirt worn with a bolero-like jacket. A long coat is sometimes worn on top.

RURAL KOREA

Even though Korea was predominantly agricultural for many years, its mountainous terrain meant that little of the land could be cultivated. Rice is the staple food grown in the foothills in paddyfields.

JAPAN IS MADE UP OF FOUR MAIN volcanic islands and over 3,900

JAPANESE

ANCIENT MEETS MODERN

smaller islands situated to the east of mainland Asia. Nearly 75 percent of the country is rugged and mountainous and virtually uninhabitable, and the

The modern city

Tokyo, the capital of Japan, is a fast-paced, energetic city that never seems to rest. It houses a population of 12 million people and covers approximately 800 sq miles (2,100 sq km). Much of the capital was destroyed in World War II and today is filled with high-rise office buildings and sprawling suburbs.

HOT SPRINGS
The islands that make up Japan are volcanic, and like a giant sponge, Japan leaks from thousands of hot springs, or *onsen*. For over 2,000 years the Japanese have enjoyed hot, outdoor baths in the naturally warm waters.

A MODERN WORLD
Japanese children and teenagers are very much a modern generation, listening to Western pop music and keeping up with fashions.

Rush hour in Tokyo.

ROBOT TECHNOLOGY
Few people in the modern world are unaffected by the technological ideas of Japan, from cars to computers. High-tech toys and games have been at the forefront of Japanese technology since the 1970s. Today about half of the world's robots are found in Japan.

majority of what is left is farmed. This means that a huge amount of the population live in urban areas. Japan is still a country of remarkable ethnic and cultural purity. Non-Japanese people make up only one percent of the population. The cities of Japan are busy with traffic and industry but old traditions still survive and deep-rooted appreciation of traditional arts flourishes throughout Japan, from the tea ceremonies to sumo wrestling.

Traditional Japan

Japan's oldest religion is Shinto, and most Japanese still observe Shinto rituals alongside Buddhist practices. Manners and customs are of utmost importance in Japan, and the old respect and humility are practiced in the home as well as in the modern office.

TEA CEREMONY

The Japanese tea ceremony, or *chanoyu*, was established in the 16th century and is much the same today. It is the ritual way of preparing and drinking green tea and is considered an art as well as a way to purify the soul.

STREET FESTIVALS

The Japanese celebrate a huge number of festivals, many of which include street parades, such as this one. In May, when the spectacular "Children's Day" is celebrated, colorful carp banners are flown.

KIMONO

The kimono is the traditional dress of Japan. Today, Japanese women rarely wear kimonos except on special occasions, such as weddings. Children's kimonos are similar to the adults ones but often much brighter in color. Because of the complex material shape, it can take an hour or more to dress a child in a kimono.

SAPPORO SNOW FESTIVAL

The Sapporo Snow Festival is one of Japan's largest winter events. For seven days in February the main street in Susukino is transformed into a myriad of ice sculptures and ice buildings. Many countries take part in the ice-sculpting competition.

Sumo

SUMO WRESTLING is the extraordinary and exciting national sport of Japan. Its roots go back nearly 1,500 years and the ritual has changed little. The sport reflects many values that the Japanese hold dear, such as respect and rank, and sumo wrestlers are considered to be living heroes. There are six Grand Tournaments every year, each one lasting for 15 days.

Large banners announce sumo tournaments.

THE WEIGHT

In sumo, the larger the man the better. There are no weight limits so it is possible for a wrestler to find himself fighting a component twice his weight. The average weight of a wrestler is about 350 lb (158 kg). One of the largest wrestlers ever was 700 lb (317 kg)!

PREPARATION

Before the match each sumo wrestler's hair is tied into a top knot, called a *mage*. The knot is slightly different according to the seniority of the wrestler. The *mawashi*, or loin cloth—the only piece of clothing worn during the match—is made from 30 ft (10 m) of black silk.

THE RITUAL OF SUMO

A sumo match is filled with symbolism, even before the
fighting starts. The rituals for the top sumos are allowed to
go on for four minutes before the judges make them begin to
fight. The ritual fires up the spectators to feverish excitement.

1 The purification
At the start, the sumo
rinses his mouth with
water, the source of purity, and
wipes his body with a paper
towel. He then scatters a handful
of salt into the ring to purify it.

2 The leg lift
The wrestler repeats
certain ritualistic motions,
such as raising his arms to the
side as well as raising a leg up
high and stamping it down
hard on the ground.

3 The glare
The contestants then face
each other and, crouching
forward, place their fists on the
floor. They then glare fiercely
at each other before hurling
themselves together for the fight.

DOHYO-IRI

The formal ceremony held in the ring at the start of the match is called the
Dohyo-iri. The sumo contestants each wear an apron made of silk, beautifully
decorated with rich embroidery and hemmed with gold, which they will
remove for the fight. The senior judge, the *gyoji*, wears a traditional kimono.
The wrestlers form a circle around the ring, then in turn, each one claps his
hands to attract the attention of the gods, before performing movements to
drive evil from the ring.

A wrestler may grip onto an
opponent's *mawashi* to force
him to the ground.

THE FIGHT

A bout of sumo is won by a wrestler
forcing his opponent out of the ring
or hurling him to the ground within
it. No part of the body may touch
the ground except the feet. Slapping,
pushing, tripping, and judo-style
flips are allowed.

PADAUNG
THE LAND OF THE GIRAFFE WOMEN

THE PADAUNG PEOPLE OF BURMA number less than 7,000, but have attracted much interest over the years due to their practice of neck-stretching. The women, commonly known as "giraffe women," start a life of neck rings at the age of five or six. The village medicine man works the first several loops around the girl's neck at this age and then one extra is added every two years until the desired length has been reached. By the time the woman is of marriageable age, the neck will have extended to about 10 in (25 cm). The custom is more than a rare, strange expression of feminine beauty—the number and value of rings indicates status and respect for the wearer's family.

THAIS

A BUDDHIST CULTURE

THE ETHNIC THAI PEOPLE ARE MADE UP OF FOUR core groups: Central Thai, Thai-Lao, Northern Thai, and Southern Thai. The 62 million Thais all descend from the natives of the Yunnan province in China and

City life

The streets of the capital city, Bangkok, are filled with traffic, from cars, bikes, and taxis, to the traditional three-wheeled vans known as *tuk-tuk*.

THAI SILK

Thailand is rich in crafts but perhaps the most famous is Thai silk, which is dyed to produce rich colors.

BUDDHISM

About 95 percent of Thais are Buddhists. They do not visit the temples regularly, but more often worship in their own homes at a shrine in front of a Buddha image. When believers are in a temple, tradition dictates that the head is lower than the Buddha image, or any Buddhist monks present, so they sit on the floor.

FLOATING MARKET

A number of narrow canals run through Bangkok. These are filled with narrow boats selling anything from food and drink to souvenirs. Almost all of the boats are paddled by women wearing blue with flat hats called *muak ngob*. The floating markets are still important commercial centers for those living along the banks.

officially emerged as a people in 1238. Other Thai-speaking people live in China, Laos, and Burma. Thailand has a royal family, whose history dates back 700 years. The monarchy of Thailand prides itself on constantly adapting to ensure that it fits in with the modern world, its people, and society. Thai culture retains a distinctiveness that the people are very proud of. Almost all share the Buddhist faith, which has helped to bind them.

Rural life

The towns of Thailand are surrounded by small farming villages, many of which have developed different traditions and styles of dress. The villages are made up of family groups or clans ruled by a headman and his council.

FARMING VILLAGES

The villagers cooperate with each other becoming like a large, extended family. Every village has a temple, or *wat*, used as a meeting place as well as for worship.

THAI BOXING

Muay Thai, or Thai boxing, is one of Thailand's most popular sports. The roots of this martial art can be traced back to medieval times, and it is not just a sport but an extravagant event. Before every match, the two fighters dance to special boxing music to honor and pay respect to the trainer, family, and to the sport.

AKHA HEADDRESS

The Akha people who live in the hilly regions of northern Thailand are known for their elaborate headdresses. These are adorned with silver balls and colored beads and are worn regularly by the women, not just on ceremonial occasions.

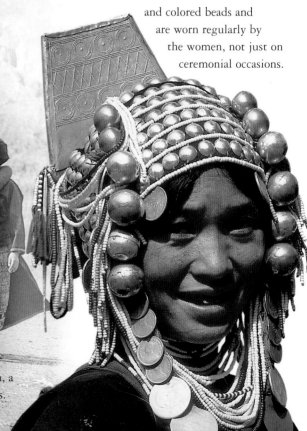

YAO PEOPLE

The Yao people are best known for their clothing. The women wear a black turban, a long tunic with a large red ruff sewn into the front, and heavily embroidered pants. The embroidery itself is a craft tradition of which the Yao are particularly proud.

IBAN

PEOPLE OF THE LONGHOUSES

THE MALAYSIAN PROVINCE OF SARAWAK on northwest Borneo Island is a maze of endless rivers making their way through dense, steamy rain forests. It is here that the Iban people live, forming

Longhouses

The Iban live in longhouses, which are at the very center of communal life in Sarawak. Most longhouses are riverside dwellings and are therefore built on stilts to prevent flooding. The entire community lives under one roof.

An Iban bride wears a full silver headdress.

VILLAGE LIFE

The longhouses are divided into apartments and when a new couple is married, often they will simply add another building to the end of the house. Some longhouses have hundreds of rooms under one roof. A long communal balcony runs along the side of the house with the doors to the apartments along it.

The *agom* is a carved wooden figure that is placed on the pathways to rice fields to protect the crop.

CARVING AND WEAVING

The Iban people learn to weave and carve from an early age. The men carve and the woman weave; the gifted continue all their lives and are highly valued. They believe the objects they make protect them from evil spirits.

JEWELRY

Large earrings and gold teeth show that a girl comes from a well-to-do family. The teeth are sometimes inlaid with precious stones. Heavy earrings create large, elongated earlobes.

30 percent of the state's population and existing by hunting, fishing, and growing rice in the thick jungle. Sarawak is known as "the land of the hornbill" after a majestic bird believed by the Iban people to be a messenger from the spirit world. Today, the majority of the Iban are Christian, but they still practice traditional rituals, which are a mixture of animistic and Hindu-Buddhist beliefs.

Hunting

The Iban hunt and eat a wide variety of forest animals, including birds, squirrels, monkeys, lizards, and barking deer. But the most prized game animal is the bearded pig. Sometimes weighing more than 220 lb (100 kg), one of these animals can supply enough meat to feed a group for several days.

To shoot the dart fast and accurately, the breath must be blown from the chest and stomach rather than just the mouth.

HEADHUNTERS

As recently as 50 years ago the Iban people were notorious headhunters. They believed that the captured heads of their enemies would bring them strength and prosperity. It is now illegal to headhunt in Sarawak.

BLOWPIPES

The traditional hunting weapon of the Iban is the blowpipe. It is lighter and more accurate than a shotgun and the darts kill silently, allowing a hunter take a second shot should he miss the first. The darts are dipped in poison made from tree sap, which kills by causing suffocation. The dose is carefully chosen to suit the prey.

LONGBOATS

The Iban travel on the rivers and waterways in longboats. They are not only for transportation, but also to show off the owner's carving skills and status among the villagers. Well-carved paddles are also used for ceremonial occasions.

BAJAU

THE PEOPLE OF THE SEA

COMMONLY KNOWN TO WESTERNERS AS SEA GYPSIES, the Bajau boat dwellers have lived scattered over the water off Philippines for thousands of years. Some live a nomadic life in outrigger houseboats and others settle in stilt houses at the water's edge. The Bajau people are famous for their pearl diving. Today, they retain rights to the pearl beds in the area, which are used by the modern pearl industry. Even these days, the Bajau divers free-dive to depths well beyond the safe limits of normal scuba diving. They can dive to depths of 125 ft (40 m).

THE ISLAND OF BALI LIES IN THE INDONESIAN ARCHIPELAGO

BALINESE

LIFE ON PARADISE ISLAND

to the east of Java. The small island is a cluster of high volcanoes that drop straight to the sea with very little flat land between. The Balinese are Hindu

COMMUNITY LIFE

Family and community ties are one of the most important factors in Balinese life. All the families in a village worship a common ancestor —the village god—who binds the community together. Villages regularly organize festivals and participate in music and dancing.

Rice culture

According to Balinese legend, the island orginally only grew sugar cane. Then, out of pity for the human race, the God of fertility and water came to Earth and delivered rice. Rice to the Balinese is therefore a gift from God and is treated with great respect. From planting to harvest, the rice is watched, tended, and worshipped.

FARMING RICE

Rice is grown on every piece of land that is accessible to water. Irrigation is difficult, but the Balinese have developed an elaborate system of canals, dams, bamboo pipes, and tunnels to control the water.

1 Watering fields
First the terraces and fields are filled to the brim with water, which makes the land look like giant mirrors reflecting the sky.

2 Planting seeds
When the earth has turned to mud, the seeds are sprinkled on the ground. They will grow into a thick green carpet.

3 Harvesting grain
As the grain ripens, the rice plants turn a golden color. Both men and women work hard to collect the rice at harvesttime.

Men carry the rice in two baskets on their shoulder and the women carry it in baskets on their heads.

THE RICE RITE

The Balinese perform many rituals and ceremonies to make the rice grow well. They pray for enough water, and the prevention of pollution to the land, and perform rituals to keep thieves, such as mice, away.

by religion, which is unusual in an area almost exclusively made up of Muslim countries. The Balinese are proud of having preserved their unique Hindu culture and this is seen in the large number of beautiful temples on the island and numerous festivals and celebrations held. The island is visited by thousands of tourists and although this has led to many changes, the Balinese have sustained a vibrant and fascinating culture.

MARKETS

The colorful Balinese markets are not only a necessity to the people, but also attract large number of tourists eager to buy their beautiful crafts.

ART
Textiles and carvings represent a mark of cultural identity to the Balinese. Their clothes are beautifully designed and famous the world over. Woodcarving is at its best as part of temple and palace architecture in Bali.

MUSIC
A traditional Balinese orchestra is known as the *gamelan*. It is almost completely made up of percussion instruments, such as gongs, cymbals, and xylophones. The Balinese believe that the *gamelan* is of divine origin and the instruments are treated with the greatest respect.

Balinese cremation

The people of Bali see a cremation ceremony as a joyous occasion rather than one of mourning. Hundreds of people carry beautifully decorated towers, sometimes 60 ft (18 m) high, containing the body to the place of cremation. The body is then placed inside a wooden casket and the whole thing, with the decorations, is set alight in order to liberate the soul to a higher world.

An impressive cremation adds greatly to the prestige of a wealthy family, giving occasion for extravagant festivities.

THE PEOPLE OF
The Pacific and Australia

aborigine *nj* original or native
inhabitant of a country, especially Australia.
aboriginal *adj* earliest, primitive, or indigenous.

pacific *adj* peacemaking; appeasing; inclining toward
peace; peaceful; mild; tranquil; of or relating to the ocean
between Asia and America, so called by Magellan, the first
European to sail on it, because he happened to cross it in
peaceful conditions.

THE PACIFIC ISLANDS AND AUSTRALIA COVER AN AREA larger

THE PACIFIC AND AUSTRALIA

than Asia but
the landmass
is smaller than

A CONTINENT OF THOUSANDS OF ISLANDS

Europe's. At over

PACIFIC AND AUSTRALIA FACTS

PLACES
Highest point ....Mt. Wilhelm, Papua New Guinea,
14,793 ft (4,509 m)
Biggest desert ....Great Australian Desert, Australia
Longest river ....Murray-Darling, Australia,
2,330 miles (3,750 km)
Biggest country ....Australia

PEOPLE
Population of continent ....30 million
Most densely populated country ....Nauru, 1,469 per
sq mile (567 people per sq km)
Most populous country ....Australia, 19 million
Most populous city ....Sydney, Australia, 4.1 million

LITERACY RATE
Male ....86 percent
Female ....71 percent

The Pacific Islands

Many of the islands in the Pacific became
European colonies in the 19th century.
Some are still colonies or are administered
under international agreements, but
most have recently grouped together
to form small independent nations.

Micronesia
This area includes the
Marshall Islands, Nauru,
and Palau.

Northern Mariana
Islands
(to US)

Wake
Islan
(to US

Mariana Islands

Saipan

*Philippine
Sea*

Guam
(to US)

Bikini Atoll

**MARSHALL
ISLANDS**

Yap

M I C R O N E S I A

Caroline Islands

Pohnpei

Chuuk

Babeldaob

Kosrae

PALAU

M e l a n e s i a

NAURU

PAPUA NEW GUINEA

*Bismarck
Sea*

New Ireland

*New
Britain*

Solomon Islands

**SOLOMON
ISLANDS**

New Guinea

*Bougainville
Island*

*Solomon
Sea*

Guadalcanal

*Santa Cruz
Islands*

Arafura Sea

Torres Strait

*Coral
Sea*

VANUAT

Efate

Coral Sea Islands
(to Australia)

New Caledonia
(to France)

*Timor
Sea*

*Joseph
Bonaparte
Gulf*

*Gulf of
Carpentaria*

P A C

Norfolk Island
(to Australia)

I N D I A N   O C E A N

NORTHERN
TERRITORY

QUEENSLAND

Lord Howe Island
(to Australia)

A U S T R A L I A

*Lake Eyre
North*

WESTERN AUSTRALIA

SOUTH AUSTRALIA
Lake Torrens

NEW
SOUTH WALES

AUSTRALIAN
CAPITAL TERRITORY

Australia
Two-thirds of
Australia is a
great plateau
of deserts and
mountains.

*Great Australian
Bight*

VICTORIA

*Tasman
Sea*

Bass Strait

TASMANIA

Tasmania

New Zealand
The country comprises
two islands—the
North Island and the
South Island.

S O U T H E R N

30 million, its population is the smallest of any continent. The area is made up of Australia, New Zealand, Papua New Guinea, and thousands of islands in the Pacific Ocean. These islands are divided into three main areas: Micronesia, Melanesia, and Polynesia. Australia is too large to be called an island and is now considered a continent in its own right, and with the other islands, is known as Oceania.

0 km 400 800
0 miles 400 800

The world's biggest atoll is Kwajalein, in the Marshall Islands. An atoll is a ring of coral enclosing a central lagoon.

Melanesia
Five main island groups make up Melanesia – Papua New Guinea, Fiji, Vanuatu, New Caledonia, and the Solomon Islands.

Polynesia
This area covers the Cook Islands, French Polynesia, Easter Island, and Pitcairn Islands, among other small island groups.

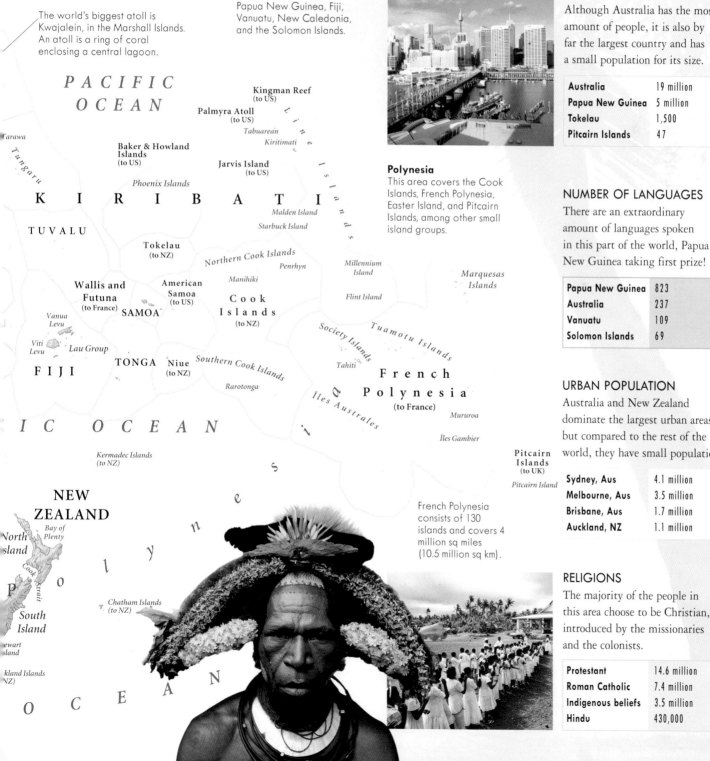

PACIFIC OCEAN

Tarawa
Tungaru
KIRIBATI
TUVALU

Kingman Reef (to US)
Palmyra Atoll (to US)
Tabuarean
Kiritimati

Baker & Howland Islands (to US)
Phoenix Islands
Jarvis Island (to US)

Line Islands

Malden Island
Starbuck Island

Tokelau (to NZ)
Northern Cook Islands
Penrhyn
Manihiki

Millennium Island
Marquesas Islands
Flint Island

Wallis and Futuna (to France)
American Samoa (to US)
SAMOA
Vanua Levu
Viti Levu Lau Group
FIJI
TONGA
Niue (to NZ)
Cook Islands (to NZ)
Society Islands
Tahiti
Southern Cook Islands
Rarotonga
Tuamotu Islands

French Polynesia (to France)

Mururoa
Iles Gambier
Iles Australes

IC OCEAN

Kermadec Islands (to NZ)

Pitcairn Islands (to UK)
Pitcairn Island

NEW ZEALAND
North Island
Bay of Plenty
Cook Strait
South Island
ewart sland
kland Islands NZ)
Chatham Islands (to NZ)

French Polynesia consists of 130 islands and covers 4 million sq miles (10.5 million sq km).

OCEAN

The Pacific and Australia statistics

POPULATION BY COUNTRY
Although Australia has the most amount of people, it is also by far the largest country and has a small population for its size.

Australia	19 million
Papua New Guinea	5 million
Tokelau	1,500
Pitcairn Islands	47

NUMBER OF LANGUAGES
There are an extraordinary amount of languages spoken in this part of the world, Papua New Guinea taking first prize!

Papua New Guinea	823
Australia	237
Vanuatu	109
Solomon Islands	69

URBAN POPULATION
Australia and New Zealand dominate the largest urban areas, but compared to the rest of the world, they have small populations.

Sydney, Aus	4.1 million
Melbourne, Aus	3.5 million
Brisbane, Aus	1.7 million
Auckland, NZ	1.1 million

RELIGIONS
The majority of the people in this area choose to be Christian, introduced by the missionaries and the colonists.

Protestant	14.6 million
Roman Catholic	7.4 million
Indigenous beliefs	3.5 million
Hindu	430,000

The People of the Pacific and Australia

THE FIRST INHABITANTS of this area were the Aborigines and Torres Strait Islanders of Australia, Tongans, Tahitians, Samoans, Micronesians, Melanesians, and the Polynesians—such as the New Zealand Maori. They are thought to have originated from Southeast Asia, arriving as far back as 40,000 years ago.

A fifth of Australia's population lives in Sydney.

COLONIZATION

During the late 18th century, Europeans started to pour into Australia, attracted by gold and "a new life," and much of the region was colonized. Today, Australia and New Zealand have a rich mixture of ethnic groups from Europe and Asia.

CITY LIFE

The amount of people in Oceania is very low. Australia is one of the least densely populated areas on Earth. Eighty percent of Australia's population live within 25 miles (40 km) of the coast, most in cities such as Melbourne, and Sydney.

SPORT

One of the popular sports in Oceanic culture is rugby. The Australian and New Zealand—"All Blacks"—teams have some of the world's best players. The Pacific Islands, such as Fiji and Samoa, also have international teams.

FARMING

Australia and New Zealand both rely on their resources for income, such as sheep and cattle farming, and mining.

Island people

Over 20,000 islands are scattered over the vast expanse of the Pacific Ocean. Some are large, such as New Guinea, others are little more than tiny coral islands. Only a few thousand are inhabited today.

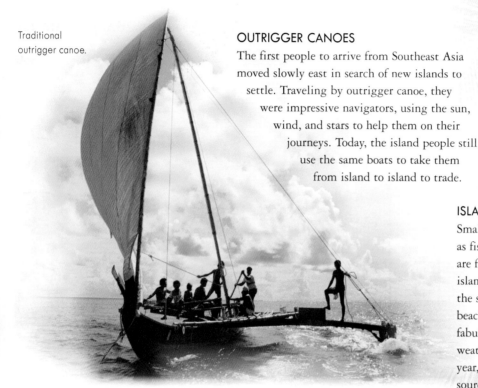

Traditional outrigger canoe.

OUTRIGGER CANOES

The first people to arrive from Southeast Asia moved slowly east in search of new islands to settle. Traveling by outrigger canoe, they were impressive navigators, using the sun, wind, and stars to help them on their journeys. Today, the island people still use the same boats to take them from island to island to trade.

ISLAND INDUSTRY

Small scale industries, such as fishing and some mining, are found on the Pacific islands. However, due to the stunningly beautiful beaches and lagoons, fabulous diving, and fine weather throughout the year, tourism is the main source of income.

Tolai dancers wearing ceremonial masks in Papua New Guinea.

FOREIGN INFLUENCE

Many islanders became Christian when the missionaries arrived in the late 18th century and have since absorbed many foreign influences. Some villages in Papua New Guinea, however, have had little contact with the outside world, and have developed totally different languages and cultures from each other.

LANGUAGE

English is widely spoken throughout Australia, New Zealand, and on many of the Pacific Islands. However, Papua New Guinea lays claim to over 800 different languages!

AUSTRALIA IS AN ENORMOUS COUNTRY. It is the sixth largest country

AUSTRALIANS

A MIXED NATION OF PEOPLE

in the world, but very little of the land is inhabited. There is less than one person per square mile and, although Australia is

A way of life

Australians enjoy a hot climate all year round and spend a lot of time outdoors playing land and sea sports. Surfing and diving are two of the most popular pastimes. Team sports, such as rugby union and cricket, are also widely played. The country's teams are world famous—sport is almost a religion.

AUSTRALIAN RULES

Australian Rules is a game unique to the country and is a mixture of rugby and Gaelic football. It is played in every state and territory, and players are household names and treated as stars.

CULTURAL MIX

For thousands of years Aborigines and Torres Strait Islanders were the only inhabitants of Australia. In the 18th century British colonists arrived and the discovery of gold in the 1850s brought a rush of people from Europe, China, and the US. After World War II more people immigrated there, and today about a quarter of Australian residents were born in another country.

THE GOLD COAST

With about 300 days of sun a year, the Gold Coast that stretches down the eastern side of Australia is a true surfers' paradise. The sprawling region has grown up around an extensive stretch of beautiful beaches, which makes the area a very attractive tourist destination.

THE BIGGEST SCHOOL IN THE WORLD

Children who do not live in the cities of Australia and grow up on farms—often hundreds of miles from a town—attend the "school of the air." The children stay at home and receive instruction over the air by radio and, more recently, over the internet. This "air school" covers thousands of square miles of Australia.

almost as big as the whole of Europe, it has less than 3 percent of the population Europe has. About 80 percent of people live in cities along the coast—mostly the east and southeast coasts—and most of the area in the center of the country is desert. Australia is proud to be a multicultural nation. The first inhabitants, the Aborigines, now make up 1.5 percent of the population.

The outback
The area between the coasts and the desert of Australia is known as the outback. It is one of the hottest, driest areas in the world and is a very difficult to raise crops. Livestock, however, such as sheep and cattle, can survive and are kept on huge farms there.

If someone on an outback farm becomes sick or injured, the flying doctor arrives by plane.

FARMING BIG STYLE
Less than 5 percent of the population are farmers, yet over half of the land is used for grazing. A single sheep or cattle station is sometimes so big that it can take three or four days to travel across it.

1 Finding the herd
Because of the huge areas that the cattle and sheep are free to roam, farmers frequently use motorcycles or quadbikes to monitor their animals.

2 Rounding up
Beef cattle graze on dry grass and drink water drawn from wells. When they need to be herded back to the station, helicopters are used.

3 Closing in
Helicopters communicate with farmers in ground vehicles and between them help to drive the cattle into large enclosures.

The great reef dive

SWIMMING AROUND THE WORLD'S LARGEST LIVING STRUCTURE

SCUBA DIVING IS ONE OF THE MOST POPULAR SPORTS in Australia. Thousands of tourists flock there each year to see the world's largest living structure, the Great Barrier Reef, which stretches down just off the east coast and covers an area about the size of New Mexico. There are 2,600 separate reefs, 1,500 varieties of fish, and 350 types of coral amid the crystal-clear waters. During the Sydney Olympic Games in 2000, the torch featured the first-ever underwater leg of its journey through the Great Barrier Reef.

FOR 60,000 YEARS THE ABORIGINES OF AUSTRALIA have

ABORIGINES

THE ANCIENT PEOPLE OF AUSTRALIA

lived in every incredibly different region of this enormous country. While all native Australians are known as Aborigines, there are

Arnhem Land

One of the areas of Australia where traditional Aboriginal culture has remained intact is Arnhem Land, situated in the far north of the Northern Territories. The land is all Aboriginal owned and outsiders may only visit with permission. Here the people choose to live in accordance with their original culture.

FAMILY LIFE
The Aboriginal family unit is large and extended. The raising of children is not just the duty of the parents, but of the entire community. These family systems are central to the way each society is organized and the close family ties ensure that the traditional culture is kept alive. Elders are treated with great respect—they are the bridge between past and present.

CITY LIFE
Not all Aboriginal Australians live a traditional way of life. Many of them now live in major cities, such as Sydney, and lead more Westernized lives.

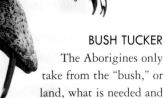

MODERN CONVENIENCES
Although the people of Arnhem Land choose to live very traditionally, they also make good use of the modern world. These men are using one recently installed telephone to check that neighbors will be coming to a ceremony.

BUSH TUCKER
The Aborigines only take from the "bush," or land, what is needed and always make sure that game and plants can regenerate. Children are taught to hunt when very young.

many different groups who, over thousands of years, have shared their ideas, practices, and experiences with each other. For this reason the groups share similarities. Due to their intimate knowledge and understanding of the harsh environment and their ability to accept change, they have survived to become some of the oldest living cultures in the world.

WEAVING

The women make mats, baskets, and other containers by weaving many materials together, such as pandanus, palm fronds, bark, grasses, and even human hair. The items are colored with natural dyes made from roots or bark and are sometimes decorated with feathers or pieces of cloth. The Aborigines are famous for their arts, and woven products as well as their paintings are sold throughout Australia.

THE NGANGIYAL

This tentlike basket is called a *ngangiyal*. It is a special tent made of woven pandanus and is used for what the Aborigines refer to as "private women's business." As these children show it's also fun to play with!

THE BOOMERANG

Boomerangs are curved wooden throwing sticks used as hunting weapons and as clapsticks during ceremonies. They are cleverly designed to return to you when thrown. They are made from many types of wood and are often decorated.

The two children on the left are accompanying the didgeridoo player with their clapsticks.

THE DIDGERIDOO

A musical instrument, the didgeridoo is a long, thin tree trunk, usually made from a eucalyptus tree that has been hollowed out by termites. The trunk is cut to 3 ft (1 m) or so in length and fitted with a waxy mouthpiece. When blown it makes low rumbling notes. It is very difficult to play, but experts can make it sound like the callings of certain birds and animals.

Dreamtime

The Aborigines believe that their knowledge, faith, and practices are linked to the stories of creation, which are known as *Dreamtime* or *Dreaming*. Ancestral spirits came to Earth and created the land, animals, and plants. They taught the people how to live with the Earth and to respect it. The Dreamtime stories are still told today and are central to Aboriginal culture.

STORYTELLING

The Dreamtime stories explain how people should behave, live, and respect the land. These stories are passed down from generation to generation and relate to a large part of everyday life. The elders take every opportunity to teach children about the way of life of their people and, through story and song, have kept alive their traditions and heritage over thousands of years.

ULURU

All over Australia there are many sacred sites and *Dreamtime tracks*, which are the paths taken by the spirits when they created the land. Uluru is a sacred rock for the Aboriginal peoples of the Central Desert. It is rich in mythology and the caves are filled with ancient rock art depicting Dreamtime stories. In 1985 the site was returned to the Aboriginal people and the caves can only be visited by initiated Aborigines.

MIMI

The Mimi are spirits believed to live in Northern Australia. They are always carved or painted as tall, thin beings. When the first people arrived in Australia it is said that the Mimi spirits taught them how to live off the land. They showed them how to hunt, cook, and respect the Earth that they live on. They also taught the people how to paint. The Mimi are believed to be mischievous, but harmless spirits.

Dreamtime today

When Australia was colonized, the Aboriginal way of living was misunderstood and the colonials made attempts to change the way the indigenous people lived. Today, the culture is accepted and many Aborigines are returning to their traditional ways.

AN ANCIENT ART
Modern painting and ancient rock art often depict the Dreamtime stories. The Rainbow Serpent is a spirit shared by many communities across Australia. It is the protector of land and people, and the source of life, but it can be destructive if it is not respected.

Uluru, or Ayers Rock as it used to be called, is the largest stone monolith on Earth.

WALKABOUT
To enter manhood a young Aborigine will take a journey alone to prove he can survive in the wilderness in the traditional Aboriginal way. It is often referred to as a "walkabout." These boys are demonstrating a traditional way of drinking that does not disturb the water.

INITIATION CEREMONY
In some Aboriginal communities in Australia, boys have to go through an initiation ceremony to enter manhood. They are taught songs and dances, they decorate their bodies, then perform rituals that can go on for weeks.

MIDDLE SEPIK

RIVER PEOPLE OF PAPUA NEW GUINEA

THE SEPIK IS A LONG RIVER THAT RUNS through mainland Papua New Guinea, from the highlands to the coast, and all along it live different clans. The people of the Middle Sepik live along the river, inland from the

LIVING ON STILTS

The houses along the Sepik river are mainly built on stilts. This is so that during the rainy season, when the water level rises, the houses are in no danger of flooding. The stilts also prevent too many mosquitoes and rats from infesting the houses.

The river

The Sepik River is roughly 700 miles (1,100 km) from source to mouth and is navigable for almost its entire length. It is vital to the local people who live on its banks—they use it for transportation, water, and food. Many of the legends in the area are connected to the river and it is regarded as a spirit itself.

COLLECTING FOOD

Men, women, and children all share the fishing jobs in the Middle Sepik area. They use long dugout canoes to catch large eels and crocodiles, and set traps in the water or use spears to catch fish. They make flour from sago palms in the swamps and keep chickens and pigs in the villages.

THE CROCODILE

The Sepik people honor the crocodile and there are many myths and legends surrounding it. The people have lots of spirits or gods and the crocodile is one such spirit of the river. When making canoes, the Sepik people often carve the head of a crocodile on the prow.

Two dugout canoes negotiate one of the many narrow waterways on the river.

coast, and their land stretches up to the beginning of the highlands. They share many cultural similarities from village to village, such as the elaborate initiation rites and the highly developed art and architectural styles. Secrecy is an important part of life; the older males get, the more they are allowed to learn. Older men often hold debates challenging each other's knowledge of the secret and magical names.

Male initiation

The process of males initiating boys into manhood is of enormous importance in Sepik societies and there are many rituals connected to it. The initiation has many levels where each boy is taught obligations and secret rituals, and learns about the mythical journeys of their ancestors. It is often years before a boy becomes a man.

HAUS TAMBARAN

Every village has a spiritual house called a *haus tambaran*. The building can have one or two stories and contains many intricate carvings. It is where the young boys learn rituals that will take them to manhood. Women are not allowed to enter.

INITIATION SCARRING

In some Sepik groups a young male must learn about pain—this involves scarring. This boy has had his skin cut deeply and made to resemble crocodile skin. Afterward the wounds are rubbed with a mixture of ashes, oil, and mud to ensure that the pattern is permanent.

Only certain powerful men may lower the *savi* masks from their storage in the *haus tambaran*.

SEPIK MASKS

The Middle Sepik people are famous for their art and carvings. Spirit houses are filled with masks depicting ancestors, mythical beings, and nature spirits. The masks each have complex meanings and many different spiritual purposes. Some masks, such as this one, have tongues sticking out as a sign of aggression toward enemies of the clan.

HULI

THE WIG PEOPLE OF THE HIGHLANDS

PAPUA NEW GUINEA IS THE EASTERN HALF of a large island in the Pacific Ocean with a number of islands surrounding it. The western half of the island is Irian Jaya—part of Indonesia. The inland central area rises

The Huli

The Huli people live in the central mountains of Papua New Guinea in rain forest that is so dense that no outsider knew they existed until the 1930s. Like many of the peoples on the island, ceremonies and festivals are a major part of life—they are not only important within the group, but also to form alliances with different clans. Self-decoration is a large part of the ceremonies.

In a nation where no written word exists, an important form of education is song and dance.

EVERYDAY LIFE

The Huli live in small scattered settlements, each with its own plot of land on which they grow food such as sweet potatoes and taro. Walls surround the area both to keep the livestock in and the evil spirits and enemies out. Men and women live in separate houses, the women traditionally living with the pigs, which are the Huli's most valued possession.

THE HULI WARRIOR

From the day a Huli boy is born he is taught how to be a warrior and to defend his family. Clans often have disagreements, mainly over land, women, or pigs, which can lead to fighting. Pigs are often exchanged to settle disputes and compensate for injury or death.

into a wide ridge of mountains known as the highlands, a territory that is so densely forested that the island's local peoples remained isolated from each other for thousands of years. As a result, incredibly,

there are as many as 800 different languages in Papua New Guinea. One of the many peoples that live in the Highlands are the extraordinary Huli, famous for their spectacular head adornments.

Huli wig school

One interesting feature about the Huli people is their elaborate wigs. As teenagers, the boys are taken from their homes to live in and attend wig school for several years. They learn to be efficient warriors and good community members but, most importantly, they grow and tend to their hair, which will one day be cut and made into spectacular wigs.

The students at wig school put cassowary wing feathers through their noses.

WIG CARE
It is essential to look after the growing hair in order to keep it in prime condition. Without magical rites, the instruction of a hair trainer, and constant grooming, men cannot grow their hair sufficiently to satisfy traditional wig requirements. They even sleep with their heads propped up to keep from flattening the shape.

THE FINISHED WIG
When the hair is considered long enough it is cut and, while still keeping the mushroom shape, it is decorated with bright feathers, daisies, and even possum fur.

SING-SING
The ceremonial wigs are worn during *sing-sings*—ceremonies that include initiation rites and weddings. Neighbors are sometimes invited to attend *sing-sings* and clans and families have a chance to show solidarity and exhibit wealth. They perform dances in their groups and feast on pigs.

These men are painting their faces—using car sideview mirrors to aid them! A small sign of modern influence.

PAPUA NEW GUINEA

A GATHERING   OF TRIBES

EACH YEAR OVER 50 DIFFERENT cultural groups from
all over Papua New Guinea gather together
in the West Highlands province for the
spectacular and flamboyant Mount Hagen
Cultural Show. It was originally started as a
way to calm tribal animosities and to celebrate
the enormous diversity of traditional ways. All the
groups dress up in their most colorful displays of
makeup and ornamentation to impress the other
clans. The whole show is such a visual extravaganza
that it has become a huge tourist attraction. Up to
50,000 people have been known to descend on the
area. The Asaro clan in this picture are famous for
their extraordinary mud masks and mud body paint.

TROBRIANDERS

THE TROBRIAND ISLANDS ARE A SPRINKLING of coral islands situated in Melanesia in the Pacific Ocean. Since 1975, the islands have been considered part of a larger area known as the Massim

THE PACIFIC ISLANDS OF PARADISE

THE KULA EXCHANGE

Kula is the inter-island, ceremonial trading network that involves the Trobriands and surrounding islands. It has been in action for over 500 years and is a means of trade. Each time a person arrives on an island to trade, they must offer either shell armbands or necklaces with elaborate ceremony. The *soulava*, shell necklaces, only ever travel in a clockwise direction around the islands and the armbands, *mwali*, only travel in a counterclockwise direction, and the same ones have been in circulation for hundreds of years.

FISHING

Outrigger canoes are used for fishing. The Trobrianders use nets, spears, and baited hooks to lure fish; they catch turtles using their hands. In deep water they dive down to incredible 30 ft (10 m) depths and cling on to coral with one hand while spearing with the other. Fish are caught as food for the village or for trade with other islands.

Ancient ways

When the Christian missionaries arrived in the early 20th century, they tried to quell many traditions on the islands, such as body decoration and the wearing of grass skirts. However, in time the islanders reverted to their old customs and, although most claim to be Christian, the religion doesn't impinge on traditional beliefs.

BANANA LEAF CURRENCY

There are many kinds of valuable items that are used as currencies in Papua New Guinea, including money made from shells. Trobrianders also have a kind of currency made from banana leaves.

District of the Nation of Papua New Guinea, although the people's culture and traditional ways are still valued. The islands are beautiful tropical paradises with bleached white sand, coconut palms, dugout canoes, thatched fishing huts, and little or no traffic. Many of the islands don't even have electricity. The islanders are best known for their extraordinary method of exchange and trade with each other, known as the *Kula*.

TROBRIAND CRICKET

Cricket was introduced to the Trobriand Islands by Christian missionaries to discourage ritual warfare. The Islanders took to it with enormous enthusiasm and added many of their own rules. They perform special dances for every point they gain and have adapted some of the rules.

YAM STORAGE

The yam is prized in the Trobriand Islands. It grows well in the thin soil and is a staple food. The islanders build elaborate and beautiful yam houses to store and show off their prized vegetables, which sometimes grow to over 3 ft (1m).

The yam houses stand in the centre of the village. More care goes into the building of these than of real houses.

THE YAM FESTIVAL

Yams are more than just a food, they represent wealth and are a symbol of life. During the annual yam festival, which lasts over a month, the yams are picked and stored and the islanders hold dance competitions and cricket matches. Beauty, body ornamentation, and magic are all a large part of the festival.

SING-SING

Dance festivals, or *sing-sings*, are an important part of Trobriand life. Often the men and women dance separately. The girls perform a seductive *cassava* dance, swaying their hips in short grass skirts and snaking their hands from side to side. The men, in contrast, stamp on the sand to the rhythmic sound of drums.

YAPESE

THE TRUE DESERT ISLANDS

SITUATED IN THE HEART OF MICRONESIA in the Pacific Ocean lie the 134 islands—most of them unpopulated—that make up the State of Yap. The islands are scattered over 600 miles (950 km) of ocean, but the

THE BUILDINGS

There are three different types of buildings on the Yap Islands—the family house, the men's house, and this one, the *pebay*, which is the community house. It is a place where people get together for dances and meetings, and it also acts as a schoolhouse.

YAP DAY

On the first of March each year the islanders celebrate Yap Day—a festival commemorating the rich culture and lifestyle of the islands. All the villages perform dances that tell stories, and contests are held to find the best sportsman and the provider of the finest local produce. The dances are prepared and practiced all year and are always performed in large groups.

Yap Island

The main town on Yap is Conolia, which is situated around a bay. Although it is the center of tourism and government, most Yapese people live in villages located outside the town, where they lead an uninfluenced lifestyle. The main occupations of the people on the island are farming and fishing.

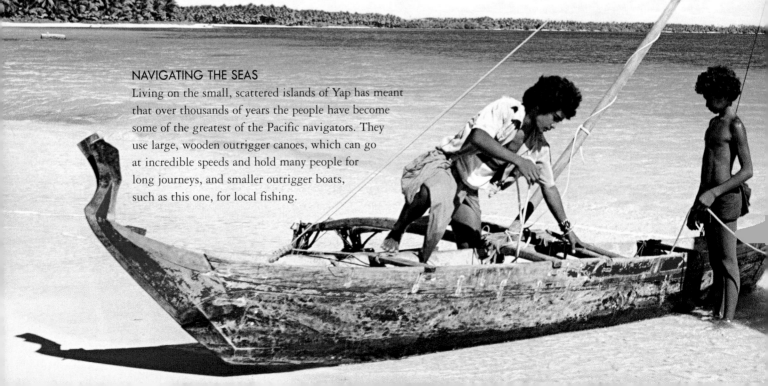

NAVIGATING THE SEAS

Living on the small, scattered islands of Yap has meant that over thousands of years the people have become some of the greatest of the Pacific navigators. They use large, wooden outrigger canoes, which can go at incredible speeds and hold many people for long journeys, and smaller outrigger boats, such as this one, for local fishing.

main four populated islands are clustered together. The temperature throughout the seasons on the islands tends to remain at approx 80°F (27°C) but in May, June, and November typhoons strike, causing huge storms. Over hundreds of years various people, such as traders and missionaries, have settled on these islands, but the Yapese have always clung with determination to their original customs and traditions.

The coins have holes in the center so they can be carried. Two people are needed to carry each coin.

STONE CURRENCY

Yap coins are the biggest in the world. They are round chunks of stone that range from 1 ft (0.3 m) to 12 ft (3.5 m) tall. But the stone does not come from the Yap Islands. It comes from volcanic islands 300 miles (550 km) away. Over hundreds of years, Yapese sailors have risked their lives to bring back the stones in outrigger canoes.

This man blows into a conch and sings to announce a successful catch.

STAR COMPASS

This simple diagram of stones and leaves is actually a star compass. The outer rim of stones represents constellations, showing when they rise and set on the horizon, and the leaves inside represent the swell of the waves and the canoe. Together they help the navigator find his way.

NI-VANUATU

THE REPUBLIC OF VANUATU IS MADE UP of 80 islands scattered over the Pacific Ocean in a "Y" shape. Most of the islands are volcanic in origin, while a few are coral islands. There are frequent earth tremors in the area

THE PEOPLE OF THE VOLCANO

Vanuatu Cultural Center

The people of Vanuatu are fiercely proud of their cultures and many value a traditional way of life. The Vanuatu Cultural Center was started in 1977 and has over 80 volunteers. They travel all over the islands collecting information about local cultures. They then write up literature about them to document and preserve them, and to promote the islands all over the world.

The preparation of kava for the men of the village.

KAVA

All over Vanuatu a favorite drink is kava. At dusk men start gathering and preparing the kava root. They chew it, then spit it into a bowl and add water. They always drink it fresh and, as it is a potent drug, it aids their sleep.

MOUNT YASUR

Tanna Island, part of Vanuatu, is a place where the culture and custom remain strong. The island is volcanic and explosions occur regularly on Mount Yasur. Most local people believe that the volcano is the house of spirits and rituals are held to honor it.

ISLAND MUSIC

The Ni-Vanuatu pride themselves on their musical instruments. This young boy, wearing a loincloth and decorative leaves, holds a long bamboo tube. While he sings, he thrusts the bamboo against a wooden board, creating rhythmic, musical sounds.

THE TOKA DANCE

The most famous dance on Tanna Island is the *toka* dance. The volcano ceremony starts with the women dancing all night, then at sunrise the men from many villages take over.

and the islands are home to nine active volcanoes. There are over 100 indigenous languages in Vanuatu, but most people speak or understand a form of pidgin, based on English. Vanuatu is home to a rich Melanesian culture full of tradition, magic, and ritual, and each tribal group on the islands has its own identity and customs.

The great Pentecost jump

Every April, when the first yam crop is ready for harvest, the inhabitants of Pentecost Island start to build a huge tower, which will end up 100 ft (30 m) high. After five weeks the tower is ready, and over the next few weeks boys and men jump from the top with only lianas vines attached to their feet. They believe that this will make the ground fertile.

LIFE OR DEATH
The men have to choose their own length of vine and, as they must aim for the vine to tighten as near to the ground as possible, the length is of vital importance. A vine just 4 in (10 cm) too long could mean serious injury or death.

1 The first jump
A boy jumps for the first time when he enters manhood, and from then on jumps regularly. His ankles are tied tightly with the vine and attached to the top of the tower.

2 Reach for the sky
The land diver always stretches his arms toward the sky before jumping. The divers believe that the higher the jumpers dive, the higher the crop will grow.

3 The jump
With the whole community watching, the diver then hurls himself off the top of the tower. It is quite common for people to die during the fall.

BUNGEE JUMPING

Modern-day bungee jumping was inspired by the ancient Pentecost jump. The only difference is that the modern jumpers use elastic, which is much safer!

SAMOANS

THE PEOPLE OF WESTERN SAMOA

THE ISLANDS OF SAMOA ARE A GROUP OF ACTIVE volcanic islands that lie in the Pacific Ocean between New Zealand and Hawaii. The only large town on the four inhabited islands is Apia, the capital.

Fa'a Samoa

The Samoan way of life, known as *fa'a Samoa,* is a moral code on how to live life. It teaches about the church, community, family, and, most importantly, respect. The *aiga*, extended family, is all important and each *aiga* is led by a *matai*—a person selected for life who runs the social, economic, and political affairs of the family.

FOOD ON SAMOA
The families all own garden plots, where they grow fruit and vegetables such as bananas and taro. They also keep chickens and pigs and marinate raw fish by a method known as *oka*.

THE HOME
Samoan homes, called *fale*, have wooden frames, thatched sugar-cane canopies, and coconut-leaf blinds that roll down the sides to shade against the sun or protect against wind and rain. They are completely open and everyone sleeps together on woven mats. Twenty or more people may all sleep in a *fale* at one time.

DANCING
One of the things the Samoans are best known for is their dancing, one area of culture that has changed little from contact with Western civilization. The dances are performed by individuals or groups either sitting or standing.

The rest of the settlements are some 400 coastal villages. In the 19th century the islands were split into two, Western and Eastern Samoa, and came under the ownership of Germany and the US. In 1962 Western Samoa became an independent nation once again. While Eastern, or American, Samoa has become industrial, Western Samoa, or Samoa, has retained a very traditional lifestyle.

SAMOAN TATTOOS

The Samoans are probably the most famous tattooists of the South Pacific with their striking patterns and designs. Not many Polynesian words have entered the English language, but one that has is *tattoo*.

1 Tattooing ceremony
Traditional tattoos are done using boar-tooth needles dipped in soot-based ink. Songs are often sung to the recipient to take their mind off the pain.

2 Soothing the tattoos
After the tattoo is finished, the tattooist rubs coconut oil into the designs. Traditional tattooing can take many weeks to complete, but these days they use methods that take a shorter time.

3 The designs
The male tattoos stretch from the knee up to the lower back and the stomach, resembling a pair of shorts. The female tattoos tend to be on the wrists or above the knee.

FISHING IN PAOPAO

Traditional fishing gear—fish hooks and octopus lures—are still used on Samoa, especially in villages. The skills are passed on through experience and practice and learned from generation to generation. The boats they use are *vaa'alo* (outriggers) and the smaller *paopao*.

RELIGION

The Samoans are devout Christians and have been ever since the Christian missionaries arrived in about 1830. Samoa's motto is "Samoa is founded on God". Churches tend to be the grandest buildings in the village and everyone wears white to the services.

TOURISM

The tourist industry is one of the most important income generators to the economy of Samoa, and the government puts heavy emphasis on it. The Samoans welcome tourists into their homes and allow them to become involved in ceremonies and the traditional way of life.

Samoan women wear traditional dresses made from woven matting or leaves.

NEW ZEALANDERS

NEW ZEALAND IS MADE UP OF TWO MAIN ISLANDS, North Island and South Island, and a scattering of smaller isles situated in the Pacific Ocean to the southeast

A LAND OF SHEEP AND SPORT

A CLEAN LAND
New Zealand has some of the most beautiful landscapes in the world, and some of the cleanest. The people do not support nuclear power. Instead they use hydroelectric power and have few industries.

CITY LIFE
Only 15 percent of the population of New Zealand live in the countryside—the rest live in towns and cities. The capital, Wellington (right), is situated on the south of the North Island. Auckland, however, is the largest city and is home to almost a third of the total population.

A LOVE OF SPORT
With over half the population belonging to sports clubs, New Zealanders are close to obsessed with playing or simply spectating—whether it is rugby union, cricket, or yacht racing. The country is also well-known for its extreme sports including bungee jumping, rafting, mountaineering, and skiing.

of Australia. It is sparsely populated with only 3.8 million people, the majority being of British descent. The indigenous Maori people make up about 14 percent of the population. The beautiful scenery in New Zealand, which ranges from towering mountains with volcanic geysers and glaciers to long beaches and lush green fields, has in recent years attracted filmmakers from all over the world who use it as a spectacular photographic location.

THE GREAT OUTDOORS

New Zealand is home to glacial mountains, huge forests, and long beaches, and is a haven for outdoor pursuits. *Tramping,* or hiking, is a very popular pastime, with many people rushing into the great outdoors on weekends.

Industry

New Zealand is an agricultural country, and its farm products are sold widely abroad. Over half the land is used as sheep pasture, with lamb and wool being major exports. Other exports include dairy products, fish, fruit, and lumber to be made into paper.

SHEEP SHEARING

There are approximately 3.8 million people living in New Zealand and an estimated 45 million sheep—that means a lot of shearing. Each year major sheep-shearing championships are held where people gather from all over the country to witness this fast and highly competitive sport— an experienced shearer can shear one sheep in just a few minutes.

KIWI FRUIT

The kiwi fruit originated in China, but was brought over to New Zealand in the 20th century and grown in domestic gardens as the Chinese gooseberry. When New Zealand began exporting it, it was given the name kiwi fruit.

Saving lives on the beaches

THE LIFEGUARDS OF NEW ZEALAND'S COASTLINE

NEW ZEALAND IS A MECCA FOR THRILL SEEKERS from all over the world, particularly those looking for thrills on or in the water. Everything from jet-skiing, white-water rafting, kayaking, and diving, to, in particular, surfing and windsurfing are experienced in all weathers nearly all year round. With so much activity on the water *Surf Life Saving New Zealand*, established in 1934, is an essential organization on the beaches. In their time the lifesavers have saved over 41,000 lives. Competitions between lifesavers are held annually, and lifeguards in this picture race across a beach in the North Island during the *Ironman Surf League* finals. The competition includes rescue events and surfboard races.

MAORI

THE MAORI WERE THE FIRST SETTLERS IN NEW ZEALAND,

A CULTURAL REVIVAL

arriving from Polynesia about 1,000 years ago. They occupied almost every area of New Zealand, and there were over 6,000 Maori villages long before European settlers first

CULTURE

The Maori culture is a heritage passed down through the generations. The people have documented their history and expressed their feelings through art for hundreds of years. The traditional Maori greeting is a nose-to-nose touch called the *hongi*.

Haka

The word *haka* means "Maori dance" and was traditionally performed at the onset of war to unite the people in anger and courage. It is a disciplined dance ritual where the hands, feet, legs, body, voice, and tongue all play their part, blending together to issue a challenge. There are several types of *haka*, but *Ka Mate* is the most popular.

This is the traditional Maori *Haka*. The New Zealand *All Blacks* rugby team has adopted the moves, which they perform before matches.

HANGI

The traditional, ancient Maori way of cooking is called *hangi*—cooking a meal underground using heated stones. The *hangi* is still popular with a lot of Maori people today.

1 Digging the pit
A large pit is dug into the ground and stones are laid at the bottom. The stones are heated and covered in cabbage leaves or watercress to stop the food from burning.

2 Into the steam
Mutton, pork, chicken, potatoes, and sweet potatoes are lowered into the pit in a wire basket. The food is covered with wet sheets and earth to keep in the steam.

3 Ready to eat
Surprisingly, the food takes about three hours to cook. When it appears it has a soft texture as if steamed, and an earthy, slightly smoked flavor.

TA MOKO

The ancient practice of Maori tattooing is called *ta moko*. The use of full facial tattoos has recently become an art form again in Maori culture, many men now tattooing their faces as well as their bodies.

arrived. The original homeland was called Hawaiiki but the European explorers renamed it New Zealand. The Maori still have a very strong culture of their own, even though many of them now live a Western lifestyle. Their numbers are now rising after a long period of decline and there are currently over 500,000 Maori, about 16 percent of the population. The Maori language is also in increasing use.

The *Marae* is often named after an ancestor. The ridgepole that holds the roof symbolizes the spine, with the rafters as ribs. Each rafter has an ancestral lineage carved into it.

THE SPIRITUAL MARAE

The center of every Maori community is the *Marae*—a meeting house with a surrounding courtyard, which may include a church. It is used as a political and ceremonial place where important decisions are made and rituals held. Within the *Marae* the Maori language, *Maoritanga*, is spoken. Even urban communities have a *Marae*.

POI DANCE

The Maori *poi* dance is generally performed by women. A *poi,* which means "ball," is attached at each end of a piece of flaxen string. The *pois* are then twirled and whirled rhythmically. The design is based on an ancient weapon and the length of them can vary from 1 ft to 3 ft (0.3 m to 1 m). They are swung around the body in various patterns that suggest forces of nature such as birds in flight, waterfalls, or summer rain. The whole effect can be very hypnotic.

The dancers wear flax skirts and traditionally woven bodices or *pari*.

A traditional greenstone, or jade, pendant.

Index

Acknowledgments

DORLING KINDERSLEY WOULD LIKE TO THANK:

Jacqueline Gooden, Sadie Thomas, and Abbie Collinson for design assistance, Margaret Parrish for editorial assistance, Lynn Bresler for compiling the index, Karen Shooter for the jacket design, and Philip Denis and Ingrid Pfrang for research assistance.

Picture Credits

1 Corbis: Robert Essel NYC. 2 Bryan And Cherry Alexander Photography: tr. 2-3c Justin Barton 2 Corbis: Patrick Ward br. 2 Getty Images: Carlos Navajas cra. 3 Alejandro Balaguer: b. 3 Corbis: Alan Schein Photography cla. 3 Getty Images: Christopher Arneson t. 6-7 Corbis: Alan Schein Photography 8-9 NASA: C. Mayhew & R. Simmon 10 Corbis: Keren Su bl, b; Martin Rogers tl. 10 Panos Pictures: Penny Tweedie tr. 11 Corbis: Bob Krist tr; Kraft Brooks/Sygma br; Richard Cummins bl. 12 Corbis: David Batterbury; Eye Ubiquitous tr; J.B.Russell/Sygma tl. 12 Still Pictures: John Maier b. 13 Corbis: Christine Osbourne bl; David Turnley br; Michael Cole tl; Roger Ressmeyer tr. 14 Bryan And Cherry Alexander Photography: tr. 14 Corbis: Benjamin Rondel tl; Bob Krist bl; Charles O'Rear crb; Dave G Houser bc; David Samuel Robbins tc; David Stoecklein cra; Dewitt Jones br; Kevin Fleming cla; Ted Spiegel clb; William Manning c. 15 Corbis: Bettmann cla; Jeff Curtes bl; W. Wayne Lockwood, M.D. tl; Warren Morgan clb. 16 Corbis:Alan Schein Photography tl; Royalty Free bl. 17 Corbis: Alan Schein Photography br; Bob Krist cl; Danny Lehman bl; Douglas Peebles cr; Michael Keller tl. 17 Magnum: Patrick Zachmann tr. 18 Corbis: Alan Schein Photography b. 18 South American Pictures: Tony Morrison tr. 19 Bryan And Cherry Alexander Photography: tl. 19 Corbis: Catherine Karnow br; Peter Turnley bl; Rose Hartman tr. 20 Corbis: Bill Ross l; Chuck Savage tr; Joseph Sohm; ChromoSohm Inc. br; Philip Gould cr. 21 Corbis: Bob Krist bl; Richard Cummins tr; Rose Hartman tr; Ted Spiegel cl. 22-23 Corbis: Adam Woolfitt 24 Alamy Images: Chuck Pefley tl. 24 Corbis: Bob Krist tr; Farrell Grehan bl, br. 25 Corbis: Joseph Sohm; ChromoSohm Inc. tr; Judy Griesedieck tl; Kevin Fleming cr; Owaki - Kulla clb, bl, br. 26 Corbis: Nik Wheeler cr; Patrick Ward tc; Philip Gould b. 26 Pa Photos: EPA cl. 27 Corbis: Buddy Mays c; Nik Wheeler bl; Owen Franken tr; William Boyce br. 28 Corbis: Kelly-Mooney Photography bl; Kevin R. Morris br; Owaki - Kulla tl; Philip Gould 29c. 29 Corbis: Kelly-Mooney Photography tr; Kevin Fleming bc; Philip Gould r. 30 Corbis: Galen Rowell tr; James Marshall cl; Rick Doyle r. 30 DK Picture Library: b, b, 30 Pa Photos: tl. 31 Corbis: Gunter Marx Photography tr; Kevin R. Morris bl; Richard A. Cooke cl; Roger Ressmeyer tl; Tom Bean br. 32-33 Getty Images: David W. Hamilton 34 Corbis: Craig Aurness 35c; Joseph Sohm; ChromoSohm Inc. b; Richard Hamilton Smith tc; Robert Holmes cl. 35 Corbis: Craig Aurness tr, bc; James A. Sugar tc, bl; Macduff Everton br; Richard Hamilton Smith c. 36-37 Bryan And Cherry Alexander Photography: 38 Alamy Images: Andre Jenny bl; Ethel Davies tl. 38 Corbis: Layne Kennedy tr. 38-39 Lonely Planet Images: Bill Bachmann c. 38 Rex Features: Jim Argo clb. 39 Corbis: David Turnley tr, cr; Joe McDonald br. 40 Corbis: Buddy Mays bc; Danny Lehman cr; Kevin Fleming bl; Ric Ergenbright br. 40 Rex Features: John Freeman tl. 41 Corbis: Peter Turnley br; Raymond Gehman bc; Richard A. Cooke c. 41 Katz/FSP: Jeff Jacobson tr. 41 Magnum: Hiroji Kubota tl. 42 Corbis: Bob Krist tr. 42 Getty Images: Cosmo Condina b. 42 South American Pictures: tr. 43 Eye Ubiquitous: James Davis tr. 43 Hutchison Library: Isabella Tree br. 43 Impact Photos: Material World cr. 43 South American Pictures: tl, cl; Tony Morrison bl. 44 Corbis: Paul A. Souders cl; Richard Cummins bl; Wally McNamee tr. 44 Hutchison Library: Robert Francis br. 45 Corbis: Dewitt Jones tl; Paul A. Souders bl; Richard Hamilton Smith bc; Richard T. Nowitz tr. 45 DK Picture Library: tr. 46-7 Getty Images: Chris Speedie 48 Corbis: Michael S. Yamashita br; Ted Spiegel bl. 48 Lonely Planet Images: Mark Lightbody tr. 49 Rolf Bettner: tc, cra, c, r. 49 Corbis: Dewitt Jones cl, b. 49 Toronto Star: tl. 50 Bryan And Cherry Alexander Photography: tl, tr, cra, c, br. 51 Bryan And Cherry Alexander Photography: tl, tr, b. 52 Bryan And Cherry Alexander Photography: cr, bl, bl. 52 Lonely Planet Images: Graeme

Cornwallis tc. 53 Bryan And Cherry Alexander Photography: bl, bc, r, t; ale c. 54 Corbis: Danny Lehman tr; David Cumming; Eye Ubiquitous; Jose Fuste Raga b. 55 Corbis: Bob Krist cba; Dave G. Houser br; Jeremy Horner bl; Tony Arruza c. 55 Getty Images: Guido Alberto Rossi t. 56 Corbis: Bob Krist tr; Owen Franken bl. 56 Panos Pictures: Jean-Leo Dugast tl; Marc French c. 57 Corbis: Macduff Everton r; Tony Arruza tr. 57 Robert Harding Picture Library: Fred Friberg bl; Sylvain Grandadam tl. 58-59 Corbis: Richard Bickel 60 Corbis: Bill Gentile bl; Jay Dickman tr, br; Kevin Schafer c. 61 Corbis: Bill Gentile tr; Kevin Schafer br. 61 Philip Dennis: tl, cla, cl, bl, bc. 62 Corbis: Buddy Mays tr; Charles & Josette Lenars bl; Danny Lehman br; David Samuel Robbins r. 63 Corbis: Bettmann c; Richard A. Cooke cl; Wolfgang Kaehler cl, r. 63 Lonely Planet Images: Alfredo Maiquez tl. 64 Corbis: Charles & Josette Lenars bl; Macduff Everton br; Roman Soumar 65c. 64 Magnum: Thomas Hoepker tc. 65 Corbis: Charles & Josette Lenars bl; Dave G. Houser tr. 65 Magnum: Burt Glinn bc; Thomas Hoepker c. 66 Corbis: Charles & Josette Lenars tl; Danny Lehman cla; Hank Whitemore/Sygma cla; Jan Butchofsky-Houser crb; Pablo Corral V tr, br. 66 DK Picture Library: Barnabas Kindersley cra. 66 Popperfoto: Bob Thomas ca. 66 South American Pictures: clb, bl. 66 Still Pictures: Nigel Dickinson cb. 67 Alejandro Balaguer: b. 67 Corbis: Ted Mahieu clb. 67 DK Picture Library: Barnabas Kindersley cra. 67 Hutchison Library: Felicity Nock crb. 67 Still Pictures: John Maier t. 68 Corbis: Galen Rowell br; Pablo Corral V l. 69 Corbis: Carl & Ann Purcell cr; Daniel Lainé tr; Galen Rowell br; Pablo Corral V tl, cl. 70 Corbis: Woolfitt bl; Alison Wright br; Tiziana and Gianni Baldizzone tl. 70 South American Pictures: tr. 70 Still Pictures: Mark Edwards cb. 71 Alejandro Balaguer: cr. 71 Corbis: Charles O'Rear tl; Stephanie Maze cra. 71 Getty Images: Andrea Booher tr; Angelo Cavalli b. 71 Robert Harding Picture Library: Victor Englebert crb. 72 Hutchison Library: Brian Moser tl; Felicity Nock tr, br; Titus Moser bl. 73 Hutchison Library: Brian Moser tl; Felicity Nock bl; Moser/Taylor r. 73 South American Pictures: Britt Dyer c. 74 Corbis: Jeremy Horner br. 74 Robert Harding Picture Library: Victor Englebert tr, l. 75 Andes Press Agency: Roberto Falck tl. 75 Alejandro Balaguer: bl. 75 Panos Pictures: tr. 75 Still Pictures: Dario Novellino br. 76-77 Corbis: Jack Fields 78 Sue Cunningham Photographic: c, cr, bl. 78 South American Pictures: Index Editora br. 78 Still Pictures: Nigel Dickinson tc. 79 Corbis: Sygma. 79 Still Pictures: Mark Edwards bc, r. 80 Sue Cunningham Photographic: 81. 82 Getty Images: Ary Diesendruck. 82 South American Pictures: tc. 82 Still Pictures: Julio Etchart bl. 83 Corbis: Jim Zuckerman br; Ricardo Azoury tl, cla; Robert Holmes cl. 83 Still Pictures: tr; Chris Martin bl. 84 Corbis: Jeremy Horner tc, tr; Owen Franken br. 84 Getty Images: Peter Adams bl. 85 Corbis: Barnabas Bosshart br; Daniel Lainé tr. 85 Sue Cunningham Photographic: cl. 85 Getty Images: David W. Hamilton bl. 86 Aspect Picture Library: Peter Carmichael br, t. 86 Corbis: Jeremy Horner cr; Kevin Schafer tl, c; Wolfgang Kaehler bl, br. 86 Hutchison Library: Eric Lawrie tr. 87 Aspect Picture Library: Peter Carmichael tl, tr, cl, br. 87 Corbis: Julie Houck tl; Wolfgang Kaehler tr. 87 Hutchison Library: Eric Lawrie br. 88 Andes Press Agency: Carlos Reyes-Manzo r. 88 Alejandro Balaguer: l. 89

Andes Press Agency: bl. 89 Alejandro Balaguer: tr. 89 Exile Images: br. 89 South American Pictures: Kathy Jarvis tl. 90 Getty Images: Geoffrey Clifford tl. 90 South American Pictures: Frank Nowikowski; Kathy Jarvis bl. 90 Zefa: Abril tr. 91 Corbis: b; Owen Franken tr. 91 South American Pictures: Tony Morrison tl. 92-3 Impact Photos: Christophe Bluntzer 94 Jacek Piwowarczyk: br. 94 Neil Gardner: tr. 94 Still Pictures: Edward Parker bl. 95 Alejandro Balaguer: tl, r. 95 Corbis: James Sparshatt bl. 96 Panos Pictures: Helen Hughes tl. 96 Rehue Foundation: c, br. 96 Rex Features: Rob Crandell l. 97 Exile Images: J Etchart br. 97 Panos Pictures: Helen Hughes tl. 97 Rehue Foundation: tr, c. 98 Aspect Picture Library: Horst Gossler br. 98 Corbis: Caroline Penn clb; Kraft Brooks/Sygma crb; Liba Taylor tr; Lindsay Hebberd cla; Owen Franken tl; Paul W. Liebhardt c; Sandro Vannini bc. 98 Impact Photos: Alain Evrard bl. 99 Corbis: Bob Krist tl; Charles O'Rear br; Earl & Nazima Kowall cla; Giraud Philippe cr; Roger De La Harpe; Gallo Images clb. 100 Corbis: Photowood Inc. 101. 100 Still Pictures: Hartmut Schwarzbach b. 101 Corbis: David Turnley tl; Jon Hicks tr; Julia Waterlow; Eye Ubiquitous cl; Lawrence Manning cr. 102 Corbis: Buddy Mays t; Jacques Langevin/Sygma bl; Wendy Stone r. 103 Bryan And Cherry Alexander Photography: tl. 103 Corbis: Charles & Josette Lenars cra; Kevin Fleming tr; Peter Turnley cr. 103 Still Pictures: Hartmut Schwarzbach b. 104 Aspect Picture Library: Peter Carmichael cl, b. 105 Aspect Picture Library: br; Peter Carmichael tl, tr, cr. 106-7 Corbis: Paul Hardy 108 Associated Press AP: bl. 108 Still Pictures: Bojan Brecel l. 109 Alamy Images: Christine Osbourne tr. 109 Corbis: Christine Osborne br; Owen Franken. 109 Getty Images: Guido Alberto Rossi bl. 109 Still Pictures: Chris Caldicott tl. 110-1 Hutchison Library: David Brimcombe 112 Africancraft.com: tl, cl, bl. 112 Robert Harding Picture Library: Jenny Pate br. 112 Hutchison Library: Nick Haslam bc. 112 Panos Pictures: tr. 113 Aspect Picture Library: Larry Burrows b. 113 Hutchison Library: Juliet Highet tl. 113 Popperfoto: Mike Hutchings/Reuters tr. 114 Bryan And Cherry Alexander Photography: tr, cl. 114 Hutchison Library: Sarah Errington c 115 Bryan And Cherry Alexander Photography: tr. 115 Hutchison Library: Mary Jelliffe l. 116 Robert Estall Photo Library: Carol Beckwith & Angela Fisher 118 Shehzad Noorani: 119 Shehzad Noorani: tl, tr, cl, clb, bl, br. 120-1 Dena Freeman: 122 Nicolas Lewis: tl, tr, bl, br. 123 Nicolas Lewis: tl, tr, cr, cr, bl, br. 124-5 Images Of Africa Photobank: David Keith Jones 124 Still Pictures: Muriel Nicolotti bl. 124 Getty Images: Joseph Van Os cl. 125 Corbis: Jim Zuckerman cr. 125 Still Pictures: Adrian Arbib br; Muriel Nicolotti tl. 126-7 Still Pictures: Adrian Arbib 128 Corbis: Roger De La Harpe; Gallo Images br. 128 Still Pictures: Roger de la Harpe t. 129 Eye Ubiquitous: Tovy Amsel bl. 129 Impact Photos: Caroline Penn tr; Gold Collection br. 129 Still Pictures: Roger de la Harpe tl. 130-131 Africa Imagery: b. 130 Corbis: Louise Gubb/SABA t. 130 Images Of Africa Photobank: Ivor Migdoll bl. 131 Africa Imagery: tl, tr. 131 Images Of Africa Photobank: Jeremy Van Riemsdyke br. 132 Corbis: Anthony Bannister; Gallo Images br. 132 N.H.P.A.: Anthony Bannister tl, c. 132 Panos Pictures: David Reed bl. 133 N.H.P.A.: Anthony Bannister tl, tr, cr, clb, b.

Picture Credits continued.

134 **Aspect Picture Library:** Horst Gossler bl, br. 134 **Giacoma Pirozzo:** t. 135 **Hutchison Library:** Christina Dodwell tr, cra. 135 **N.H.P.A.:** Daniel Heuclin br. 135 **Panos Pictures:** Jean-Leo Dugast crb, l. 136-7 N.H.P.A.: Martin Harvey 138 **Corbis:** Brian A. Vikander cla; Jan Butchofsky-Houser ca; Royalty Free crb. 138 cra **Getty Images:** Jorn Georg Tomter 138 bl **Corbis:** Christine Osbourne/138 **DK Picture Library:** Peter Wilson clb, cb, br. 138 **Eye Ubiquitous:** James Davis tl. 138 **Popperfoto:** Desmond Boylan/Reuters tr. 139 **Corbis:** SETBOUN bl. 139 **DK Picture Library:** tl, cl. 140 **DK Picture Library:** l. 140 **Getty Images:** Steve Satushek br. 141 **Corbis:** David Turnley tr; Georgina Bowater cr; Hubert Stadler tl; Owen Franken cl; Ron Watts br. 142 **Corbis:** Matthias Kulka bc; Peter Turnley t; Ray Juno bl. 142 **Panos Pictures:** J. C. Tordai br. 143 **Alamy Images:** Chad Ehlers cl. 143 **Corbis:** Palmer/Kane, Inc. br; Patrick Ward clb; Peter Turnley tr; TempSport bl. 143 **Rex Features:** Action Press tl. 144-145 **Corbis:** Catherine Karnow b. 144 **Getty Images:** Harald Sund tr. 144 **Hutchison Library:** Robert Francis tl. 144 **Artic Images:** bl. 145 **Corbis:** Catherine Karnow bl; Dave G. Houser tl. 145 **Eye Ubiquitous:** Judith Platt tr. 146 **Corbis:** Adam Woolfitt bl; Anthony Nex tl; Dallas and John Heaton c. 146 **Scotland in Focus:** Willbir r. 147 **Corbis:** Bo Zaunders br; Farrell Grehan bc; Hubert Stadler tl. 147 **Scotland in Focus:** MacSween Haggis tr. 148 **Corbis:** Chris North; Cordaiy Photo Library Ltd. bc; David Cumming; Eye Ubiquitous tr; Michael S. Yamashita c; Robert Estall bl. 148 **Foodpix:** tr. 149 **Corbis:** Adam Woolfitt tl; Michael Nicholson br. 150-1 **Charles Tait Photographic:** 152 **Corbis:** Chris Lisle bl; Galen Rowell tl; Hubert Stadler tr. 152 **DK Picture Library:** Barnabas Kindersley br. 153 **Corbis:** Stephanie Maze tl. 153 **Lonely Planet Images:** Anders Blomqvist b; Martin Moos cl. 153 **David McCreery:** /davidm.net tr. 154 **Bryan And Cherry Alexander Photography:** bl, bc, br. 155 **Bryan And Cherry Alexander Photography:** tr, cr, br, l. 156 **Corbis:** Charles & Josette Lenars br; Michael S. Yamashita cr. 156 **Getty Images:** Monica Dalmasso bl. 156 **Rex Features:** Kainulainen; Lehtikuva Oy/ Ritola tr. 157 **Corbis:** Layne Kennedy tr; Stephanie Maze cr, crb. 157 **Lehtikuva Oy:** Matti Kolho tl; Pekka Sakki br. 158-9 **Corbis:** John Garrett 160 **Corbis:** James A. Sugar bl; Owen Franken br. 160 **Lonely Planet Images:** Guy Moberly t. 161 **Corbis:** Dave G. Houser cl; Galen Rowell bl; Jose Fuste Raga tr. 161 **Lonely Planet Images:** Guy Moberly br. 161 **Zefa:** J. A. Raga tl. 162-3 **Corbis:** Hans Georg Roth 164 **Alamy Images:** Photolocate cr. 164 **Corbis:** Stephanie Maze tl. 164 **Getty Images:** Bruno De Hogues r; Ian Shaw bl. 165 **Corbis:** Peter Turnley tl; Richard Bickel bl. 165 **Rex Features:** Action Press cl. 166 **Corbis:** Craig Aurness l; Owen Franken tr, br. 167 **Alamy Images:** Robert Harding World Imagery tr. 167 **Corbis:** Owen Franken tl. 167 **Getty Images:** Jean-Pierre Pieuchot b. 168 **Bryan And Cherry Alexander Photography:** tl. 168 **Corbis:** Uwe Walz tl. 168 **Lonely Planet Images:** David Peevers br. 168-9 **Rex Features:** Action Press 168 **Still Pictures:** Andreas Riedmiller bl. 169 **Corbis:** Bob Krist br; Dave G. Houser tr. 169 **Getty Images:** Michael Rosenfeld bl. 170 **Corbis:** Gideon Mendel br; Richard Klune bl. 170 **Still Pictures:** Andreas Riedmiller tr. 171 **Corbis:** Gunter Marx Photography tl; Jose Fuste Raga tr. 171 **Still Pictures:** Andreas Riedmiller cl, cr, b. 172-3 **Sean Gallup:** 174 **Getty Images:** Frans Lemmens tl. 174 **Christof Sonderegger, Fotograf:** bl, br. 175 **Bryan And Cherry Alexander Photography:** bl. 175 **Eye Ubiquitous:** James Davis tl. 175 **Getty Images:** Hans Wolf cr. 176 **Christof Sonderegger, Fotograf:** tl, cr, 177b. 177 **Eye Ubiquitous:** tl. 177 **Robert Harding Picture Library:** cr. 177 **Magnum:** Fred Mayer cl. 178 **Bryan And Cherry Alexander Photography:** tr. 178 **Associated Press AP:** Dmitry Lovetsky br. 178 **DK Picture Library:** cl. 178-9 **Impact Photos:** Andy Johnstone 178 **Magnum:** Martin Parr bl. 179 **Bryan And Cherry Alexander Photography:** cl. 179 **Associated Press AP:** Mikhail Metzel tl. 179 **Eye Ubiquitous:** James Davis bl. 179 **Robert Harding Picture Library:** Ellen Rooney r. 180 **Popperfoto:** Sergei Venyavsky/Reuters 181 br. 180 **Art Directors & TRIP:** N. Chesnokov tr. 181 **Associated Press AP:** Maxim Marmur tr. 181 **Popperfoto:** Vladimir Suvorov/Reuters tl. 181 **Art Directors & TRIP:** N. Chesnokov c. 182 **Corbis:** Bernard Bisson/SYGMA tr; David Turnley bl; James Marshall br. 183 **Corbis:** Raymond Gehman t; Setboun br. 183 **Lonely Planet Images:** Krzysztof Dydynski bl. 184 **Network Photographers Ltd.:** Laurie Sparham bl. 184 **Panos Pictures:** Peter Barker tl. 184 **Art Directors & TRIP:** J. Bartos br. 185 **Popperfoto:** Dimitar Dilkoff/Reuters br; Petr Josek/Reuters l. 185 **Art Directors & TRIP:** M. Maclaren tr. 186 **Corbis:** Gary Trotter; Eye Ubiquitous tr; Richard Bickel b. 186 br. **Corbis:** Richard Bickel 186 **James Kyllo:** cr. 186 Rod Shone: tl. 187 **Corbis:** Richard Bickel b. 187 **Rod Shone:** tl, tr. 188 **Corbis:** Bettmann tc; David Hanover bl; Enzo & Paolo Ragazzini c; Pasquero Luca/Sygma br; Vittoriano Rastelli bc. 189 **Corbis:** David Lees tl; Geray Sweeney bl; Owen Franken r; Vittoriano Rastelli c. 190 **Corbis:** Jeffrey L. Rotman tr. 190 **Getty Images:** Francesco Ruggeri br. 190 **Magnum:** Ferdinando Scianna l. 191 **Corbis:** Jonathan Blair cl; Vittoriano Rastelli bl, bc. 191 **Lonely Planet Images:** Ionas Kaltenbach tl. 191 **Rex Features:** Camilla Morandi bl. 192 **Corbis:** Sheldan Collins bl. 192-3 **Eye Ubiquitous:** James Davis 192 **Impact Photos:** Jeremy Nicholl tr. 192 **Rex Features:** Patrick Frilet tl. 193 **Getty Images:** Bernard Grilly tr. 193 **Impact Photos:** David Slimings bcr. 193 **Art Directors & TRIP:** M. Nichols cr. 194 **Alamy Images:** D Lomax/Robert Harding World Imagery br; John Henry Claude Wilson tl. 194 **Bryan And Cherry Alexander Photography:** bc. 194 **Bruce Coleman Ltd:** c. 194 **Corbis:** Baldev/Sygma cr; Bettmann tr; Keren Su ca; Lindsay Hebberd cla; Tiziana and Gianni Baldizzone bl. 194 **Popperfoto:** AFP photo/Yoshikazu Tsuno cl. 195 **Corbis:** Catherine Karnow cl; Dean Conger tl; John Hicks cl. 195 **Panos Pictures:** John Miles bc. 196 **Corbis:** Keren Su bl, b. 197 **Corbis:** Jed & Kaoru Share tl; Jose Fuste Raga cr; Michael Freeman cl; Steve Raymer tr. 198 **Corbis:** Arthur Thévenart br; Caroline Penn tr; Helen King bl. 198 Pa Photos: EPA tl. 199 **Corbis:** Chris Lisle br; David H. Wells c; Lindsay Hebberd bl; Richard Powers t. 199 **Lonely Planet Images:** Peter Davis clb. 200 **Corbis:** Annie Griffiths Belt tl, tr; Hanan Isachar bl, br. 201 **Associated Press AP:** Nati Harnik tr. 201 **Corbis:** Hanan Isachar tl. 201 **Rex Features:** ASAP b. 202 **Corbis:** Charles & Josette Lenars bl. 202 **Magnum:** Ian Berry c, br. 202 **Art Directors & TRIP:** V Kolpakov tr. 203 **Armenia Week:** cr, br. 203 **Corbis:** David Turnley cl; Jon Spaull tl. 203 **Jon Spaull:** tr. 204-5 **Corbis:** Nik Wheeler 206 **Associated Press AP:** Hasan Sarbakhshian cr; Vahid Salemi tr; Xinhua News Agency, Ainiwar l. 206 **DK Picture Library:** br. 207 **Alamy Images:** Christine Osborne/World Religions b. 207 **Associated Press AP:** tr; Enric Marti c; Hasan Sarbakhshian tl. 208 **Associated Press AP:** Ruth Fremson tc. 208 **Getty Images:** Nevada Wier cl, bl. 209 **Alamy Images:** D Lomax/Robert Harding World Imagery t. 209 **Getty Images:** Frans Lemmens bl. 209 **Jon Spaull:** br. 210 **Hutchison Library:** Sarah Errington tr. 210 **Panos Pictures:** Alain le Garsmeur b. 211 **Corbis:** Keren Su tr; Nevada Wier bl. 211 **Hutchison Library:** Sarah Errington cl, br; Trevor Page tl. 212 **Bryan And Cherry Alexander Photography:** tr, cl, bl, br. 213 **Bryan And Cherry Alexander Photography:** tl, tr, c, br. 214-5 **Bryan And Cherry Alexander Photography:** 216 **Corbis:** Alison Wright tr; Christine Kolisch br; Tiziana and Gianni Baldizzone cr. 216 **Still Pictures:** Hartmut Schwarzbach bl. 217 **Corbis:** Galen Rowell tl; John Noble b; Kurt Stier tr. 218 **Robert Harding Picture Library:** Christopher Rennie bl, c; James Strachan cl, bc. 219 **Robert Harding Picture Library:** David Beatty tr, br; Maurice Joseph tc. 219 **Panos Pictures:** Dermot Tatlow bc. 220 **Corbis:** Bennett Dean/Eye Ubiquitous bc. 220 **Robert Harding Picture Library:** F Jackson c. 220 **Saif Saifuddin:** tr. 221 **Corbis:** Earl & Nazima Kowall tr; Ric Ergenbright bc. 221 **Robert Harding Picture Library:** F. Jackson tl, bl. 221 **Lonely Planet Images:** Richard L'Anson br. 222 **Corbis:** Baldev/Sygma tr; Brian A. Vikander tl, bl; Martin Jones; Ecoscene br. 223 **Corbis:** Brian A. Vikander cl. 223 **Lonely Planet Images:** Sara-Jane Cleland tl; Stephen Saks r. 224 **Hutchison Library:** Jeremy Horner cr, bl. 224 **Panos Pictures:** Jeremy Horner tr; Peter Barker tc. 224 **Still Pictures:** Shehzad Noorani br. 225 **Hutchison Library:** Nancy Durrell McKenna cr, cbr; Shahidul Alam tr. 225 **Panos Pictures:** Paul Smith tl. 225 **Still Pictures:** Shehzad Noorani b. 226-7 **Still Pictures:** Hartmut Schwarzbach 228 **Corbis:** Jeremy Horner tr; Lindsay Hebberd br; Michael Busselle tl; Sheldan Collins tl; Wolfgang Kaehler c. 229 **Corbis:** Chris Lisle tc; Lindsay Hebberd cl, bl, br. 230-1 **Corbis:** Jeremy Horner 232 **Corbis:** David Ball tl; Keren Su tr, br. 232 **Hutchison Library:** Michael Macintyre bl. 233 **Corbis:** Alison Wright br; Keren Su tr; Patrick Ward bl; Paul A. Souders bl. 234 **Corbis:** Tiziana and Gianni Baldizzone bc. 234 **Hutchison Library:** tr. 234 **Impact Photos:** Christophe Bluntzer c. 234 **Still Pictures:** Thomas Kelly l. 235 **Corbis:** Michael S. Yamashita b; Tiziana and Gianni Baldizzone tl. 235 **Impact Photos:** Christophe Bluntzer tr. 235 **Still Pictures:** Thomas Kelly cr. 236 **Hutchison Library:** Sarah Murray c; Stephen Pern tc. 236 **Impact Photos:** David Gallant bl. 236-7 **Still Pictures:** Stephen Pern 237 **Corbis:** Adrian Arbib cra; Jacques Langevin/Sygma tl. 237 **Hutchison Library:** Stephen Pern tr. 237 **Still Pictures:** Adrian Arbib cla; Stephen Pern bl. 238 **DK Picture Library:** bl. 238-9 **Still Pictures:** Adrian Arbib 240 **Bryan And Cherry Alexander Photography:** tr, br, l. 241 **Bryan And Cherry Alexander Photography:** tl, tr, cr, b. 242 **Bryan And Cherry Alexander Photography:** tl, tr, b. 243 **Bryan And Cherry Alexander Photography:** tr, cl, cr, bl, br. 244 **Corbis:** c; Bill Varie bl; Keren Su tl; Liu Liqun tr; Michael S. Yamashita br. 245 **Corbis:** John Slater c; Keren Su br; Robert van der Hilst bl. 245 **Lonely Planet Images:** Bradley Mayhew tr. 246 **Corbis:** Keren Su tl, tr, bl. 246-7 **Panos Pictures:** Penny Tweedie 247 **Alamy Images:** Robert Harding World Imagery tr. 247 **Corbis:** Keren Su tl, br; Steve Raymer bl. 248 **Robert Harding Picture Library:** Sassoon tr. 248 **Impact Photos:** Philip Gordon cl, b. 249 **Corbis:** Dave Bartruff bl, br. 249 **DK Picture Library:** Barnabas Kindersley cr. 249 **Hutchison Library:** Michael Macintyre tr. 249 tl **popperfoto.com:** Marwan Naamani/**AFP250 Corbis:** Bettmann c; John Dakers/Eye Ubiquitous tl; Michael S. Yamashita tr; Oyashiki Miyoko/Sygma bl. 250 **Popperfoto:** AFP photo/Yoshikazu Tsuno br. 251 **Corbis:** Bob Krist c; HARUYOSHI YAMAGUCHI/SYGMA br; Michael Freeman bl; Michael S. Yamashita tc. 252 **Corbis:** Bernard Bisson/Sygma tr. 252 **DK Picture Library:** l. 252 **Robert Harding Picture Library:** br. 253 **Corbis:** Michael S. Yamashita tl; Steve Crise clb. 253 **Robert Harding Picture Library:** tr. 253 **Still Pictures:** Kyodo News cl, b. 254-5 **Impact Photos:** M. Huteau/ana 256 **Robert Harding Picture Library:** tr. 256 **Hutchison Library:** Jeremy Horner c; Liba Taylor l. 256 **Lonely Planet Images:** Chris Mellor br. 257 **Corbis:** Wolfgang Kaehler br. 257 **Impact Photos:** Alain Evrard bl; Robert Hind tl. 257 **Panos Pictures:** Jean-Leo Dugast tr. 258 **Corbis:** Chris Hellier tr; Reinhard Eisele bc. 258 **Robert Harding Picture Library:** l; Richard Ashworth c. 258 **Panos Pictures:** Chris Stowers bl. 259 **Corbis:** Dallas and John Heaton tr. 259 **Hutchison Library:** Michael Macintyre br. 259 **Panos Pictures:** Chris Stowers tl. 259 **Still Pictures:** Chris Caldicott bl. 260-1 **Corbis:** Albrecht G. Schaefer 262 **Corbis:** Ludovic Maisant cr; Patrick Ward br; Paul A. Souders bl. 262 **Robert Harding Picture Library:** Maurice Joseph cra. 262 **Hutchison Library:** Jakum Brown tl. 262 **Panos Pictures:** Chris Stowers tr. 263 **Robert Harding Picture Library:** Sylvain Grandadam tr. 263 **Hutchison Library:** J.G. Fuller tl; Michael Macintyre b. 263 **Lonely Planet Images:** Gregory Adams tc. 264 **Corbis:** ca; Craig Lovell clb; Dallas & John Heaton br; Dimitri Lundt; TempSport bl; Jack Fields bc; Mark A. Johnson tl; Owen Franken cra; Paul A. Souders tr. 264 **Focus New Zealand:** cr. 264 **Hutchison Library:** Isabella Tree c. 264 **Panos Pictures:** Penny Tweedie cla, crb. 265 **Corbis:** Anders Ryman cla; Casa Productions bl; Wayne Lawler; Ecoscene cl. 265 **Getty Images:** tl. 266 **Corbis:** Mark A. Johnson bl. 267 **Corbis:** Anders Ryman br; Benjamin Rondel r; Casa Productions tr; Wendy Stone br. 268 **Corbis:** Albrecht G. Schaefer bc; Paul A. Souders tr; Royalty-free tl. 268 **Popperfoto:** Reuters bl. 269 **Bryan And Cherry Alexander Photography:** tl. 269 **Corbis:** Charles & Josette Lenars bl. 269 **Getty Images:** Michael Coyne bc. 270 **Corbis:** Dimitri Lundt; TempSport tl. 270 **Getty Images:** Zigy Kaluzny c. 270 **Panos Pictures:** Penny Tweedie. 270 **Pa Photos:** tr. 271 **Corbis:** Michael S. Yamashita bl; Patrick Ward crb; Paul A. Souders cr, br, t. 272-3 **Lonely Planet Images:** Nigel Marsh 274 **Panos Pictures:** Penny Tweedie tr, c, bl. 274 **Getty Images:** Louis Grandadam cl. 275 **Corbis:** Dallas & John Heaton bl. 275 **Panos Pictures:** Penny Tweedie tl, tr, br. 276 **Corbis:** Yann Arthus-Bertrand c. 276 **Panos Pictures:** Penny Tweedie bl, br. 277 **Panos Pictures:** Penny Tweedie tr, cr, br. 278 **Corbis:** Arne Hodalic tr; Michael S. Yamashita tl; Wayne Lawler; Ecoscene br, b. 279 **Corbis:** Bob Krist tr; Bojan Brecelj cl; Chris Rainier b. 280 **Corbis:** Chris Rainier br. 280 **Hutchison Library:** Isabella Tree bl. 280 **Michele Westmorland:** tr. 281 **Corbis:** Albrecht G. Schaefer bl; Kevin Schafer cl. 281 **Michele Westmorland:** tc, tr. 282-3 **Corbis:** Chris Rainier 284 **Corbis:** Caroline Penn c, br. 284 **Hutchison Library:** Andre Singer tl. 285 **Corbis:** Caroline Penn br. 285 **Eye Ubiquitous:** James Davis bl. 285 **Robert Harding Picture Library:** tl. 285 **Impact Photos:** Caroline Penn tr. 286 **Bryan And Cherry Alexander Photography:** tl, tr, b. 287 **Bryan And Cherry Alexander Photography:** tr, br. 287 **Corbis:** Anders Ryman bl; Charles O'Rear tc. 288 **Corbis:** Anders Ryman bl; Roger Ressmeyer tl, tr, br. 289 **Corbis:** Anders Ryman tl, cl, bl, r; Paul A. Souders bc. 290 **Corbis:** Catherine Karnow tl; Earl & Nazima Kowall tr. 290 **Eye Ubiquitous:** James Davis bl, b. 291 **Corbis:** Anders Ryman tl, cla, cl; Jack Fields tr, br. 292 **Corbis:** Paul A. Souders c, b. 292 **Getty Images:** Jess Stock tl. 292 **Lonely Planet Images:** Grant Somers tr. 293 **Corbis:** Craig Lovell tl; Kevin Fleming tr, br. 294-5 **Corbis:** Paul A. Souders 296 **Corbis:** Anders Ryman bl; Neil Rabinowitz br; Paul Almasy crb. 296 **Eye Ubiquitous:** James Davis tr. 296 **Focus New Zealand:** tl. 296 **Robert Harding Picture Library:** Caroline Washington cra. 297 **Corbis:** Anders Ryman b; Macduff Everton tr; Wolfgang Kaehler tl. 299 **Bryan And Cherry Alexander Photography:** . 300 **Robert Harding Picture Library:** G. Corrigan. 303 **Hutchison Library:** Isabella Tree.